Anna Krämling
Tyranny of the Majority?

Anna Krämling

Tyranny of the Majority?

Implications of Direct Democracy
for Oppressed Groups in Europe

Budrich Academic Press
Opladen • Berlin • Toronto 2024

All rights reserved. No part of this publication may be reproduced, stored in or introduced into a retrieval system, or transmitted, in any form, or by any means (electronic, mechanical, photocopying, recording or otherwise) without the prior written permission of Barbara Budrich Publishers. Any person who does any unauthorized act in relation to this publication may be liable to criminal prosecution and civil claims for damages.
You must not circulate this book in any other binding or cover and you must impose this same condition on any acquirer.

A CIP catalogue record for this book is available from Die Deutsche Nationalbibliothek (The German National Library): https://portal.dnb.de.

Carbon compensated production

© 2024 by Budrich Academic Press GmbH, Opladen, Berlin & Toronto
www.budrich.eu

     ISBN   978-3-96665-084-7 (Paperback)
     eISBN 978-3-96665-913-0 (PDF)
     DOI   10.3224/96665084

Budrich Academic Press
Stauffenbergstr. 7. D-51379 Leverkusen Opladen, Germany
www.budrich-academic-press.de

86 Delma Drive. Toronto, ON M8W 4P6 Canada
www.budrich.eu

Cover design by Bettina Lehfeldt, Kleinmachnow – www.lehfeldtgraphic.de
Typesetting by Angelika Schulz, Zülpich, Germany
Printed in Europe on FSC®-certified paper by Books on Demand GmbH, Norderstedt, Germany

Acknowledgements

This dissertation would not have been possible without the support of many great people. First of all, I want to thank Brigitte Geißel, who believed in me when I did not believe in myself. She has always been supportive and offered critical thinking and reading to improve my work. Thank you for providing me with the opportunity to do this! Many thanks to Adrian Vatter, whose work on direct democracy and minorities inspired me to write this dissertation, and who fortunately agreed to serve as my second supervisor.

I also owe thanks to all my current and former colleagues in the Democratic Innovations Research Unit at Goethe University. I could not have wished for a better team, who have been like a family at work as well as critical challengers of my thinking. In addition to their feedback, I am also grateful for the feedback received from the Doctoral Colloquium in Comparative Politics at Goethe University, Gary Schaal and his team at Helmut Schmidt University Hamburg, Archon Fung and my co-fellows at the Democracy Seminar of the Ash Center at Harvard Kennedy School, and all the helpful comments at numerous workshops and conferences. Thank you Jenny Mansbridge for your excellent ideas on my PhD project, its theoretical framework, and the interpretation of my results. Additionally, I received very helpful support on my analyses from the Institute for Quantitative Social Science at Harvard University. Providing academic exchange, but also a much-needed break from it during the day, I owe thanks to all my wonderful colleagues at the Faculty of Social Sciences at Goethe University – especially, but not only throughout the pandemic. Melanie Dietz deserves special credit for providing enormous support and making the effort to proofread the whole thesis. Thank you to everyone at Budrich Academic Press for your work throughout the process of publishing this book.

Finally, I want to thank my friends and my family for all their love and support. I am beyond grateful for having such great people in my life. I never could have done any of this without you! In loving memory of my Grandpa Rudi, who sparked my interest in politics. To Alexander, with love – "all's well that ends well to end up with you" (Swift, 2019).

Anna Krämling

Contents

Acknowledgements 5
Tables 11
Figures 15
Abbreviations 17

1　Introduction **19**
1.1　Approach of this Dissertation 21
1.2　Research Questions 23
1.3　Roadmap of the Dissertation 24

2　Conceptual Frame and Definitions **27**
2.1　The Concept of Oppressed Groups 27
　　2.1.1　Criticism and Use in the Social Sciences 29
　　2.1.2　Application in this Dissertation 31
2.2　The Definition of Direct Democracy 33
　　2.2.1　Pro- and Contra-Bills and -Outputs and Direct Democratic Instruments 34
　　2.2.2　Other Stages of the Direct Democratic Process 36
2.3　Direct Democracy and the Tyranny of the Majority 37
　　2.3.1　Reasons to Expect a Tyranny of the Majority 37
　　2.3.2　Reasons to Expect Empowerment 39
　　2.3.3　Different Implications for Different Oppressed Groups 40
　　2.3.4　Explaining Variables for the Probability of Pro- and Contra-Bills and –Outputs: Institutions 44
　　2.3.5　Explaining Variables for the Probability of Pro- and Contra-Bills and -Outputs: Socio-Economic Variables 46
2.4　Summary 47

3　State of the Art: Findings on Direct Democracy and Oppressed Groups **49**
3.1　Negative Implications of Direct Democracy for Oppressed Groups 49

3.2	Positive Implications of Direct Democracy for Oppressed Groups		52
3.3	Explaining Variables		54
	3.3.1	Institutional Effects	54
	3.3.2	Attitudinal Effects	56
	3.3.3	Socio-Economic Effects	60
3.4	Gaps in Existing Research		62
4	**Hypotheses**		**65**
4.1	Different Impacts for Different Groups		65
4.2	Explaining Variables: Institutional Effects		66
	4.2.1	Direct Democratic Instruments	66
	4.2.2	Quora	66
4.3	Explaining Variables: Attitudinal Effects		67
	4.3.1	Negative Attitudes towards Outgroups	67
	4.3.2	Support for Equality	67
4.4	Explaining Variables: Socio-Economic Effects		68
	4.4.1	Education	68
	4.4.2	Economic Growth	68
	4.4.3	Ethnic Fractionalization	69
5	**Methods and Data**		**71**
5.1	Data		71
5.2	Methods		75
6	**Descriptive Results**		**79**
6.1	Oppressed Groups and Direct Democratic Bills		79
6.2	Oppressed Groups and Direct Democratic Outputs		82
6.3	Explaining Variables		85
	6.3.1	Institutional Explaining Variables, Switzerland	85
	6.3.2	Attitudinal and Socio-Economic Explaining Variables	93
6.4	Summary: Descriptive Results on Hypotheses		95
7	**Bivariate Statistics**		**99**
7.1	Explaining Variables and Pro- and Contra-Bills		99
7.2	Explaining Variables and Pro-Outputs		101

7.3	Explaining Variables and Contra-Outputs		104
7.4	Correlations between Explaining Variables		106
7.5	Summary: Bivariate Results on Hypotheses		107

8 Multivariate Statistics 111

8.1	The Probability of Pro-Bills		112
	8.1.1	Variation between Countries and Years	114
	8.1.2	Institutional Explaining Variables, Switzerland	115
	8.1.3	Attitudinal Explaining Variable	116
	8.1.4	Socio-Economic Explaining Variables	116
8.2	The Probability of Pro-Outputs		118
	8.2.1	Variation between Countries and Years	121
	8.2.2	Institutional Explaining Variables, Switzerland	122
	8.2.3	Attitudinal Explaining Variable	123
	8.2.4	Socio-Economic Explaining Variables	123
8.3	The Probability of Contra-Outputs		126
	8.3.1	Variation between Countries and Years	128
	8.3.2	Institutional Explaining Variables, Switzerland	129
	8.3.3	Attitudinal Explaining Variable	130
	8.3.4	Socio-Economic Explaining Variables	130
8.4	Diagnostics		133
8.5	Summary: What Determines the Fate of Oppressed Groups in Direct Democracy?		133

9 Discussion 135

9.1	Overview: Hypotheses and Results		135
9.2	Hypotheses 1a-c: Low SES Groups		136
9.3	Explaining Variables: Institutional Effects		139
	9.3.1	Hypotheses 2a-c: Direct Democratic Instruments	139
	9.3.2	Hypotheses 3a and b: Quora	140
	9.3.3	Explorative Analyses: Binding Vote Results and Switzerland	142
9.4	Explaining Variables: Attitudinal Effects		144
	9.4.1	Hypotheses 4a-c: Negative Attitudes	144
	9.4.2	Hypotheses 5a-c: Support for Equality	144

9.5	Explaining Variables: Socio-Economic Effects		147
	9.5.1	Hypotheses 6a-c: Education	147
	9.5.2	Hypotheses 7a-c: Economic Growth	150
	9.5.3	Hypotheses 8a-c: Ethnic Fractionalization	152
9.6	Summary: What Works Best for Oppressed Groups in Direct Democracy?		153
9.7	The Concept of Oppressed Groups in Direct Democracy		155

10 Conclusions 159

10.1	Oppressed Groups can Benefit from Direct Democracy		159
	10.1.1	Addressing the Gap: A Quantitative, Comparative Analysis of Oppressed Groups in Direct Democracy	160
	10.1.2	Results: Pro-Bills and –Outputs Outnumber Contra-Bills and -Outputs	162
	10.1.3	Limitations and Avenues for Future Research	163
10.2	Binding Votes and Absence of Quora Benefit Oppressed Groups		165
	10.2.1	Addressing the Gap: Multilevel Logistic Regressions	165
	10.2.2	Results: Institutional Variables are Key	166
	10.2.3	Limitations and Avenues for Future Research	168
10.3	It Depends on the Resources and Attitudes		170
	10.3.1	Addressing the Gap: A Differentiated Analysis of Direct Democratic Votes	170
	10.3.2	Results: Different Implications for Different Groups	170
	10.3.3	Limitations and Avenues for Future Research	172
10.4	A Tyranny of the Majority?		175

Appendix 177
Appendix A: Codebook 177
Appendix B: Additional Analyses 183

Bibliography 197
Name Index 207

Tables

Table 1:	Group Characteristics and Direct Democracy	43
Table 2:	Oppressed Groups and Direct Democratic Bills in European Democracies 1990-2015	80
Table 3:	Pro- and Contra-Outputs in European Democracies 1990-2015	83
Table 4:	Oppressed Groups and Direct Democracy in European Democracies 1990-2015	85
Table 5:	Direct Democratic Bills and Outputs and Instruments, 1990-2015	86
Table 6:	Direct Democratic Bills and Outputs and Bottom-Up-Instruments, 1990-2015	87
Table 7:	Direct Democratic Bills and Outputs, Binding and Not Binding, 1990-2015	87
Table 8:	Direct Democratic Bills and Outputs and Quora, 1990-2015	88
Table 9:	Direct Democratic Bills and Outputs and Approval Quora, 1990-2015	89
Table 10:	Direct Democratic Bills and Outputs and Turnout Quora, 1990-2015	89
Table 11:	Direct Democratic Bills and Outputs and "Ständemehr", 1990-2015	89
Table 12:	Direct Democratic Bills and Outputs in- and outside Switzerland, 1990-2015	91
Table 13:	Direct Democratic Bills and Outputs and Instruments in- and outside Switzerland (CH)	92
Table 14:	Direct Democratic Bills and Outputs and Quora in- and outside Switzerland (CH)	92
Table 15:	Tests of Hypotheses in Descriptive Analyses	96
Table 16:	Direct Democratic Bills and Nominal Explaining Variables, Cramér's V	100
Table 17:	Pro-Bills and Explaining Variables, logistic regression coefficients from single models with standard errors in brackets	101
Table 18:	Pro-Outputs and Nominal Explaining Variables, Cramér's V	102

Table 19:	Pro-Outputs and Explaining Variables, logistic regression coefficients from single models with standard errors in brackets	103
Table 20:	Contra-Outputs and Nominal Explaining Variables, Cramér's V	104
Table 21:	Contra-Outputs and Explaining Variables, logistic regression coefficients from single models with standard errors in brackets	105
Table 22:	Tests of Hypotheses in Bivariate Analyses	108
Table 23:	The Probability of Pro-Bills I, Bayesian multilevel logistic regressions	112
Table 24:	The Probability of Pro-Bills II, Bayesian multilevel logistic regressions	113
Table 25:	The Probability of Pro-Bills III, Bayesian multilevel logistic regressions	114
Table 26:	The Probability of Pro-Outputs I, Bayesian multilevel logistic regressions	119
Table 27:	The Probability of Pro-Outputs II, Bayesian multilevel logistic regressions	120
Table 28:	The Probability of Pro-Outputs III, Bayesian multilevel logistic regressions	121
Table 29:	The Probability of Contra-Outputs I, Bayesian multilevel logistic regressions	126
Table 30:	The Probability of Contra-Outputs II, Bayesian multilevel logistic regressions	127
Table 31:	The Probability of Contra-Outputs III, Bayesian multilevel logistic regressions	128
Table 32:	Tests of Hypotheses in Descriptive (H1), Bivariate (H4) and Multilevel Logistic Analyses	136
Table 33:	Education and the Probability of Pro-Outputs without low SES bills, Bayesian multilevel logistic regressions	149
Table 34:	GDP Growth and the Probability of Pro-Outputs without low SES bills, Bayesian multilevel logistic regressions	152
Table 35:	Direct Democratic Bills, Outputs and Success Rates in European Democracies 1990-2015	163
Table 36:	Effects on the Probabilities of Pro-Bills, Pro-Outputs and Contra-Outputs	168
Table 37:	Different Oppressed Groups and Direct Democracy in European Democracies 1990-2015	172
Table 38:	Direct Democratic Bills and Outputs and Attitudes, 1990-2015, means of attitudes	183

Table 39:	Direct Democratic Bills and Outputs and Context, 1990-2015, means	183
Table 40:	Votes in Switzerland and Institutional Explaining Variables, Cramér's V	184
Table 41:	Votes in Switzerland and Attitudinal and Socio-Economic Explaining Variables, means (ttests)	184
Table 42:	Direct Democratic Instrument and Institutional Explaining Variables, Cramér's V	185
Table 43:	Direct Democratic Instrument and Attitudinal and Socio-Economic Explaining Variables, means (anova)	185
Table 44:	Binding Votes and Quora, Cramér's V	186
Table 45:	Binding Votes and Attitudinal and Socio-Economic Explaining Variables, means (ttests)	186
Table 46:	Correlations between Attitudinal and Socio-Economic Variables I, correlation coefficients	187
Table 47:	Correlations between Attitudinal and Socio-Economic Variables II, correlation coefficients	188
Table 48:	Correlations between Attitudinal and Socio-Economic Variables III, correlation coefficients	188

Figures

Figure 1:	Direct Democratic Instruments	35
Figure 2:	Number of Direct Democratic Votes per Year, 1990-2015	73
Figure 3:	Number of Direct Democratic Votes per Country	74
Figure 4:	Multilevel Structure of Data	76
Figure 5:	Institutional Factors, Switzerland and Pro-Bills, Model 5 (mean coefficients, credible intervals)	115
Figure 6:	Equality and Pro-Bills, Model 6 (mean coefficients, credible intervals)	116
Figure 7:	Education and Pro-Bills, Model 7 (mean coefficients, credible intervals)	117
Figure 8:	GDP Growth and Pro-Bills, Model 8 (mean coefficients, credible intervals)	117
Figure 9:	Ethnic Fractionalization and Pro-Bills, Model 9 (mean coefficients, credible intervals)	118
Figure 10:	Institutional Factors, Switzerland and Pro-Outputs, Model 5 (mean coefficients, credible intervals)	122
Figure 11:	Equality and Pro-Outputs, Model 6 (mean coefficients, credible intervals)	123
Figure 12:	Education and Pro-Outputs, Model 7 (mean coefficients, credible intervals)	124
Figure 13:	GDP Growth and Pro-Outputs, Model 8 (mean coefficients, credible intervals)	124
Figure 14:	Ethnic Fractionalization and Pro-Outputs, Model 9 (mean coefficients, credible intervals)	125
Figure 15:	Institutional Factors, Switzerland and Contra-Outputs, Model 5 (mean coefficients, credible intervals)	129
Figure 16:	Equality and Contra-Outputs, Model 6 (mean coefficients, credible intervals)	130
Figure 17:	Education and Contra-Outputs, Model 7 (mean coefficients, credible intervals)	131
Figure 18:	GDP Growth and Contra-Outputs, Model 8 (mean coefficients, credible intervals)	132
Figure 19:	Ethnic Fractionalization and Contra-Outputs, Model 9 (mean coefficients, credible intervals)	132
Figure 20:	Support for Equal Treatment and Opportunities per Country	145
Figure 21:	Support for Equal Treatment and Opportunities per Year	146

Figure 22:	Number of Votes Affecting Different Oppressed Groups, 1990-2015	189
Figure 23:	Means of Agreement "No neighbors of a different race"	190
Figure 24:	Means of Agreement "No neighbors with mental problems"	190
Figure 25:	Means of Agreement "No neighbors of Muslim religion"	191
Figure 26:	Means of Agreement "No neighbors of different religion"	191
Figure 27:	Means of Agreement "No immigrant neighbors"	192
Figure 28:	Means of Agreement "No homosexual neighbors"	192
Figure 29:	Means of Agreement "When jobs are scarce, men should be advantaged"	193
Figure 30:	Means of Agreement "Larger income differences are necessary"	193
Figure 31:	Means of Negative Attitude towards Affected Group	194
Figure 32:	Means of Agreement "Important that people are treated equally & have equal opportunities"	194
Figure 33:	Means of Share of People with University Degree	195
Figure 34:	Means of Growth of GDP per capita	195
Figure 35:	Means of Levels of Ethnic Fractionalization	196

Abbreviations

AfD	Alternative for Germany
approx.	approximately
DFG	German Research Foundation
e.g.	for example
etc.	et cetera
GDP	Gross Domestic Product
ICC	intra class correlation
i.e.	id est (*Engl.* that is)
LGBTQ	lesbian, gay, bisexual, transgender, queer
MP	member of parliament
SES	socio-economic status
SVP	Swiss Peoples Party
U.S.	United States of America

1 Introduction

> "I regard as impious and detestable this maxim that in matters of government the majority of a people has the right to do anything"
>
> "So what is a majority taken as a whole, if not an individual who has opinions and, most often, interests contrary to another individual called the minority. Now, if you admit that an individual vested with omnipotence can abuse it against his adversaries, why would you not admit the same thing for the majority?"
>
> *Tocqueville, Democracy in America* (2012, pp. 410, 411)
>
> "It is of great importance in a republic […] to guard one part of the society against the injustice of the other part."
>
> *Madison, The Federalist, 51* (2008, p. 258)

Direct democratic votes, where a majority of voters usually directly decides on policies, have gained popularity all over the world in recent decades. While portrayed as a potential cure for the malaises of current representative democracies by some, others fear that the absence of representative filters in direct democratic votes bears the risk of a *Tyranny of the Majority* as described by Tocqueville (2012). In light of the growing popularity of direct democratic votes, this dissertation analyzes quantitatively and cross-nationally the real implications of these votes for minorities, thereby addressing a gap in research on direct democracy as well as the ongoing political debate.

The potential advantages and disadvantages of direct democracy are the subject of fierce debate in the contexts of politics and political science, and the few existing studies on single countries offer no clear picture. From a theoretical perspective, the inclusion of as many citizens as possible in political decision-making can be seen as a democratic value in itself (e.g., Barber, 1984; Pateman, 1970). Scholars of participatory democracy regard direct democratic decision-making as a possible cure for the current "crisis of democracy", with declining participation and trust in representative institutions. Especially in regard to minorities, direct democratic votes might offer new channels to bring their interests onto the political agenda (e.g., Bowler et al., 2017; Dalton, 2004). In the late 19th century United States (U.S.), direct democracy was already seen as a counterbalance to decision-making by corrupt legislators driven by special interests (Lewis, 2013). Based on these arguments, some political scientists as well as parties and interest groups call for the extension of direct democratic options worldwide. Likewise, the use of initiatives and referenda has been increasing globally for the last 30 years.[1] However, amplifying theoretical concerns about the consequences of direct democracy, direct democratic votes in the U.S. especially have proven to be difficult for minorities. For example, eleven out of twelve ballot measures concerning the rights of minority groups were decided against the minority in 2006 (Lewis, 2013). In Switzerland, where direct democratic votes are most widespread, results seem to depend on the minority concerned: Muslims and foreigners in particular tended to lose in direct democratic votes during recent years, whereas for instance linguistic minorities did not encounter similar disadvantages (Christmann & Danaci, 2012; Vatter & Danaci, 2010). Yet quantitative and especially cross-national analyses that could shed greater light on these differences are missing.

Corresponding to the academic discourse, political parties are debating the up- and downsides of direct democracy as well. Additionally, recent surveys have witnessed a growing skepticism amongst citizens. Regarding parties, the debate in Germany provides an interesting example. Four out of six parties currently represented in the German Bundestag campaigned for the introduction of direct democratic votes at the federal level in Germany before the Bundestag election in 2017. Support for extending direct democratic options ranged across the whole ideological spectrum, from the Left to Alternative for Germany (AfD).[2] However, during the election campaign in 2021, the German Greens – historically the party most in favor of direct democracy – replaced their long-standing claim for extension of direct democracy to the German federal level with a call for more citizens' councils.[3] This mirrors a growing awareness of the risks of direct democracy and the potential for it to lead to *Tyranny of the Majority,* among center-left parties in recent years, while demands for and use of direct democratic options have been increasing among right-wing populists (see Chapter 3). A trend towards fading enthusiasm for direct democracy is also evident in citizen surveys: in Rounds 6 and 10 of the European Social Survey (conducted in 2012 and 2020) respondents were asked whether it is important for a democracy that citizens have the final say on political issues by voting directly in a referendum. Whereas overall support for referenda was high in both rounds, the share of people choosing the two most supportive options 9 or 10 decreased by roughly 5.5 % from 2012 to 2020. Although the decline is small, it never-

---

1 https://www.washingtonpost.com/amphtml/news/theworldpost/wp/2018/05/08/direct-democracy-is-thriving/?noredirect=on&__twitter_impression=true (29.02.24)
2 https://www.tagesschau.de/inland/btw17/programmvergleich/programmvergleich-demokratie-101.html (29.02.24)
3 https://cms.gruene.de/uploads/documents/Wahlprogramm_Englisch_DIE_GRUENEN_Bundestagswahl_2021.pdf (29.02.24)

theless hints at growing skepticism about direct democracy in a previously very enthusiastic citizenry.[4]

1.1 Approach of this Dissertation

In light of the current debate on extending direct democratic options in many countries, a cross-national analysis of the outputs of the votes so far is much needed to test empirically the validity of people's hopes and fears about such processes. However, with the lack of a common definition of minorities and an encompassing dataset on direct democratic votes, quantitative and above all comparative research on the results of minority-related votes outside of Switzerland and the U.S. is scarce. This dissertation addresses this research gap by analyzing all direct democratic votes on a national level in European democracies from 1990 to 2015.

Focusing on European democracies, where direct democracy has a long-standing tradition in Switzerland and has gained prominence in many other countries since the 1990s, allows for a comparative design as well as for a certain contextual stability. The timeframe from 1990 onwards enables the inclusion of Central and Eastern European countries whose new constitutions introduced direct democratic options in the early 1990s. Based on data gathered in our project "Inequality and direct democracy in Europe" funded by the German Research Foundation (DFG), the timeframe ends with 2015 but could easily be extended for future research. Analyzing votes from all European democracies over 25 years enables robust conclusions based on a large amount of data to be drawn for the first time.

Analyses to date have used the term minorities in different and often not well-specified ways (e.g., Haider-Markel et al., 2007; Hajnal et al., 2002). Instead, I draw on the concept of "oppressed groups" described by Iris Marion Young (Young, 1990), which I will outline in more detail in Chapter 2. Applying Young's concept permits the investigation of more groups and thereby broader differentiation. While some groups, such as women or people of low socio-economic status (SES), might not be a numerical minority, they are included by Young as they nonetheless face forms of oppression. Therefore, they might be at a disadvantage in direct democratic votes as well. At the same time, a common criticism of Young's concept is that it is too broad (Kymlicka, 1995). In my dissertation, I test whether a broad concept such as

---

[4] Own calculations using European Social Survey Round 6 Data (2012) and European Social Survey Round 10 Data (2020) (ESS6 – Integrated File, Edition 2.4 [Data Set], 2018; ESS10 – Integrated File, Edition 2.1 [Data Set], 2022).
Countries include Belgium, Switzerland, Czechia, Estonia, Finland, France, Hungary, Iceland, Italy, Lithuania, Netherlands, Norway, Portugal, Slovenia, Slovakia.

this works in the context of direct democracy or whether a narrower definition, like the previous application of the term minorities, is more useful for analyzing the implications of direct democratic voting.

For the first time in research on direct democratic votes and oppressed groups,[5] my analyses cover two stages of the direct democratic process – the so-called bill- and output-levels (see also Geißel et al., 2019b, 2019a; Krämling et al., 2022). Again, I shall introduce these terms briefly here then describe them in more detail in the next chapter. At the bill-level, a direct democratic bill brought to a vote can either support the interests of an oppressed group or disadvantage them. The former is the case if a bill aims at benefitting the affected group by improving its legal, political or socio-economic status or by preventing a deterioration of this status (called pro-bill in the following), while the latter is true if a bill aims at preventing an improvement of the group's status or aims at further deteriorating it (called contra-bill in the following). At the output-level, if a pro-bill wins a majority of votes and passes a potential quorum, it generates a pro-output. In contrast, if a contra-bill wins a majority of votes and passes a potential quorum, it generates a contra-output. This dual focus on the bill- and the output-levels enables a thorough investigation of what actually happens in direct democratic voting.

Summing up, this dissertation represents an important contribution to the literature on direct democracy and oppressed groups. For the first time, a dataset covering all national-level votes in European democracies between 1990 and 2015 allows for an encompassing analysis of the implications of direct democratic votes for various oppressed groups. In the first quantitative and cross-national analysis on the topic, I identify the influence of various institutional, attitudinal and socio-economic variables in this regard. In the process, relevant factors emerge that foster the success of oppressed groups in direct democracy as well as factors that prevent discrimination. Finally, the first application of the concept of oppressed groups in research on direct democracy enables the analysis to be extended to groups such as low SES groups and political minorities who are also likely to be disadvantaged in direct democratic votes but have to date been largely neglected in studies on direct democracy and minorities.

---

5   I mainly use the term "oppressed groups" from here on when referring to previous research on direct democracy and what it refers to as "minorities".

1.2   Research Questions

The main aims of my dissertation are threefold: determining the record of oppressed groups in direct democratic votes on the bill- as well as on the output-level, revealing explanations for pro- and contra-bills and their respective success at the ballot, and identifying possible differences between different groups. Based on this, by investigating the fate of oppressed groups in direct democracy cross-nationally, this thesis aims to answer the following research questions:

1. Do direct democratic bills and outputs support or disadvantage the interests of oppressed groups (pro-bills/-outputs or contra-bills/-outputs)?
2. What explains whether supportive rather than disadvantaging bills come to a vote (pro- instead of contra-bills)? What explains supportive and disadvantaging outputs (pro- and contra-outputs), respectively?
3. Can we observe differences in bills and outputs depending on which oppressed group is affected by the vote? Based on this, what constitutes the concept of oppressed groups in direct democracy?

The first question hints at the record of oppressed groups in direct democratic votes in Europe: how many direct democratic bills aim at supporting the interests of oppressed groups and how many aim at disadvantaging them? The results will reveal how successful oppressed groups are in bringing their interests to a vote and thereby onto the public agenda, as well as how successful their opponents are in doing the same. To evaluate the direct impact of these bills, i.e., the impact of their adoption, we must look at the output-level: how many direct democratic outputs aim at supporting the interests of oppressed groups and how many aim at disadvantaging them? Do pro-bills and contra-bills differ in their chances of succeeding?

Regarding the second question, of particular interest is the role of institutional, attitudinal and socio-economic factors. Which circumstances promote the interests of oppressed groups in direct democracy by increasing the probability of pro-bills and pro-outputs? And which circumstances contribute to a potential *Tyranny of the Majority* by increasing the probability of contra-outputs?

The third question entails similar questions to the first one, but now focuses on differences between oppressed groups. Do we find a higher share of pro-bills for some groups while others face contra-bills more often? Are pro-bills for some groups more likely to succeed than pro-bills for others and, vice versa, is adoption easier for bills targeting certain groups compared to bills targeting others? Based on the results, I will evaluate whether all of the groups defined as oppressed by Young and others[6] are actually so in direct

---

6   Outlined in Chapter 3.

democracy. If differences emerge, I will identify which groups should count as oppressed as well as which group characteristics might explain this, thereby refining the application of the concept of oppressed groups in research on direct democracy. This will reveal whether a broad concept of oppressed groups is useful in analyzing direct democratic votes or whether research should stick to a narrower notion of (well-specified) minorities.

1.3 Roadmap of the Dissertation

In answering these research questions, the thesis proceeds as follows: Chapter 2, "Conceptual Frame and Definitions" introduces the concept of oppressed groups by Iris M. Young and the advantages of applying this concept instead of the concept of minorities, as well as how Young's concept has been operationalized in the social sciences thus far and how it is applied here. Furthermore, I outline my definition of direct democracy and the terms pro- and contra-bills and –outputs. The chapter continues by presenting theoretical reasons why direct democracy might result in a *Tyranny of the Majority* versus why it might instead empower oppressed groups. Lastly, I introduce group characteristics that I expect to be influential for a group's fate in direct democratic votes, as well as institutional factors relating to the vote, attitudes among the electorate, and the socio-economic characteristics of the country that may be relevant.

In Chapter 3, "State of the Art: Findings on Direct Democracy and Oppressed Groups", I summarize the existing research on the negative implications of direct democracy for oppressed groups as well as on positive implications. For a more differentiated view, I present previous results on institutional, attitudinal, and socio-economic effects influencing direct democratic outputs for oppressed groups. Based on this, I identify the gaps in existing research on direct democracy and oppressed groups that my thesis aims to address.

Building on the theoretical arguments and empirical findings presented in Chapters 2 and 3, I formulate the hypotheses guiding my analyses in Chapter 4, "Hypotheses". This includes assumptions about different impacts for different groups. Additionally, I formulate hypotheses about the institutional effects of direct democratic instruments and quora; the attitudinal effects of negative attitudes towards the group affected by a vote and support for equality more general; and the socio-economic effects of the levels of education, economic growth and ethnic fractionalization at the time and in the country of a vote.

In Chapter 5, "Methods and Data", I detail the data I gathered on all national votes in European democracies between 1990 and 2015 and how I coded direct democratic bills according to their possible impact on oppressed groups. In addition, I provide information about the data for the explaining variables. Afterwards, I outline the methods for my descriptive and bivariate analyses and explain in more detail why I perform Bayesian multilevel logistic regressions in my multivariate analyses.

Chapter 6, "Descriptive Results", contains descriptive statistics on the direct democratic bills and outputs for different oppressed groups as well as on the institutional explaining variables and on the characteristics of Swiss votes (given the importance of direct democracy in Switzerland), and describes the data on attitudinal and socio-economic explaining variables. The chapter concludes by outlining whether the descriptive results support or contradict the hypotheses formulated in Chapter 4.

In Chapter 7, "Bivariate Statistics", I present findings on the correlations between the explaining variables and pro-and contra-bills, pro-outputs, and contra-outputs. Furthermore, this chapter explores how the explaining variables correlate with each other. It concludes with the implications of the bivariate results for my hypotheses.

Chapter 8, "Multivariate Statistics", represents the heart of my analysis: the results of multivariate, multilevel logistic regressions investigating what affects the probability that a pro-bill will come to a vote, the probability of a pro-output, and the probability of a contra-output. Here, I outline the results of models for each of these three dependent variables, carving out the effects of the institutional, attitudinal and socio-economic explaining variables. Taken together, these analyses provide insights into the factors that determine the fate of oppressed groups in direct democracy.

In Chapter 9, "Discussion", I discuss the results of my analyses in light of the theoretical assumptions and previous findings that led to my hypotheses. For the most surprising and counter-intuitive results I perform additional analyses to test possible causal mechanisms that might explain them. The chapter concludes with a recipe of what works best for oppressed groups in direct democracy – i.e., which steps can be taken to support oppressed groups in direct democratic votes according to my analyses. In addition, I elaborate how Young's concept of oppressed groups can be applied in research on direct democracy.

Finally, Chapter 10, "Conclusions", provides an overview of my work, testing the value of the concept of oppressed groups for research on direct democracy and analyzing the implications of direct democratic votes for these groups as well as identifying relevant explaining variables. I present the key results of this undertaking and provide answers on my research questions while also outlining the limitations of my analyses and suggesting avenues for future research on oppressed groups in direct democracy. At the end, the thesis returns to its starting point: do empirical findings substantiate a *Tyranny of the Majority* over oppressed groups in direct democracy? What can be done to prevent such a tyranny? My answers provide ideas for ways in which we can potentially heal the malaises of current representative democracies through providing options for direct democratic participation without endangering the most vulnerable groups in our societies.

2 Conceptual Frame and Definitions

To prepare the ground for my analysis of direct democratic bills and outputs for oppressed groups, this chapter presents the conceptual frame and most important terms I use. First, starting with the new conceptual ground this thesis touches upon, I present the concept of "oppressed groups" defined by Iris M. Young, outline why it is useful for investigating patterns of direct democracy, and describe how I apply it in this dissertation. Second, the chapter contains the definition of direct democracy used in this thesis. I introduce the differentiation between pro- and contra-bills as well as between pro- and contra-outputs in more detail and define different direct democratic instruments. Third, the chapter deals with theoretical reasons given in the literature for why direct democracy might result in a *Tyranny of the Majority* – or why it could empower oppressed groups instead. I outline the characteristics of oppressed groups that I expect to influence a group's fate in direct democratic votes. In addition, I present theoretical assumptions about the effects of direct democratic instruments, quora and a binding vote result, as well as the effects of the education levels, economic growth and ethnic fractionalization in the country and year of a vote.

2.1 The Concept of Oppressed Groups

Why is the concept of oppressed groups useful for the purpose of this dissertation? The following section presents the concept, reasons for applying it, criticism and use of the concept in the social sciences, and its application in this thesis.

Most of the literature on the possible tyrannical effects of direct democracy uses the term "minorities" to refer to groups that might be in particular danger (e.g., Christmann & Danaci, 2012; Haider-Markel et al., 2007; Lewis, 2013; Vatter & Danaci, 2010). For example, in Lewis' (2013) analysis of direct democracy in the U.S., he refers to "the concept of 'political minorities' that focusses on discrimination and political rights […]. […] These widely protected classes include minority groups defined by race, color, religion, ethnicity, and national origin. More recently other groups have also gained recognition as valid 'political minorities', including groups defined by their sexual orientation, gender identity, age, gender, and disabilities."

(Lewis, 2013, p. 13). The term (political) minorities contains the conception of a group that differs from the majority of the population due to a certain characteristic, excluding for example women (as they do not represent a numerical minority). In addition, low SES groups in particular have been proven to be disadvantaged in case studies on direct democratic votes (Schäfer & Schoen, 2013; Töller & Vollmer, 2013). Yet, these groups are usually excluded when research on direct democracy refers to its impact on minorities. Finally, being a minority does not necessarily mean that a group is in a disadvantaged position – resourceful minorities are often influential, very likely to mobilize voting majorities and thereby able to benefit from direct democracy. Besides these major downsides, there has been no discussion of nor presentation of alternatives to the concept of minorities in research on direct democracy so far.

Therefore, I am using the concept of an "oppressed social group" as coined by Iris Marion Young (1990) to identify relevant groups that can be expected to be especially vulnerable in direct democracy. For Young, "it is identification with a certain social status, the common history that social status produces, and self-identification that define the group as a group" (Young, 1990, p. 44). For my purposes, it is crucial that others perceive its members as a group and judge them accordingly – or, as Young puts it, "our identities are defined in relation to how others identify us, and they do so in terms of groups which are always already associated with specific attributes, stereotypes, and norms" (Young, 1990, p. 46). For example, she explicitly includes poor people and women (Young, 1989). Applying her concept to research on direct democratic votes thereby allows for an investigation of their implications for a wider variety of groups which can be assumed to be disadvantaged by direct democracy.

For Young, oppression has five faces: exploitation, marginalization, powerlessness, cultural imperialism, and violence (Young, 1990). Young explains the focus on these five aspects pointedly in her own words as follows: On *exploitation*: "The injustice of exploitation consists in social processes that bring about a transfer of energies from one group to another to produce unequal distributions, and in the way in which social institutions enable a few to accumulate while they constrain many more." (Young, 1990, p. 53). On *marginalization*: "Marginals are people the system of labor cannot or will not use. […] A whole category of people is expelled from useful participation in social life and thus potentially subjected to severe material deprivation and even extermination." (ibid.) "Two categories of injustice beyond distribution are associated with marginality in advanced capitalist societies. First, the provision of welfare itself produces new injustice by depriving those dependent on it of rights and freedoms that others have. Second, even when material deprivation is somewhat mitigated by the welfare state, marginalization is unjust because it blocks the opportunity to exercise capacities in socially defined and recognized ways." (ibid., 54) "…it also involves the deprivation of cultural, practical, and institutionalized conditions for exercising capacities in a context of recognition and interaction." (ibid., 55). On *powerlessness*: "The powerless are those who lack authority or power even in this mediated sense, those over whom power is exercised without their exercising it; the powerless are situated so that they must take orders and rarely have the right to give them." (ibid., 56) "I have discussed several injustices associated with powerlessness: inhibition in the development of one's capacities, lack of decisionmaking power in one's working life, and exposure to disrespectful treatment because of the status one occupies." (ibid., 58). On *cultural imperialism*: "To experience cultural imperialism means to experience how the dominant meanings of a society render the particular perspective of one's own group invisible at the same time as they stereotype one's group and mark it out as the Other." (ibid., 58-59). On *violence*: "Members of some groups live with the knowledge that they must fear random, unprovoked attacks on their persons or property, which have no motive but to damage, humiliate, or destroy the person. […] I also include in this category less severe incidents of harassment, intimidation, or ridicule simply for the purpose of degrading, humiliating, or stigmatizing group members." (ibid., 61) "The oppression of violence consists not only in direct victimization, but in the daily knowledge shared by all members of oppressed groups that they are liable to violation, solely on account of their group identity. Just living under such a threat of attack on oneself or family or friends deprives the oppressed of freedom and dignity, and needlessly expends their energy." (ibid., 62).

Applied to this dissertation, every group that suffers from one or more of these faces of oppression or has done so in the recent past is considered to be potentially vulnerable in majoritarian decision-making. Given that the focus of this dissertation is on democracies, oppression of violence should be less common. However, forms of exploitation, marginalization, powerlessness, and cultural imperialism can and do persist in democracies.

2.1.1 Criticism and Use in the Social Sciences

The publication of Young's *Justice and the Politics of Difference* with its definitions of oppression and social groups as well as the five faces of oppression and the policies she recommends sparked a debate in Political Theory. In the following, I provide a short overview of the major critiques and explain why I nevertheless use her conceptualization here. Afterwards, I summarize previous operationalizations of the concept in the social sciences.

Nancy Fraser, for example, has criticized Young for differentiating too strictly between cultural and political-economic phenomena when it comes to groups, the forms of oppression they suffer, and therefore the remedies for oppression – thereby often favoring the cultural dimension (Fraser, 1997a, 1997b). Instead, Fraser calls for a more "differentiated view of difference" (Fraser, 1997b, p. 204). According to her, the roots of the oppression experienced are decisive for defining the remedy – for example, cultural forms of oppression might have economic roots, resulting in redistribution being the right remedy rather than recognition of the group's difference. In some cases, such redistribution might even lead to the abolishment of the group as such. Therefore, rather than always applying a politics of difference, one should differentiate between differences that need to be erased, those that should be universalized, and those that should be enjoyed (Fraser, 1997b). Yet this interpretation of Young's concept has also been called into question, with Lima e Silva and Silva arguing that Young (1990, 2000) does address economic injustices to the same degree as cultural ones, for example by focusing on the role of distribution and division of labor (Lima e Silva & Silva, 2019).

As a reaction to Young's concept, Melissa Williams developed her own concept of marginalized groups. According to her, these have four characteristic features: "(1) patterns of social and political inequality are structured along the lines of group membership; (2) membership in these groups is not usually experienced as voluntary; (3) membership in these groups is not usually experienced as mutable; and (4) generally, negative meanings are assigned to group identity by the broader society or the dominant culture." (M. S. Williams, 2000, pp. 15–16). Who counts as a marginalized group may be the subject of political disagreement, as it depends on their history of exclusion from citizenship and state-sponsored discrimination, changing social circumstances and intergroup relations (M. S. Williams, 2000). Compared to Young's concept, this concept of marginalized groups therefore allows for greater flexibility. Yet while this concept has a great value in itself, the last point especially makes it difficult to use for the purpose of this dissertation. Although one can expect changes over space and time in terms of which groups are oppressed and which are not, political disagreement as implied by the concept itself would disable any clear-cut operationalization and application in quantitative comparative analysis.

Given the diverse faces of oppression and the numerous groups that have since been defined as oppressed (see below), Kymlicka (1995) criticizes the breadth of the concept, stating that applying the concept to the U.S. would result in about 80 percent of its population being classed as oppressed. I build on this critique by analyzing whether a concept as broad as this is useful in investigating the implications of direct democratic votes.

Another point of potential criticism might be whether describing a group as oppressed is not too harsh a word, describing the group as an object rather than a subject of actions, and posing the question of who the oppressor is. While I especially agree with the second point, one focus of this dissertation is to investigate whether these groups really are oppressed in direct democratic votes, i.e., whether groups that are worse off regarding the topic of a bill are put at further disadvantage by its adoption or rejection at the ballot box. A finding of more bills being brought to and adopted in a vote that support a group's interests would support the claim that calling that group oppressed does not hold in the context of direct democracy. I also do not question the ability of so-called oppressed groups to stand up against oppression – they do so every day, often encountering numerous barriers in the process. Rather, this dissertation will specifically offer insights into whether said groups are *successful* in taking action via the direct democratic route. Finally, the existence of oppressed groups requires the existence of an oppressor as well. However, who constitutes an oppressing group depends on the oppressed group and the circumstances of their oppression. Therefore, for the purpose of this dissertation, oppressing groups are diverse coalitions of different people aiming at disadvantaging oppressed groups even further or inhibiting improvements in their situation via direct democratic votes.

Young's concept has since been used to refer to several different groups in different contexts. She herself provides an encompassing list of oppressed social groups in the U.S. today, including women, Blacks, Native Americans, Chicanos, Puerto-Ricans and other Spanish-speaking Americans, Asian Americans, gays and lesbians, working-class people, poor people, old people, people with mental health issues, and those with physical disabilities. In addition, she points to the historical exclusion of Jews in Europe (Young, 1989). Recently, several studies have focused on LGBTQ (lesbian, gay, bisexual, transgender, queer persons), women, people with disabilities and low SES groups as oppressed groups (Mancenido-Bolaños, 2020; Pineda, 2020; Tempels et al., 2020; C. C. Williams et al., 2020).

2.1.2 Application in this Dissertation

Following her definition of the five faces of oppression and the past operationalizations of Young's concept outlined above, for the purpose of my descriptive analyses and discussion of the concept I differentiate between three clusters of oppressed groups. First, "classic oppressed groups" include members of the LGBTQ+ community, non-citizens, people with disabilities and those suffering from mental health issues, members of linguistic minorities, members of religious minorities, and women. Previous research on the effects of direct democracy on minorities mostly focuses on one or several of these groups. This cluster also includes direct democratic bills that contain bans on discrimination more generally and bills strengthening the rule of law and fundamental rights. Second, low SES groups represent another cluster – reflecting the debate mentioned above on whether Young's concept also includes a socio-economic dimension. This cluster includes different areas of policies, such as housing, welfare, education, healthcare, and transport. I expect bills on these topics to affect low SES groups in particular. Third, oppression of powerlessness especially can persist because of the concentration of political power. When political power is highly concentrated and the political system is closed in the sense that it is hard for new actors to gain access to power, power is exercised over oppressed groups and they "must take orders and rarely have the right to give them" (Young, 1990, p. 56), just like Young defines the face of powerlessness. A third cluster called "political groups" therefore includes bills on the rights of parliamentary opposition, on the voting system, and on division of power. For example, a direct democratic bill proposing more investigative powers for parliamentary commissions (and thereby potentially strengthening the parliamentary opposition) was voted upon in Ireland in 2011. While parliamentary oppositions can rarely be called oppressed in democracies, reducing their rights can result in a lower probability of them ever exercising power, and, in extreme cases, can actually lead to oppression.

The differentiation between classic oppressed groups, low SES groups and political groups serves as a framework for the descriptive analyses, investigating which (clusters of) groups benefit from or lose out in direct democratic votes. Therefore, there are no clear-cut theoretical expectations about direct democratic bills and outputs impacting the clusters of groups in specific ways. I will outline the characteristics of oppressed groups that I assume to make a difference in terms of their fate in direct democracy in the last section of this chapter. However, these characteristics do not correspond directly to the descriptive clusters introduced here, as the same group might have different characteristics depending on the country or the time of a vote.

One could question whether there is something like a group's interest[7] at all – yet I argue that at least in the case of direct democratic votes affecting a group, we can assume that there is. Young emphasizes the internal heterogeneity of groups (Young, 1990), and I acknowledge that members of groups can and do have different interests. However, the direct democratic bills analyzed in this dissertation contain measures that improve or worsen the situation of whole groups. I therefore assume that it is in the interest of most group members to see these bills adopted in the first case or not adopted in the second. For example, a bill that aims at decreasing costs for housing or energy benefits most people of low socio-economic status and is therefore assumed to be in this group's interest. In a similar vein, an individual can of course belong to several oppressed groups, e.g., non-citizens in same-sex relationships. In most of the votes analyzed in this thesis, the measures

---

7   Interests in this dissertation entail material interests as well as rights. The codebook in the Appendix gives an overview of ways in which direct democratic bills can touch upon oppressed groups' interests.

proposed in a bill clearly affect one group in particular, e.g. by increasing hurdles for obtaining citizenship or by introducing same-sex marriage. Therefore, I am able to assign these bills to one category despite the intersectionality of individual group members. Chapter 5, "Methods and Data", contains more details on the coding procedure, including for the bills which actually contain various measures from different categories, and provides other examples of bills for illustration.

As mentioned above, another critique of Young's concept is that it encompasses too many groups, and thus about 80 percent of the U.S. population would have to be considered oppressed (Kymlicka, 1995). I take up this criticism in the following and, by comparing bills and outputs for different groups, examine whether Young's broad concept is helpful in analyzing the fate of oppressed groups in direct democracy. This would be the case if similar patterns emerge across the groups she addresses. If, however, different patterns emerge depending on the group concerned, this argues for a more differentiated approach. Young's concept might nevertheless be of use as a framework, if groups previously unaccounted for in research on direct democracy and minorities prove to be affected in a specific way. Based on my empirical findings, I will re-assess the use of the concept of oppressed groups in direct democracy in Chapter 9.

2.2 The Definition of Direct Democracy

What do I mean when I write about direct democracy? The following outlines the definition of direct democracy used here and provides reasons for this choice of terms.

Direct democracy is defined here as popular votes on certain issues – excluding direct elections or recalls of politicians. Strictly speaking, none of the countries under investigation in this dissertation is a "direct democracy", as direct democratic votes are only one form of political decision-making in use alongside other, mostly representative forms. These countries do not have direct democratic political systems but rather single or several direct democratic votes. There is large variety in direct democratic instruments as well as in how they are combined with representative or deliberative decision-making. As a result, for example el-Wakil and McKay (2020) call for a democratic systems approach instead of a direct democracy approach. Rather than analyzing what they term "popular vote processes" as direct democracy as opposed to representative democracy, they argue that research should acknowledge this variety more fully and help find constructive ways to better implement popular votes in democratic systems.

I stick to the term direct democracy for three reasons. First, while there certainly is significant diversity in direct democratic options and the ways in which they connect to the democratic system at large, they share certain characteristics that differentiate them from representative or deliberative procedures and deserve investigation. All citizens and sometimes all inhabitants are eligible to vote on bill proposals, and, at least in the votes under analysis here, a majority of votes decides. This differs from elections of persons or parties in representative procedures and from the consensus-oriented deliberation in smaller groups involved in deliberative procedures. Second, using the established concept of direct democracy facilitates conversation with existing literature on the topic and contributes to the ongoing discussion (e.g., Christmann & Danaci, 2012; Geißel et al., 2019b; Krämling et al., 2022; Lewis, 2013; Vatter & Danaci, 2010). Third, and maybe most important, although it is not possible in quantitative comparative analysis to identify the effects of every potential way in which a direct democratic vote connects to the democratic system at large, I do differentiate between certain characteristics that might be influential in this regard. Outlined in greater detail in 2.3, these are: who initiates the vote, does the bill have to fulfill a quorum, and whether the vote result is binding. Analyzing the effects of these factors can help identify the best way to implement direct democratic options that protect oppressed groups and potentially even improve their situation.

Before turning to the theoretical reasons given in the literature for why direct democracy should disadvantage or empower oppressed groups, the next section includes the differentiation between direct democratic bills and outputs in more detail. They represent the focus of this dissertation. Future research can build on this and investigate the effects of direct democracy both before a bill comes to the ballot and after it has been adopted, as outlined further in 2.2.2. In addition, I also define different direct democratic instruments in the next section.

2.2.1 Pro- and Contra-Bills and -Outputs and Direct Democratic Instruments

As mentioned in the Introduction, I distinguish between direct democratic bills, i.e., all bills that come to a direct democratic vote, and direct democratic outputs, i.e., bills that are adopted at the ballot (see also Geißel et al., 2019a, 2019b; Krämling et al., 2022). A *pro-bill* contains measures to support oppressed groups or is a veto referendum against a law that disadvantages them. A *pro-output* is a pro-bill that gains a majority at the ballot and passes a possible quorum, i.e., is adopted in the direct democratic vote. In contrast, a *contra-bill* contains measures to disadvantage oppressed groups or is a veto

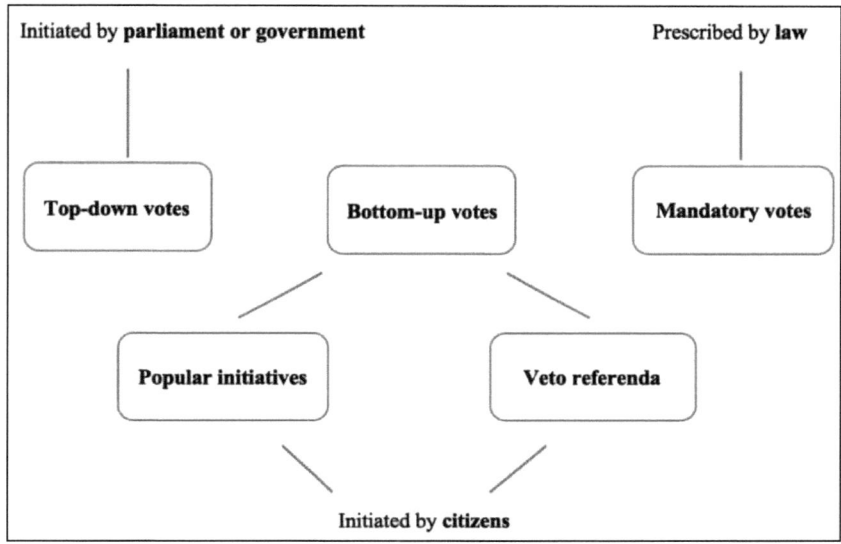

Figure 1: Direct Democratic Instruments. Source: own diagram

referendum against a law that supports them. A *contra-output* is a contra-bill adopted at the ballot, i.e., that gains a majority of votes and passes a possible quorum.

Direct democratic votes come in a variety of forms in the countries under investigation in this dissertation. I differentiate between these direct democratic instruments based on who initiates them: popular initiatives and veto referenda initiated by citizens on parliamentary bills are coded as bottom-up votes, optional referenda initiated by a majority of parliament or government are coded as top-down votes, and votes prescribed by law are coded as mandatory votes (see also Geißel et al., 2019a). Figure 1 illustrates this distinction.

These direct democratic instruments fulfill different roles in a political system. First, citizens can use bottom-up votes to bring measures to the ballot that parliament is unlikely to adopt, or to repeal a law passed by parliament. In the first case – the popular initiative – citizens act as agenda-setters, while in the second case (the veto referendum) they can be a popular check on parliamentary power (Lacey, 2021; Leemann, 2015; Serdült & Welp, 2012). Second, parliament or government can use top-down votes to (for example) bypass legislative gridlock, resolve conflicts within a governing party or coalition, gain electoral advantages, or enhance the legitimacy of a policy (Gherghina, 2019; Morel, 2007; Qvortrup, 2006; Rahat, 2009; Welp & Ruth, 2017). Third, mandatory votes are often on constitutional amendments. Here, the necessity of popular approval is to ensure that there is broad support in society for constitutional change. In subchapter 2.3.4.1, I introduce assumptions about how these different instruments might affect oppressed groups in diverse ways.

As outlined in more detail in subchapter 2.3.1, there are obstacles for every group, but especially for oppressed groups at the bill- as well as at the output-level. At the bill-level, to bring a popular initiative to a vote that supports their interests, oppressed groups must be familiar with the procedure, draft the bill, and gather signatures. Depending on the signature requirements, this might already involve using networks to find influential allies with human and financial resources, for example interest groups or (opposition) parties. Similar mechanisms are at work to initiate a veto referendum on a parliamentary bill. For top-down votes on bills supporting their interests, oppressed groups need enough members of parliament (MPs) that are either part of the group or in another way motivated to draft such a bill and organize a parliamentary majority in favor of bringing it to the ballot. This applies to mandatory bills as well. At the output-level, to gain a majority for a bill supporting their interests or to prevent a majority for a bill disadvantaging them, oppressed groups again need powerful allies and networks, resources for campaigning, and access to media. Especially for those groups that are perceived as not belonging by a majority of voters, effective campaigns are required to counter negative stereotypes, while low SES groups may need convincing calls for solidarity even though this might involve financial costs for others. In many of these regards, the opponents of oppressed groups potentially have advantages.

2.2.2 Other Stages of the Direct Democratic Process

Beyond the scope of this dissertation are the so-called indirect effects of direct democracy – bills that are either adopted or not adopted by the legislature to prevent a direct democratic vote. In this case, the mere existence of direct democratic options affects legislation in at least four ways. First, because parliament may soften or even drop measures to avoid a veto referendum. Second, because parliament behaves similarly to avoid defeat in a mandatory vote. Third, because parliament includes additional measures it assumes to be popular to pass a mandatory vote. Fourth, because parliament agrees to adopt measures demanded by an initiative in exchange for the initiators withdrawing from the direct democratic vote. These pre-ballot scenarios can be highly influential for legislation in terms of the interests of oppressed groups – either supporting or disadvantaging them, depending on how legislators perceive the likely voting behavior of the electorate (e.g., Kousser & McCubbins, 2005; Matsusaka, 2014; Morel, 2001). Therefore, while this dissertation focuses on what happens at the ballot, future research that analyzes the stages before the vote is necessary to comprehensively understand the full implications of direct democratic options for oppressed groups.

The focus on direct democratic bills and outputs also excludes an investigation of the real or measurable outcomes of these votes – which might deviate significantly from the bills' content. This next step towards an encompassing evaluation of the topic requires in-depth analysis of which bills are actually implemented and how, as well as their mid- to long-term effects for oppressed groups. This would include, for example, an investigation of the important role bureaucracy plays in implementing laws (e.g., Boswell, 2016), or possible changes to adopted bills by parliament as part of the process of implementation (Lupia & Matsusaka, 2004).

The following section deals with theoretical reasons supplied in the literature for why direct democracy in general could either result in a *Tyranny of the Majority* or might in fact empower oppressed groups. Afterwards, I discuss different potential implications based on the specific oppressed group affected by a bill as well as based on characteristics of the direct democratic vote and on socio-economic circumstances at the time and in the country of the vote.

2.3 Direct Democracy and the Tyranny of the Majority

Before discussing potential explaining variables for the probability of pro- and contra-bills and -outputs, I provide an overview of the theoretical arguments for why direct democracy might disadvantage versus empower oppressed groups.

2.3.1 Reasons to Expect a Tyranny of the Majority

First of all, it is important to mention that *Tyranny of the Majority* in this regard means a potential discriminatory majority at the polls that puts the interests of oppressed groups at risk in direct democratic votes (see also Vatter & Danaci, 2010). The U.S. Founding Fathers' representative democracy might well have been afraid of the lower-class masses overthrowing the political elite in majoritarian popular votes. However, today's understanding in research on direct democracy on the contrary involves (for instance) the possibility of better off groups mobilizing a majority of voters to discriminate against low SES groups, or of politically powerful actors diminishing the influence of their less powerful opponents.

Indeed, concerns about the dangers of majoritarian decision-making for oppressed groups were one of the main reasons for establishing a representative system in the U.S. as well as for implementing a separation of power and emphasizing the Bill of Rights (Eule, 1990; Gamble, 1997). In contrast, direct democracy is said to entail the danger that racial beliefs, for example, are directly translated into policies in the case of votes affecting non-citizens or Blacks. Even in the 19th century, a number of votes excluded free Blacks and limited Black immigration to the U.S.; today, a homogenous middle-class electorate might use direct democracy to prevent greater heterogeneity. In addition, direct democratic campaigns are often criticized for exploiting prejudices and oversimplifying topics (Bell, 1978; Eule, 1990; Kobach, 1993). This should affect classic oppressed groups especially.

Other critiques of direct democracy point to its potential ability to prevent the contestation of opinions and complicate the revision of decisions. As Tocqueville put it, "as long as the majority is uncertain, people speak; but as soon as the majority has irrevocably decided, everyone is silent and friends as well as enemies then seem to climb on board together." (Tocqueville, 2012, p. 417). In direct democracy, the direct translation of opinions into laws would leave room for demagogy – "the majority's passions" according to Tocqueville (2012, p. 415) – , which could then pave the way for tyranny (Lacey, 2021; Lafont, 2020; Miller, 2016; Urbinati, 2014). Following this, especially direct democratic votes on matters of polity (in this case affecting mostly political groups) should be handled with caution. Another common criticism, which could affect low SES groups in particular, is the large influence of resourceful groups in direct democracy and the prevalence of established actors (Lacey, 2021; Parkinson, 2020) – although Gerber (1999) points to the more conservative influence of economic groups. Bellamy (2018) criticizes direct democracy for ignoring the plurality in the opinions of individuals and groups, and even accuses it of always resulting in domination. According to Haskell (2001), the dichotomous choices offered in direct democratic votes could disregard historically vulnerable oppressed groups. In a similar vein, Eule (1990) calls for increased judicial review of initiatives and veto referenda that repeal parliamentary decisions, as the lack of representative filters in direct democracy put oppressed groups' rights at risk. Following that, Kobach (1993) names the absence of a bill of rights in Switzerland as one reason why oppressed groups are particularly vulnerable in Swiss direct democratic votes.

In contrast to these risks of direct democracy, critiques frequently mention that the representative democracy ideal encompasses several mechanisms for protecting oppressed groups: if MPs vote in public, they have to justify their decisions and therefore should avoid openly racist motivations and discriminatory voting targeting classic oppressed groups. Electoral incentives to protect oppressed groups in an MP's district might add to that effect in first-past-the-post systems. In hearings, MPs might be confronted with representatives of oppressed groups and their interests, voices that are easily missed or actively shouted down in public debates. In addition, the diversity of parliament itself might raise awareness of the interests of oppressed groups among MPs. Hearings and the necessity to compromise to ensure widespread support often result in multiple changes to bills during the long parliamentary process until they are enacted. This could offer several opportunities for oppressed groups to influence the content of the final bill and veto harmful proposals. Because representatives might need the support of their colleagues who represent oppressed groups for other bills, there is an incentive to act on their behalf if interests of these oppressed groups are concerned. MPs are in aggregate also better educated and more involved in international relations than the average citizen, ideally making discrimination of oppressed groups less probable (Christmann & Danaci, 2012; Vatter & Danaci, 2010). Without these checks, which are absent in direct democracy, a *Tyranny of the Majority* that seriously endangers the rights and interests of oppressed groups may be more likely to arise (Bell, 1978; Bellamy, 2018; Eule, 1990; Gamble, 1997; Gerber, 1999; Haider-Markel et al., 2007; Haskell, 2001; Lewis, 2013; Merkel, 2011; Moeckli, 2018; Schmidt, 2010).

Finally, Young herself criticizes the ideal of the civic public promoted by many participatory democrats for excluding women and other groups that are perceived as different, because it prioritizes rationality and universalism. In contrast, she argues for inclusion in a way that acknowledges and respects differences (Young, 1990). This corresponds to Bellamy's (2018) critique of direct democracy as ignoring plurality, mentioned above.

2.3.2 Reasons to Expect Empowerment

However, supporters of direct democracy stress its potential to empower oppressed groups instead. Especially those groups lacking access to representatives might be given the opportunity to bring their issues onto the agenda in bottom-up votes, and rally support for their cause. Even if they do not win in the direct democratic vote, the mere fact of the public discussing their interests might trigger progress (e.g., Lacey, 2021; Leemann, 2015; Serdült & Welp, 2012; Stojanović, 2021). In the same vein as Lafont's (2020) discussion of the right to legal contestation as empowering citizens to put a topic on the public agenda and enable discussion about arguments in support of and against certain opinions, direct democracy might act as an instrument of empowerment as well.

Similarly, direct democratic options are said to often entail mechanisms to reverse previous direct democratic decisions, thereby countering the above-mentioned fears of harmful, definite votes (Trechsel, 2010). The veto referendum was actually introduced in Switzerland as a mechanism to protect oppressed groups: in the case that parliament adopts a bill that harms their interests, if a group's vote is unified against it and able to raise skepticism among some members of the majority, oppressed groups could veto the bill and thereby protect themselves. In addition, direct democratic votes would prevent the consolidation of fixed majorities in a society, because everyone is said to be a member of the majority on some issues and a member of the minority on others (Kobach, 1993). Finally, literature on political representation argues that descriptive representation in parliaments enhances substantive representation of oppressed groups' interests because shared experiences result in MPs pushing for policies supporting these groups (Allen, 2021; Mansbridge, 1999). Involving as many groups in political decision-making as possible via direct democratic votes would approximate an ideal of descriptive representation. It should therefore lead to the adoption of bills improving the position of groups often excluded from parliamentary decision-making, as their shared experiences are brought into the process of lawmaking.

As the next chapter presents in more detail, previous empirical research finds evidence for direct democracy both disadvantaging oppressed groups and empowering them. These contrasting findings mostly stem from differences in research design – the topics under investigation; whether vote results or the mere existence of direct democratic options are analyzed; and the countries, states and timeframes under analysis. The encompassing comparative analyses in this thesis will resolve these issues and provide reliable results on the merits and downsides of direct democracy for oppressed groups.

2.3.3 Different Implications for Different Oppressed Groups

In addition to the different findings mentioned above, studies from Switzerland suggest that the fate of oppressed groups in direct democracy might depend on the characteristics of the group affected by a vote. The following section lays out expectations about which oppressed groups might be in particular danger from direct democratic votes by discussing three different group characteristics: ingroups/outgroups, size, and resources.

2.3.3.1 Ingroups and Outgroups – the Role of Attitudes

Not every oppressed group that has experienced discrimination in a long distant past is necessarily still discriminated against by direct democratic outputs today. Therefore, for the timeframe analyzed in this dissertation (1990-2015) it is necessary to identify oppressed groups towards which discrimination is more probable than towards others. For this purpose, research from Switzerland suggests a crucial differentiation: the discriminating effect of direct democracy could depend on the status of the oppressed group as an ingroup or an outgroup in the respective society (Vatter & Danaci, 2010).

This builds on assumptions of the theory of social identities: members of a group see their membership as part of their identity and therefore frame their group (the so-called "ingroup") as positively as possible, above all in comparison with other groups (so-called "outgroups"). Discriminating against outgroups in any way is assumed to increase one's self-esteem and decrease social uncertainty (especially if the outgroup is perceived as a threat). It might also be used as a proof of loyalty towards the ingroup (Gibson & Gouws, 2000; Hogg & Abrams, 2003; Weldon, 2006). In a similar vein, supporting benefits for the ingroup or denying them for the outgroup would make the groups more distinguishable and enhance the status of the ingroup – thereby facilitating identification with it and favoring a positive self-image (Billig & Tajfel, 1973; Haselswerdt, 2020; Shayo, 2009; Tajfel, 1970).

Following this, in direct democratic votes we might expect there to be an incentive to disadvantage groups that are perceived as outgroups by large parts of the electorate. Taking these theoretical assumptions into account, part of this dissertation is testing whether direct democratic decisions really have different effects on oppressed groups perceived as ingroups than on those perceived as outgroups, a topic that has received only little attention in the literature so far. Yet, which groups are perceived as outgroups differs between countries and changes over time. For instance, the rise in post-materialist values has resulted in increasing support for the rights of members of the LGBTQ+ community during the last decades – but at the same time provoked a backlash in some Central Eastern European countries (Guasti & Bustikova, 2020). Linguistic groups are another example; they are part of the national identity in Switzerland, while tensions are much greater in Belgium (Bellamy, 2018). These differences require me to include attitudes as a factor in my analyses instead of assuming certain groups to always be outgroups and therefore disadvantaged in direct democratic votes in general.

2.3.3.2 Size of Oppressed Groups

The majoritarian logic of direct democratic votes implies that the size of the group affected by a vote should matter – larger groups should benefit more often, while smaller groups are at a disadvantage. The use of the term minorities in research on a possible *Tyranny of the Majority* in direct democracy points to the important role of group size (e.g., Lewis, 2013). For instance, women make up roughly half of the electorate. Therefore, it should be easier for them to collect the necessary signatures to bring a bill to the ballot that supports their interests, as well as to gain a majority of votes. A similar logic could apply to broad bills guaranteeing fundamental rights or banning discrimination, as large parts of the electorate would benefit from them. Following this line of thought, one could expect people of low socio-economic status to benefit from direct democratic votes as well, at least in countries where wealth is unequally distributed and this group represents a large part of the electorate. Yet, this leads us to the important role of resources in direct democratic votes.

2.3.3.3 Resources of Oppressed Groups

Drafting a direct democratic bill, bringing it to the ballot, mobilizing voters to support it, and finally winning the vote requires resources – money, but also time, education, civic skills, networks, and access to the media. Therefore, established, resourceful actors are at an advantage in the direct democratic arena (e.g., Lacey, 2021; Parkinson, 2020). People of low socio-economic status, on the other hand, lack these resources, and thereby are not only less likely to benefit from direct democratic votes, but also more likely to be put at further disadvantage by them. Unless they can find resourceful allies, they cannot compete with large campaigns against their interests. In addition, voting itself entails higher costs for such groups, resulting in lower turnout (Schäfer & Schoen, 2013; Töller & Vollmer, 2013). When it comes to topics such as the education system or healthcare, direct democratic votes therefore potentially put the interests of low SES groups in danger, regardless of the groups' size.

Added to this is the fact that measures to support low SES groups often come at a financial price, while (to give just one example) extending the rights of the LGBTQ+ community less frequently involves material costs. As a result, whereas postmaterialist values are spreading in many European countries (e.g., Inglehart & Norris, 2017) and populations are becoming increasingly willing to grant these rights, they might be far less willing to pay higher taxes. Especially when people of medium or high SES believe poor people are poor because they are lazy, the better off might be inclined to think they earned exclusive access to high-class education or healthcare. This type of potential for discrimination in direct democracy might further contribute to what Young describes as oppression of exploitation and marginalization (Young, 1990).

Summing up the last three sections, which groups can we expect to be in greatest danger from direct democracy, and which groups might benefit from it? Table 1 gives examples of different combinations of group characteristics and expectations about their fate in direct democratic ballots.

Whereas Table 1 for practical reasons displays only the interaction of two characteristics at the same time, a combination of three characteristics is of course possible as well. As a result, the groups probably most at risk are

Table 1: Group Characteristics and Direct Democracy

		Size		Resources		Ingroup/Outgroup	
		Large	Small	High	Low	Ingroup	Outgroup
Size	Large	+					
	Small		–				
Resources	High	+ +	+ –	+			
	Low	+ –	– –		–		
Ingroup / Outgroup	Ingroup	+ +	+ –	+ +	+ –	+	
	Outgroup	+ –	– –	+ –	– –		–

+, ++ = might benefit; –, –– = might be disadvantaged; + – = no clear expectations

those combining a small group size with low resources and perceived as an outgroup by large parts of the electorate. An example might be non-citizens in xenophobic countries without a large community of rich non-citizens. Another example could be low SES groups in meritocratic societies where poverty is not widespread. In contrast, large, resourceful groups that are perceived as ingroups are those most likely to benefit from direct democracy. A large group of well-equipped women in countries with high gender equality could be an example of this – although these women could hardly be described as oppressed according to Young's definition.

In reality, most groups fall in the middle categories, combining beneficial with disadvantaging characteristics. To return to the example mentioned above, low SES groups might be large and even represent a majority in a country – but given that they lack resources to use direct democratic tools effectively, they might come under pressure anyway. In contrast, members of the LGBTQ+ community might be in a numerical minority. However, a significant number of them may be well equipped and thus successfully use direct democracy to extend their rights in tolerant societies.

Additionally, the examples illustrate that presumably much depends on country-specific factors such as attitudes among the electorate. Therefore, clear-cut assumptions like "group X always benefits, group Y always loses" are impossible to make in a comparative analysis. Nonetheless, for the reasons formulated above, we can expect low SES groups to be at a disadvantage in direct democracy, as they by definition lack beneficial resources. Regarding the other groups, attitudes towards them are likely to be decisive – with women probably at an advantage given the sheer size of their group. As characteristics like size and resources differ for groups depending on the country and the year of a vote, I do not have data for every example and therefore cannot fully analyze their impact. This is also why there will be no hypotheses on impacts for the clusters of oppressed groups besides low SES groups here. However, data on attitudes towards the group affected by a direct democratic bill is available for some votes and will be investigated. The impact of resources will be accounted for in a set of hypotheses on bills and outputs for low SES groups. Finally, the interplay between ingroup/outgroup, resources and size will serve as a heuristic to explain patterns in the descriptive analysis.

Table 1 will also serve as a framework to evaluate the concept of oppressed groups in direct democracy in Chapter 9. If these characteristics prove to be decisive for the fate of oppressed groups in direct democracy, the concept will be refined for research on direct democracy accordingly. If other patterns emerge in the analyses, this calls for a search for alternative explanations, based on which the concept's use for the direct democratic context can be evaluated. Both routes will provide an essential evaluation of the use of the concept of oppressed groups in research on direct democracy.

Besides the characteristics of the oppressed group affected in a vote, I also expect the characteristics of the direct democratic vote itself to influence the bill's content and outputs for oppressed groups – effects that can actually be analyzed based on the dataset I will build. Outlined below, the characteristics analyzed in this dissertation are the direct democratic instrument in play, the quora requirements, and whether a vote result is binding.

2.3.4 Explaining Variables for the Probability of Pro- and Contra-Bills and -Outputs: Institutions

Before turning to socio-economic variables that might be influential regarding the implications of direct democratic votes for oppressed groups, this section deals with the institutional characteristics of the vote itself. As mentioned below, there are numerous theoretical reasons to expect the specific direct democratic instrument used, the existence of quora requirements, and whether a vote result has to be turned into law to influence its impact.

2.3.4.1 Direct Democratic Instruments

First, I assume bills and outputs to differ depending on the direct democratic instrument used in a vote. As mentioned above, mandatory bills such as constitutional amendments are usually of a more general kind, without obvious material costs for implementation. As a result, they might more often support oppressed groups than work to their disadvantage. Following the theoretical reasoning of bottom-up votes as instruments of empowerment for extra-parliamentary actors and top-down votes as instruments of already established parliamentary majorities, the former should be more protective of the interests of oppressed groups than the latter (Eder & Magin, 2008; Kobach, 1993). In addition, pro-bills should be more likely to succeed in bottom-up votes than in mandatory or top-down votes, because a unified minority was already necessary to fulfill the requirements to initiate the vote. Assuming voters to be risk averse, initiatives should be less likely to succeed than veto referenda, since whereas the former aim to change the status quo, the latter aim to preserve it (see also Kriesi, 2005).

2.3.4.2 Quora as Possible Mechanisms of Protection

Second, while many of the protective mechanisms of representative democracy are absent in direct democratic votes, quora are one way to increase hurdles for a *Tyranny of the Majority*. These might include the requirement for a certain percentage of the electorate to participate in the vote (turnout quorum), the requirement for a certain percentage of the electorate to approve the bill (approval quorum), the requirement for approval in a majority of territorial regions ("Ständemehr" in Switzerland), or even a combination of these. In order for a bill to pass, it potentially needs the support of the group affected by it (e.g., Merkel & Ritzi, 2017). As a result, for example Eder and Magin (2008) expect quora to protect oppressed groups.

2.3.4.3 Mixed Expectations about (Non-)Binding Vote Results

Third, a final important vote characteristic under investigation in this dissertation is whether the vote result is binding, i.e., whether a majority of voters makes the final decision (binding) or whether another institution (e.g., parliament) has the final decision-making power (non-binding) (see also Jäske & Setälä, 2019; Merkel & Ritzi, 2017). Besides the electoral costs of not implementing a successful bill even in a non-binding vote, both types of votes connect differently to representative decision-making, at least in theory. Whereas binding vote results substitute for a representative decision, non-binding ones must overcome the parliamentary hurdle. Even if we assume the electoral costs of not adopting them to be too high in general, this "bindingness" signals to voters the consequences of their vote choice. Regarding the implications for oppressed groups, this might work in both directions. On the one hand, a vote result not being binding could protect oppressed groups by placing representative mechanisms prior to its ultimate adoption. On the other hand, oppressed groups might be less motivated to initiate, campaign for and vote for a bill if the result is not binding. In this case, bills supporting the interests of oppressed groups would be less commonly adopted at the direct democratic ballot. Additionally, discriminatory voting behavior might be more common when voters perceive the results of their vote choices as not being binding. Therefore, I do not have clear-cut theoretical assumptions about the effect of this vote characteristic.

2.3.5 Explaining Variables for the Probability of Pro- and Contra-Bills and -Outputs: Socio-Economic Variables

Finally, I expect several socio-economic variables at the country-level to affect whether oppressed groups benefit at the ballot. Chapter 3 presents previous research on this and related findings that will serve to inform my hypotheses. For now, I outline a few theoretical arguments as to why these variables could be important.

The first is the level of academic (tertiary) *education* in a country at the time of a vote. According to Christmann and Danaci (2012), higher educated people tend to be more tolerant. This should then work to benefit oppressed groups in direct democratic votes. In contrast, one could argue that higher educated people might be reluctant to share their privileges – in this case, a higher level of tertiary education could result in more contra-bills and – outputs. Whatever the effects will be, education is an important variable to consider in research on oppressed groups in direct democracy.

The second socio-economic variable of potential influence is the level of *economic growth* in a country at the time of a vote. Here again, two different mechanisms might come into play. On the one hand, in times of economic growth, people are better off and have more to share, presumably making them more willing to support oppressed groups. In addition, with their material needs satisfied, people might turn to post-materialist values such as tolerance (Inglehart & Norris, 2017). On the other hand, and similar to the reasoning outlined above, people might not be willing to share the benefits of economic growth with other people they potentially perceive as less deserving. Contributing to that might be that people who own more also have more to lose – potentially resulting in them being more protective of what they have.

Finally, the level of *ethnic fractionalization* in a country at the time of a vote might affect the experiences of oppressed groups in direct democracy. Higher fractionalization might result in more groups fighting for their interests and being able to put them on the direct democratic agenda. Through coalitions with other groups, they also might be able to win at the ballot or defeat contra-bills. Assumptions like these lead scholars such as Landemore (2020) to expect participatory practices to be of special value in fractionalized societies, promoting the integration of groups such as linguistic minorities (Stojanović, 2021). Yet, higher fractionalization could also increase tensions between groups and prevent rallying behind a common cause, thereby decreasing chances for any direct democratic bill to gain a majority of votes.

Taken together, these theoretical considerations about the effects of socio-economic variables do not result in clear-cut expectations. In the next chapter, I will present previous research on these and related mechanisms, thereby providing the ground for the formulation of hypotheses in Chapter 4. Before turning to the state of the art, the following section summarizes the key points in Chapter 2.

2.4 Summary

Summing up, this dissertation establishes new conceptual ground by applying the concept of oppressed groups to the analysis of direct democracy and assessing the use of the concept in research on direct democracy based on empirical results. Compared to previous research, which mostly used the term minorities, this has several advantages: first, Young's five faces of oppression and recent operationalizations of the concept provide a clear-cut definition of which groups can count as oppressed and might be in particular danger of being tyrannized by a majority in direct democracy. Second, the concept is broad enough to include a variety of groups that might not be in a numerical minority but could still be at a potential disadvantage in direct democracy. Group size is one important characteristic among others – low SES groups might lose out in direct democracy even if they constitute a large part of the electorate. Resulting from this is an encompassing analysis of direct democratic bills and outputs. Finally, the variety in oppressed groups allows investigation of broader patterns as well as the possible differences between groups, thereby hinting at which group characteristics might be beneficial and which might be disadvantaging in direct democratic processes. In addition, theoretical considerations about the impact of various institutional, attitudinal, and socio-economic explaining variables provide the ground for identifying relevant factors for the success of oppressed groups in direct democracy in my analyses. The following chapter presents the state of the art in research on direct democracy and oppressed groups.

3 State of the Art: Findings on Direct Democracy and Oppressed Groups

Research on the relationship between direct democracy and the interests of oppressed groups up to now focuses mainly on the U.S. and Switzerland and results are mixed. In the following, I first present the findings on negative and positive implications for oppressed groups. Second, I present findings on possibly influential factors – i.e., institutions, attitudes, and the socio-economic characteristics of the electorate. Afterwards, gaps in existing research that this dissertation addresses are identified.

3.1 Negative Implications of Direct Democracy for Oppressed Groups

Are theoretical claims about the danger of a *Tyranny of the Majority* backed by empirical investigations? One body of literature, mostly focusing on the U.S. and Switzerland, indeed primarily found that direct democracy had negative implications for classic oppressed groups and low SES groups.

Looking at Switzerland, there are some famous direct democratic defeats for classic oppressed groups that are often quoted by critics of popular decision-making. For example, Merkel refers to the Swiss referenda on the prohibition of minarets and easier deportation of criminal immigrants or asylum seekers to underscore his claim that direct democracy is dangerous for minorities (Merkel, 2011, 2015). Additionally, French Swiss are often outvoted by German Swiss in controversial referenda, and referenda on naturalizations up to 2003 decreased the probability of applications being accepted[8] (Helbling & Kriesi, 2004; Schmidt, 2010). In the latter case, the clash of two different norms becomes apparent: the protection of the interests of non-citizens as an oppressed group on the one hand, and the norm of citizenship on the other hand, which naturally needs criteria of exclusion if you do not want to grant citizenship to everybody living in a country. In a similar vein, a more recent investigation of naturalizations in Swiss municipalities between 1990 and 2010 shows a significant increase in naturalization rates after a shift from direct democratic to representative decision-

---

8 Compared to cities where other procedures were used to decide on naturalizations.

making. Expert interviews reveal that politicians shy away from discriminatory behavior as they have to justify their decisions – in contrast to voters in referenda. This supports one of the main theoretical arguments about mechanisms of protection in representative democracy. Analyzing direct democratic procedures relating to naturalizations more closely reveals that the applicant's country of origin had the largest effect, whereas language skills or how well s/he is integrated played almost no role. Especially applicants from Turkey and Yugoslavia, as the most marginalized groups, suffered most from this discriminatory behavior. Consequently, the effect of switching the procedure was larger in municipalities with a higher level of xenophobia (measured by the local vote share of the right-wing Swiss Peoples Party (SVP)) (Hainmueller & Hangartner, 2019). Regarding people of low socioeconomic status, findings on lower tax rates and state expenditure in Swiss cantons with more direct democratic options hint towards negative implications of direct democracy for people who depend on social welfare as well (Feld & Kirchgässner, 2000).

In Germany, legal rules make openly discriminatory direct democratic votes difficult. Yet, interests of oppressed groups can also be endangered in more subtle ways, especially when it comes to low SES groups. Schäfer and Schoen (2013) suggest that the benefits of more opportunities to participate through direct democratic procedures mostly result in more influence for groups that are influential anyway, at the expense of others. As an example, they name the bottom-up vote on the Hamburg school reform in 2010, where disproportionate participation prevented school reform fostering equal opportunities.[9] A case study from Germany by Töller and Vollmer (2013) also shows that resourceful groups are better able to enforce their interests and hinder redistribution – mirroring the negative effect of direct democracy on redistribution in Switzerland since the late 1990s (Feld et al., 2010).

Direct democracy seems to have slowed down the accommodation of classic oppressed groups in Liechtenstein – especially female suffrage, which was not introduced until 1984. However, there is no proof of discrimination and a backlash on rights, as institutional hurdles to do so are high. Above all, checking the constitutionality of ballot proposals is important here, which does not take place in Switzerland (Marxer, 2012).

Most analyses that found direct democracy had overtly negative implications for classic oppressed groups and low SES groups, however, stem from the U.S. context. The first, widely-recognized analysis on the topic by Gamble (1997) seemed to confirm theoretical concerns for the U.S., with the

---

9   Participation was disproportionately high in districts with high income and low unemployment rates and disproportionately low in districts with low income, high unemployment rates and many non-citizen inhabitants. This led to success for the opponents of the reform, which would have raised equality of opportunity in the education system for pupils of all social backgrounds.

great majority of initiatives resulting in losses for classic oppressed groups. Most of the time, initiators thereby hindered measures of minority protection by parliament or government. Following this track, a number of other studies found overall negative implications of direct democratic options and decisions for classic oppressed groups in the U.S. (Haider-Markel et al., 2007; Heußner, 2012; Lewis, 2013; Moore & Ravishankar, 2012). For example, conservative religious groups in the U.S. used as many as 39 direct democratic votes only between 1998 and 2015 to ban same-sex marriage. Simon et al. (2018) provide evidence that these groups are especially successful in mobilizing opponents of same-sex marriage – support for bans in votes exceeds support in surveys, and it actually decreases with rising voter turnout. In addition, direct democratic campaigns are found to enforce negative stereotypes about oppressed groups and portray them as a threat, increasingly also targeting institutions protecting their rights (Donovan, 2013; Donovan & Tolbert, 2013; Haskell, 2001).

Using the direct democratic experience of California as an example, where campaigns would poison the social climate and infrastructure would deteriorate as a consequence of direct democratic decisions, Haskell (2001) states that oppressed groups refrain to use direct democracy to fight for their interests. In contrast, these groups successfully use parliamentary venues to do so (Haskell, 2001). Regarding low SES groups, it is important to note the large influence of established, resourceful actors in direct democratic campaigns – especially in the U.S., but also in Switzerland. Therefore, direct democratic votes far from automatically present an opportunity for agenda-setting by groups whose voices are unheard in the representative system – a function that is often prescribed to direct democracy by its supporters (Parkinson, 2020). Rosenbluth and Shapiro (2018), building on the Californian experience, even observe that ballot initiatives prevent parties from enacting policies that represent all voters' interests comprehensively, as issues are taken off the parliamentary agenda and decided in ways that promote organized interests.

To sum up, there are a number of negative findings on the effect of direct democracy on the interests of classic oppressed groups and low SES groups – mainly in the U.S., but also in Switzerland, Germany, and Liechtenstein. Nevertheless, there are also positive results for oppressed groups from direct democratic votes. The following subchapter presents these findings.

3.2 Positive Implications of Direct Democracy for Oppressed Groups

In Switzerland, there are a number of positive findings concerning the outputs of direct democratic votes on civil rights and minority issues as well as on the frequency of French and Italian Swiss being outvoted (Benedikter, 2012; Bolliger, 2007; Frey & Goette, 1998). In addition, according to a Swiss study, even when oppressed groups lose in direct democratic votes, their interests are at least well voiced by the media – although newspapers often focus on statements of established political actors instead of presenting members of the affected group as advocates of their own affairs (Marcinkowski & Donk, 2012). In more general terms, Moeckli (2018) states that Swiss direct democracy, and especially the threat of bottom-up votes, has led to an early integration of minorities into the political system. This corresponds to Kriesi's (2005) conclusion that direct democracy in Switzerland did not lead to uncontrollable risks, but instead opens up new opportunities for participation while at the same time preserving a key role for elites in the political system.

According to Stojanović (2021), direct democracy contains several features that work to integrate the different Swiss linguistic groups. First, bottom-up votes give voice to minorities' interests. Second, frequent voting brings cross-cutting cleavages to the surface, which prevents an 'us vs. them' rhetoric (see also Kobach, 1993). Third, regular decisions by 'the people' enhance the feeling of being a common demos. Finally, nationwide debates and campaigns aiming at cross-regional coalitions work to integrate the country horizontally. While direct democracy is not the only reason for the stability of Swiss democracy, Stojanović calls it a very important one, structuring other institutions like the system of concordance and the emergence of multilingual parties and interest groups. His four case studies of direct democratic votes that were particularly salient for linguistic groups in the Swiss multilingual cantons point to the opportunity for ethnolinguistic tensions which are driven by the media, while the secret ballot furthers aversion-based voting. However, Stojanović stresses that these were the only examples he could find that caused tensions among the many Swiss votes, that even there the tensions did not escalate, and that one case also serves as an example of how the threat of a direct democratic vote can result in the protection of linguistic groups in parliamentary bills. So, whereas particularly sensitive issues might be better decided by parliament, direct democracy in general could enhance democratic stability in multilingual countries by supporting oppressed groups such as linguistic minorities (Stojanović, 2021).

Turning to other European countries, an investigation of recent referenda in Ireland by Kissane (2012) reveals no majoritarian outcomes but a strengthening of minority rights. In a similar vein, Pállinger (2012) states that no important direct democratic decisions discriminated against ethnic and political minorities in Hungary up to 2012.

At least when it comes to the Finnish Citizens' Initiative, there is evidence that direct democratic options are able to mobilize otherwise politically inactive groups – in this case, young citizens (Christensen et al., 2017). This might hint at the potential to mobilize oppressed groups in direct democratic votes as well, ideally increasing the probability of pro- while decreasing the probability of contra-outputs. Likewise, Kim (2019) finds the existence of direct democratic meetings at the local level increasing female turnout in Sweden after the introduction of universal suffrage in the early 20th century, as this signaled to women that their opinion is valued as much as men's.

As noted above, conditions for the protection of classic oppressed groups in direct democracy are much better in Germany than in Switzerland or the U.S.: fundamental rights cannot be changed and the federal constitutional court assesses the constitutionality of every initiative before a vote. Therefore, no rights of classic oppressed groups have been taken away by direct democracy at the German Länder level between 1946 and 2008, with some votes actually increasing protection (Magin et al., 2008; Vatter & Danaci, 2010).[10]

Even in the U.S., there are some findings on positive direct democratic outputs for classic oppressed groups. Analyzing all direct democratic votes in California between 1978 and 2000, according to Hajnal, Gerber, and Louch (2002) Latinos, Blacks and Asian Americans are more likely to be on the winning side than to lose (although they are less likely to win than whites). The only significant difference they find is between Latinos and non-Latinos in votes that target Latinos' rights (Hajnal et al., 2002).

Questioning some of the positive evaluations of direct democracy in Switzerland outlined above, Barry (1975) notes that it is not the direct democratic votes themselves that prevent conflicts between socio-cultural groups in Switzerland, but the decision of the Swiss people not to use them as instruments of oppression. In and of themselves, initiatives and referenda are the opposite of amicable agreements. In his view, the party system not being structured along the socio-cultural cleavage further diminishes the potential for conflict (Barry, 1975). In addition, Bolliger points to the special role of linguistic groups in Switzerland, which are seen as part of the national identity and are therefore constitutionally protected. This would limit the generalizability of his results to other oppressed groups (Bolliger, 2007). Stojanović (2021) raises this point as well and also mentions that direct democracy in Switzerland has had a long time to evolve – successful export of Swiss insti-

---

10 Nevertheless, this does not guarantee that minority rights will not be targeted by direct democratic votes in Germany in the future. As Lewis points out, if an initiative enjoyed broad public support, courts might be reluctant to stop it (Lewis, 2013).

tutions to other multilingual societies is therefore far from guaranteed, and measures to protect minorities would have to be taken. These arguments hint at the important role of contextual factors, outlined in more detail in the next subchapter. Nevertheless, Switzerland seems to have a better record of respecting the interests of classic oppressed groups via direct democracy than the U.S.[11]

Summing up, direct democratic votes have had positive as well as negative implications for oppressed groups in Western democracies to date. With a heavy focus on Switzerland and the U.S., these studies mainly analyzed impacts on classic oppressed groups. In addition to the research outlined above, some findings suggest that implications of direct democracy for oppressed groups are more nuanced, depending on various factors. The following sections present results on institutional, attitudinal, and socio-economic influences.

3.3 Explaining Variables

3.3.1 Institutional Effects

A first institutional factor that might be influential is the *direct democratic instrument* in use. Theoretically, Eder and Magin (2008) expect bottom-up instruments to be friendlier towards oppressed groups than top-down ones, as outlined in Chapter 2. Likewise, Vatter (2007) states that, above all, veto referenda and popular initiatives offer less integrated but well-organized groups channels of influence in Switzerland. If we assume that left-wing parties and interest groups pursue more oppressed group-friendly policies, Kriesi's (2005) finding that popular initiatives were mostly used by the left in Switzerland in the 1980s and 1990s corresponds to that assumption. According to his research, veto referenda have been used almost equally by the two ends of the Swiss political spectrum in this period, whereas they had been primarily an instrument of the right wing during the immediate post-war period (Kriesi, 2005). In contrast, Vatter and Danaci (2010) and Gamble (1997) empirically find that veto referenda and popular initiatives significantly hinder minority protection in Switzerland and the U.S. compared to mandatory votes. Similarly, bottom-up votes produced more contra-equality

---

11 Concerning a possible explanation for this pattern, Lewis mentions the necessity to present initiatives to parliament before voting on them in Switzerland – which enables parliament to create its own, often more successful draft and thereby puts some representative hurdles in the way of a potential *Tyranny of the Majority* compared to the U.S. process (Lewis, 2013).

outputs and fewer pro-equality ones than top-down and mandatory votes did in Europe up to 2015 (Geißel et al., 2019a).

A second possibly influential factor are *quora* that must be fulfilled in order for a direct democratic bill to be adopted. Eder and Magin (2008) expect high thresholds to protect oppressed groups because for the passing of the bill these groups have to vote for it as well in order to fulfill the quorum. The case of a direct democratic vote in Slovakia in 2015 points to this potential protective effect. When measures to ban same-sex marriage, adoption by same-sex couples, and sex education were put to a vote, supporters of LGBTQ+ interests successfully called for abstention. As a result, although a large majority voted in favor of the bill, it failed to reach the necessary turnout quorum of 50 % (Guasti & Bustikova, 2020). Yet, this can also work against the interests of oppressed groups if they promote an initiative and their opponents successfully campaign to boycott the vote (Vatter & Danaci, 2010). Comparative tests of the impact of quora do not exist thus far.

A couple of studies investigated the effect of quora on voter turnout in general, but results are mixed and it remains unclear whether high turnout benefits or disadvantages oppressed groups. Thomeczek (2021) finds a significantly negative effect of the existence of a quorum on voter turnout in all direct democratic votes in the German states between 1946 and 2019. This would imply that bills are less likely to be adopted when a quorum is in place. Yet when controlling for various other factors, the effect fails to reach significance (Thomeczek, 2021). Similarly, Marx and Leininger detect a negative effect of approval quora on turnout in bottom-up votes in the German states. They contribute this mainly to the incentive for opponents of a bill to abstain from the vote if quora are in place, so the vote does not fulfill the quorum and the bill therefore is not adopted (Marx & Leininger, 2022). In a comparative analysis of all national direct democratic votes in the countries of the European Union between 1970 and 2007, Aguiar-Conraria and Magalhães (2010) detect a significant negative effect for the existence of a turnout quorum on turnout if a majority of voters supports a bill. In this case, opponents assume that the bill only fails if the quorum is not reached, presenting an incentive for them to abstain. In contrast, a turnout quorum has no significant effect on turnout if a majority rejects the proposal. Approval quora in general do not significantly affect turnout (Aguiar-Conraria & Magalhães, 2010). However, it is unclear which groups benefit from low turnout. In votes with high turnout in Switzerland, people with right-wing/conservative attitudes seem to turn out in disproportionately high numbers, putting the interests of oppressed groups at a disadvantage (Lutz, 2007). Yet, research on the policy effects of turnout in other countries is missing.

3.3.2 Attitudinal Effects

Attitudes of the electorate heavily influence voting behavior in general – a pattern that has been confirmed by some studies for direct democracy and the interests of oppressed groups as well. This includes both attitudes towards the group that is particularly affected by a direct democratic bill as well as more general liberal, conservative or populist attitudes in a constituency.

First, a number of studies from Switzerland suggest that *attitudes in the constituency towards the group concerned* by a direct democratic bill are important. First to mention this was Vatter (2007), who noted more discrimination against less integrated groups (non-citizens, supporters of rare ideologies) in the outputs of Swiss direct democratic decisions than against ethnic minorities. An extensive analysis of referenda related to classic oppressed groups in Switzerland confirms this.[12] The authors explain these findings with the theory of social identity presented in the conceptual section: upgrading one's own group and/or downgrading an outgroup – in this case by (not) discriminating against it in direct democratic votes – increases one's self-esteem. This results in a significantly better protection of Christian and well-integrated language minorities compared to non-citizens and women in Switzerland.[13] Like Gamble (1997) found for the U.S., the extension of minority rights, as well as a top-down vote or a popular initiative (in contrast to mandatory votes) decreased the probability of protection of the oppressed group significantly (Vatter & Danaci, 2010). The positive effect of direct democratic votes for in- versus outgroups in Switzerland is replicated by Vatter, Stadelmann-Steffen, and Danaci (2014). A bill affecting an ingroup, defined as a non-ethnic minority, increases the probability of pro-minority voting. In addition, the influence of education on voting behavior in referenda on minority rights is largest when rights of outgroups, defined as ethnic minorities, shall be extended, whereas education has no effect at all when a bill proposes the restriction of ingroup rights. Besides the difference the targeted group makes, the effect of education being stronger when rights of outgroups shall be extended compared to when they shall be restricted can be attributed to a status-quo bias in voting behavior (Vatter et al., 2014).

The discriminating effect against Muslims is also apparent in Christmann and Danaci's (2012) analysis of the extension of rights of religious minorities in Switzerland between 1963 and 2007, where the authors compare the results of Swiss referenda to parliamentary debates on the recognition of religious communities. If Muslims were mobilized against during the campaign,

---

12 Foreigners suffered most from discrimination, followed by language minorities, deniers of military service, women and Muslims. In contrast, Christians, Jews, homosexuals or persons with disabilities have never been discriminated against (Vatter & Danaci, 2010).
13 Women in Switzerland had no voting rights up to 1971 and are therefore considered as a discriminated "minority" in this study.

all direct democratic bills that would have extended their rights were rejected.[14] The minaret initiative was an exception insofar as it aimed at the restriction of already existing rights, whereas most anti-Muslim votes "only" prevented an extension of rights. In addition, parliament enacted stricter rules on the recognition of religious minorities if a direct democratic vote was feared (Danaci, 2012).

Zurlinden (2015) points at another reason why some outgroups might be disadvantaged in direct democratic votes: comparing small religious communities in Switzerland, she finds their opportunity to participate to be higher the more they are institutionalized and connected to the wider society. Especially Muslim and Jewish communities would shy away from public campaigning based on their current and historical experiences as marginalized groups (Zurlinden, 2015). Research on material benefits also suggests that people are more willing to grant welfare programs to groups they perceive as deserving – for example families or sick people. In contrast, support for groups perceived as less deserving (e.g. unemployed, poor, non-citizens) is less popular (Ennser-Jedenastik, 2021).

Second, and in more general terms, Milic, Rousselot, and Vatter (2014) argue that, as direct democratic decisions are supposed to mirror the median voter more closely than parliamentary ones do, the positive/negative effect for oppressed groups compared to pure representative systems depends on *how liberal/conservative* public opinion in the constituency is. This is indeed the result of a comparison between U.S. states with and without direct democratic options regarding their overall legislation on selected issues affecting classic oppressed groups, carried out by Gerber and Hug (2002).[15] The authors conclude that direct democracy is not per se hostile to oppressed groups, but increases the influence of majority preferences on pro-/anti-minority legislation. In liberal states, this leads to protection of oppressed groups, while their rights are endangered in more conservative direct democratic states (see also Lewis, 2013). The results of the only cross-national study on the topic so far (comparing minority and civil rights in 52 demo-

---

14 In the representative arena, liberal rules for religious minorities were only passed if no direct democratic vote was feared by the MPs and if those rules were embedded in a total revision. Restrictive rules were passed either a) if the possibility of a direct democratic vote or Islam were present as topics in the debate (pointing to the indirect effect of direct democracy mentioned in Chapter 2), or b) if the rules were not embedded in a total revision, the right SVP was strong and there was no debate about a popular vote. Assuming a more minority-friendly position among MPs compared to "lay" citizens, Christmann and Danaci (2012) name the embedding of liberal rules for religious minorities in a total revision as a parliamentary strategy to enforce minorities' interests despite a more conservative electorate.
15 After controlling for ideology, direct democracy alone does not have a significant effect but increases the effect of majority preferences on the existence of English-only laws and on laws protecting gays and lesbians against discrimination. This link weakens with higher signature requirements for initiatives.

cracies worldwide between 2005 and 2008) point in a similar direction. Direct democracy does not endanger or protect those rights in general, but significantly increases the influence of the median voter's preference when it comes to women's social rights and freedom of assembly (Bochsler & Hug, 2015).

The importance of attitudes is also highlighted by Christmann (2012). In her analysis of all the direct democratic votes in Switzerland between 1990 and 2010 that have been problematic in terms of fundamental rights, she finds several attitudes that significantly influence the probability that legal reasoning is given for the voting decision – assuming that legal reasoning promotes voting behavior protecting oppressed groups: legal reasoning is more likely if a person identifies with a left-wing party, regards a modern and open Switzerland as something positive, and supports equal opportunities for non-citizens. In contrast, it is less likely if someone identifies with the right-wing SVP or supports more direct democratic options. Christmann performs an experiment further investigating the relationship between reasoning and voting behavior. In the Swiss context, mentioning legal arguments in a fictional voting brochure does indeed increase the number of no-votes for bills that are problematic in terms of fundamental rights. However, there is no significant effect for reasoning in the Californian version of the experiment (Christmann, 2012).

Voting behavior in referenda is also influenced by what is operationalized as *populist attitudes*. As survey data on a Dutch referendum shows, more populist respondents not only favored direct democracy more, but were also more likely to cast an anti-establishment vote (Jacobs et al., 2018). Insofar as the assumption by Christmann and Danaci (2012) holds that the political elite is on average more liberal than citizens, this should favor votes against the interests of oppressed groups. For Germany, Grotz and Lewandowsky (2020) find that support for direct democratic instruments differs according to party affiliation: whereas supporters of the Greens and the Left prefer the introduction of a popular initiative at the federal level, right-wing AfD supporters favor mandatory votes on constitutional changes to control the establishment. However, according to Trüdinger and Bächtiger (2022), while citizens with populist attitudes are more likely to demand direct democratic options at the federal level in Germany, voters of AfD are actually less likely to cast a direct democratic vote. In contrast, voters in direct democracy are mostly those with high political interest and education and post-materialist values (Trüdinger & Bächtiger, 2022). This might actually result in direct democratic outputs in favor of oppressed groups.

A paper by Ackermann et al. (2021) investigates the opposite direction of effect – does the use of direct democratic options foster populist attitudes, thereby potentially increasing discriminatory behavior? Analyzing a survey from the German Länder, their findings indicate that the frequency of direct democratic votes does not increase populist attitudes per se. However, it does so for respondents placing themselves on the far right, while anti-elitist sentiments actually decrease with frequent votes for respondents who place themselves on the far left (Ackermann et al., 2021). These findings point to a possible negative effect of direct democracy for oppressed groups – elites have been found to be more favorable towards these groups than the general public (Christmann & Danaci, 2012), so spreading anti-elitism among the far right through direct democratic votes might increase anti-oppressed group sentiments as well.[16]

Correspondingly, populists regard direct democratic votes as representing the true "will of the people". For example in Hungary, the populist government uses direct democratic consultations to legitimize its policies, thereby further increasing xenophobia through costly media campaigns (Batory & Svensson, 2019). Although my analyses do not investigate changes in attitudes due to direct democratic votes, we should bear in mind these potential negative effects as well.

Summing up, supporters of right-wing populist parties also favor majoritarian decision-making in direct democratic votes. Likewise, populist parties demand more direct democratic options and use direct democratic votes to rally support for their policies – in the case of right-wing populists, often including discrimination against classic oppressed groups. Studies on the results of direct democratic votes for groups regarded as outgroups suggest that attitudes are not only influential in terms of whether someone supports direct democracy, but also impact the fate of classic oppressed groups in direct democracy. Results on the importance of the median voter in direct democracy further underscore the relevance of attitudes for direct democratic outputs.

---

16 According to Gherghina and Pilet (2021), previous contrasting findings on the topic might be explained by some problems in the research on populist attitudes and support for direct democracy. Besides neglecting literature on public support for direct democracy and citizens' preferences for different models of democracy as well as failing to analyze which role people envision for direct democratic decision-making in the political system, the authors criticize a common overlap between the measurement of populist attitudes and support for direct democracy, causing severe problems of tautology (Gherghina & Pilet, 2021). Consequently, Steiner and Landwehr (2018) list favor for majoritarianism as one dimension of a populist conception of democracy – a clear preference for majoritarian rule over minority interests. According to their analysis of panel data from Germany, this populist conception fosters voting for AfD. In addition, it correlates negatively with items such as support for welfare for asylum seekers and cultural diversity (Steiner & Landwehr, 2018). If these respondents are not only in favor of majoritarian decision-making, but also turn out to vote at the ballot, the interests of oppressed groups might be in danger.

3.3.3 Socio-Economic Effects

Finally, socio-economic factors relating to a constituency could influence the outputs of direct democratic votes for oppressed groups. First, *higher education* has generally been found to correlate with more liberal attitudes (Christmann & Danaci, 2012). For national direct democratic votes affecting minority rights in Switzerland, Vatter, Stadelmann-Steffen, and Danaci (2014) detect a positive effect of the level of education on pro-minority voting when rights of outgroups were voted upon. The authors assume that the tolerance promoting effect of education is especially important when a bill affects outgroups and aims at extending their rights, as less educated voters perceive outgroups as cultural or economic threats. Findings on lower educated voters being more likely to support right populist parties, which in turn often campaign for discriminatory policies, point in a similar direction (e.g., Gidron & Hall, 2017; Inglehart & Norris, 2017).

Second, the *state of the economy* might affect whether oppressed groups benefit or are disadvantaged in direct democratic votes. Although no research on exactly this effect yet exists, findings on voting for far-right parties suggest a pattern. Given that these parties often promote anti-oppressed group policies, the results indicate under which conditions discriminatory voting behavior in direct democracy might be more likely as well. For example, Rao, Raschky, and Tombazos (2018) find a negative effect for growth in Gross Domestic Product (GDP) per capita on the vote share of extremist parties in Europe. In elections in 16 European countries between 1990 and 2016, the regional GDP per capita declining by one percent leads to an increase in the vote share of extremist parties by 0.53 percentage points – mainly driven by far-right parties, whereas the effect is insignificant for far-left ones (Rao et al., 2018). Inglehart and Norris (2017) link times of economic decline with a rise of materialist values, while economic prosperity fueled post-materialist values such as tolerance. According to them, especially less educated people have experienced decreasing incomes and thereby less existential security during the past decades, resulting in rising support for populist authoritarian parties. Furthermore, declining income in general led to more support for populist authoritarian parties (Inglehart & Norris, 2017). Similarly, Gidron and Hall (2017) find lower levels of perceived social status increase support for right populist parties in twenty developed democracies. As the relative social status of men without a college education has declined since 1987, their support for right-wing populism has risen (Gidron & Hall, 2017). In terms of votes affecting low SES groups, a large group of wealthy voters might actually have the opposite effect, voting against welfare policies as they do not want to share benefits (Gerber, 1999).

Third, a final influential factor might be the degree of *ethnic fractionalization* in the country of a vote. Again, no empirical study has investigated the effect of ethnic fractionalization on direct democratic outputs so far, but a number of scholars have developed claims based on anecdotic observations. For example, Landemore (2020) expects that while ethnic homogeneity is often regarded as a prerequisite for participatory democracy to work, diversity might actually be more manageable with participatory practices. She demonstrates this by contrasting Belgium and Switzerland. Sometimes, homogeneity might even be the result of participatory democracy – for example in Iceland, where a public debate resulted in the country's conversion to Christianity in the 12th century (Landemore, 2020). This would imply that direct democracy works in support of classic oppressed groups. Similarly, as outlined above, Stojanović (2021) points to the integrating impact of direct democracy in Switzerland, especially for the different linguistic groups. In contrast, Bellamy (2018) argues that this only works because linguistic, religious and cleavages in wealth are cross-cutting in Switzerland. On the contrary, in Belgium the difference between rich and poor regions would be reinforced by the linguistic cleavage. In this context of vertical cleavages, direct democracy would run the risk of creating persisting minorities (Bellamy, 2018).

Regarding direct democratic bills and outputs for low SES groups in fractionalized countries, literature on the relationship between fractionalization and welfare spending can be informative. Alesina and Glaeser (2004), for example, show that ethnic fractionalization and redistribution are negatively correlated in the U.S. and Europe. In addition, the amount of welfare spending and support for welfare policies are lower in U.S. states where a higher percentage of the population is black (Alesina & Glaeser, 2004). While Dincer and Lambert (2012) provide evidence that the relationship between ethnic fractionalization and welfare spending is in fact U-shaped in the U.S., i.e. welfare spending is lower when fractionalization is at a moderate level and increases with higher levels, Gisselquist (2014) finds a negative relationship at least for spending on education. Mollerstrom (2015) traces the pattern of lower support for redistribution in fractionalized regions back to the theory of social identity – people are more willing to give benefits to others that they perceive as similar to themselves. Put differently, they are less willing to grant welfare to groups perceived as different. This should also manifest in voting behavior in direct democratic votes. In contrast to the hopes for direct democracy to bring people together in ethnically fractionalized countries mentioned above, these findings suggest less beneficial outputs especially for low SES groups, who benefit most from redistribution, welfare and spending on education.

3.4 Gaps in Existing Research

Summing up, although the theoretical fear that direct democracy discriminates against oppressed groups is rather old and direct democracy has been spreading all over the world during the last decades, empirical evidence is surprisingly limited. Up to now, the focus has been almost exclusively on the U.S. and Switzerland, and results are rather mixed in their conclusions, depending on the groups, timeframe and system levels investigated as well as on the controls used (if there are controls at all).

This dissertation therefore addresses a number of research gaps: first of all, it is the first analysis *comparatively analyzing direct democratic bills and outputs for oppressed groups and testing the influence of several institutional, attitudinal and socio-economic factors on these bills and outputs*. In contrast to previous research, I move beyond analyzing single countries or comparing states within Switzerland or the U.S. and provide a full picture of direct democratic votes on the national level in European democracies between 1990 and 2015.

Second, while most of the existing research investigates the implications of direct democracy for (some) classic oppressed groups, often termed minorities, I offer an *encompassing analysis by applying the concept of oppressed groups*. This enables me to analyze the implications for low SES groups and political groups as well, for which theoretical considerations and research from other areas suggest potential harmful effects from direct democracy. In addition, it represents an opportunity to test whether and how the theoretical concept of oppressed groups is informative for research on direct democracy.

Third, in contrast to the only cross-national study so far on the implications of direct democracy for oppressed groups by Bochsler and Hug (2015), this dissertation *analyzes actual outputs* of direct democratic votes instead of the existence of direct democratic options and of legislation on a topic. Thereby, it is assured that it is the use of direct democracy that results in certain pro- or contra-oppressed group laws and not a third variable influencing both the introduction/enlargement of direct democratic options (which might be never used) and legislation on the interests of oppressed groups.

Fourth, it can be assumed that attitudes towards equality should predict the output of direct democratic votes on those issues better than broad ideological categories like liberal or conservative, as used by Gerber and Hug (2002) and Lewis (2013). The discrimination of oppressed groups in popular votes should be less probable if values like equality are regarded as very important in a society. The *effect of those attitudes* on direct democratic votes concerning oppressed groups has not been analyzed at all.

Fifth, there are some contradictions between theoretical assumptions on the *effects of different direct democratic instruments* and empirical results from Switzerland and the U.S. The dissertation will investigate this pattern in the first analysis of those effects that looks beyond these two countries. Furthermore, it is the first to investigate the *effects of other institutional variables*, i.e., quora and binding votes, on direct democratic bills and outputs for oppressed groups.

Finally, the comparative design allows for an analysis of the *effects of different socio-economic variables*. Whereas previous research investigated the effect of education on direct democratic outputs for classic oppressed groups only in Switzerland, the effects of economic growth and ethnic fractionalization have not been analyzed at all. My research provides the first insights into the conditions that favor pro-bills and –outputs in contrast to conditions promoting contra-bills and –outputs in the country and year of a vote.

As demands for the implementation and extension of direct democracy are occurring worldwide, recent outputs for the interests of oppressed groups clearly need to be analyzed covering a range of countries, differentiating between groups, and analyzing the impact of attitudes regarding equality and oppressed groups, of institutional settings as well as of socio-economic variables. Only a comprehensive analysis like this enables profound statements about an important possible downside of popular decision-making: the risk of a majority tyrannizing minorities. This dissertation addresses the gaps mentioned above by analyzing all direct democratic votes affecting the interests of oppressed groups in European democracies between 1990 and 2015 at the national level. Hypotheses for analysis are outlined in the next chapter.

4 Hypotheses

This chapter formulates assumptions on impacts of direct democracy for oppressed groups which I test using data from all the national direct democratic votes held in European democracies between 1990 and 2015. Based on theoretical considerations and previous empirical results, the first part deals with possible different impacts for different categories of oppressed groups. The second part presents hypotheses on the effects of institutional, attitudinal and socio-economic explaining variables on direct democratic bills and outputs concerning oppressed groups in general.

4.1 Different Impacts for Different Groups

First, the specific characteristics of oppressed groups presumably make a difference for whether direct democratic bills and outputs support their interests. As outlined in Chapter 2, especially low SES groups are potentially at a disadvantage in direct democratic votes. Whereas outputs for other groups probably depend on how large the groups are and whether the electorate perceives them as in- or outgroups, low SES groups lack the resources to successfully use direct democratic votes in their interest. They cannot finance large campaigns, they lack the resources for collecting signatures, they often lack access to the media, and they also turn out in fewer numbers (e.g., Schäfer & Schoen, 2013). In addition, bills favoring low SES groups often involve financial costs to better off groups – thereby creating an incentive for the latter to campaign and vote against them. Findings on Switzerland in relation to lower tax rates and state expenditures in cantons with more direct democratic options support this assumption (Feld & Kirchgässner, 2000). As a result, the first set of hypotheses for descriptive analysis is:

H1a: There are more contra-bills at the ballot affecting low SES groups than there are pro-bills.

H1b: The success rate for pro-bills is lower for low SES groups compared to all other oppressed groups.

H1c: The success rate for contra-bills is higher for low SES groups compared to all other oppressed groups.

4.2 Explaining Variables: Institutional Effects

4.2.1 Direct Democratic Instruments

Different direct democratic instruments might have different effects on the interests of oppressed groups; while bottom-up instruments are theoretically assumed to be more protective, empirical insights revealed that veto referenda and especially popular initiatives affect oppressed groups negatively compared to mandatory votes (Eder & Magin, 2008; Gamble, 1997; Kobach, 1993; Kriesi, 2005; Vatter, 2007; Vatter & Danaci, 2010). By initiating a direct democratic vote, citizens might be seeking to enforce anti-oppressed group measures or hinder parliamentary action to protect oppressed groups. This also fits the assumption that MPs are in general more tolerant towards oppressed groups than the citizenry as a whole, as well as findings on bottom-up votes producing more contra-equality outputs than mandatory and top-down votes (Christmann & Danaci, 2012; Geißel et al., 2019a; Vatter & Danaci, 2010). Following this line, I assume that the interests of oppressed groups are more likely to be disadvantaged in bottom-up votes compared to top-down or mandatory votes. Therefore, the first set of hypotheses on institutional effects is:

H2a: Top-down and mandatory bills are more likely to be pro-bills than bottom-up bills are.

H2b: Compared to bottom-up votes, top-down and mandatory votes are more likely to result in pro-outputs.

H2c: Compared to bottom-up votes, top-down and mandatory votes are less likely to result in contra-outputs.

4.2.2 Quora

Quora that need to be fulfilled in order for a bill to pass at the ballot are a potential instrument that is frequently claimed to protect oppressed groups from being disadvantaged in direct democratic votes (e.g., Eder & Magin, 2008; Merkel & Ritzi, 2017). However, quora might also make it more difficult for bills to be adopted that support oppressed groups' interests. Accordingly, the chance of adoption should decrease for any bill requiring fulfilment of a quorum, regardless of whether said bill supports or disadvantages oppressed groups. At the bill-level, oppressed groups might shy away from initiating votes in their interests if quora are in place, as they might assume lower chances of success. Yet, the same reasoning might hold for opponents of oppressed groups. Therefore, I do not formulate a hypothesis on the effect of quora at the bill-level. This results in the following hypotheses:

H3a: The existence of a quorum decreases the probability of pro-outputs.

H3b: The existence of a quorum decreases the probability of contra-outputs.

4.3 Explaining Variables: Attitudinal Effects

4.3.1 Negative Attitudes towards Outgroups

As explained above, the effect of direct democracy on oppressed groups is assumed to differ depending on attitudes towards the group in the constituency (Vatter & Danaci, 2010). The first set of hypotheses on attitudinal effects is therefore:

H4a: A more negative attitude among the constituency towards the group affected by a bill increases the probability of contra- compared to pro-bills.

H4b: A more negative attitude among the constituency towards the group affected by a bill decreases the probability of pro-outputs.

H4c: A more negative attitude among the constituency towards the group affected by a bill increases the probability of contra-outputs.

4.3.2 Support for Equality

The discriminatory effect of direct democratic votes on oppressed groups is also assumed to depend on more general liberal/conservative attitudes in the electorate (Bochsler & Hug, 2015; Gerber & Hug, 2002; Lewis, 2013; Milic et al., 2014). In the case of bills affecting oppressed groups, I suggest that support for equality has a decisive influence:

H5a: Higher support for equality in a constituency increases the probability of pro- compared to contra-bills.

H5b: Higher support for equality in a constituency increases the probability of pro-outputs.

H5c: Higher support for equality in a constituency decreases the probability of contra-outputs.

4.4 Explaining Variables: Socio-Economic Effects

4.4.1 Education

Several of a constituency's socio-economic characteristics can be assumed to influence the impact of direct democracy for oppressed groups. Following Vatter et al. (2014) and Christmann and Danaci (2012), higher educated people are more tolerant and higher education should make discriminatory voting behavior less likely. Research on lower educated people being more likely to support far-right parties points in a similar direction (Gidron & Hall, 2017; Inglehart & Norris, 2017). Accordingly, the first set of hypotheses on socio-economic effects is:

H6a: Higher levels of education in the constituency increase the probability of pro- compared to contra-bills.

H6b: Higher levels of education in the constituency increase the probability of pro-outputs.

H6c: Higher levels of education in the constituency decrease the probability of contra-outputs.

4.4.2 Economic Growth

Another socio-economic factor of interest is the state of the economy at the time of a vote. It can be assumed that people are more willing to grant benefits to oppressed groups in times of economic growth, while economic decline should lead to less beneficial and more discriminating voting behavior towards the same categories (Gidron & Hall, 2017; Inglehart & Norris, 2017; Rao et al., 2018). A stronger economy should therefore result in more support for oppressed groups in general. Therefore, another set of hypotheses is:

H7a: Higher levels of economic growth increase the probability of pro- compared to contra-bills.

H7b: Higher levels of economic growth increase the probability of pro-outputs.

H7c: Higher levels of economic growth decrease the probability of contra-outputs.

4.4.3 Ethnic Fractionalization

Finally, the level of ethnic fractionalization in a country might influence how direct democracy impacts oppressed groups. This has not yet been investigated. Scholars disagree as to whether high fractionalization calls for more or less participatory democracy – assuming it to have both negative and positive effects for oppressed groups. While some cite the example of Switzerland to suggest that direct democracy might be beneficial in diverse societies, no quantitative comparative research exists which puts these assumptions to an empirical test (Landemore, 2020; Stojanović, 2021). Specifically, in direct democratic votes, one could suggest that higher fractionalization results in more groups seeking support for their interests at the ballot and thereby more pro-bills, but also making it more difficult to mobilize majorities in heavily fractionalized constituencies. Therefore, bills in general should be less likely to succeed at the ballot, regardless of the way they would affect oppressed groups. Research on the relationship between fractionalization and welfare spending suggests a negative effect, especially for pro-outputs for low SES groups (Alesina & Glaeser, 2004; Gisselquist, 2014; Mollerstrom, 2015). This results in the final set of hypotheses investigated in this dissertation:

H8a: Higher levels of ethnic fractionalization increase the probability of pro- compared to contra-bills.

H8b: Higher levels of ethnic fractionalization decrease the probability of pro-outputs.

H8c: Higher levels of ethnic fractionalization decrease the probability of contra-outputs.

The next chapter outlines the data and methods employed to put these hypotheses to the empirical test. Chapters 6, 7, and 8 will present the results of descriptive, bivariate, and multivariate analyses. These results will be further discussed in light of theoretical assumptions and previous research in Chapter 9.

5 Methods and Data

This chapter presents the dataset collected on direct democratic votes and the methods employed to test the hypotheses outlined above. Analyzing the data with the methods described here will provide answers to the research questions posed in this dissertation.

5.1 Data

The hypotheses are tested using data on all the national direct democratic decisions from European democracies[17] between 1990 and 2015. This high number of votes allows for profound conclusions and extends existing studies on the U.S. and Switzerland to a significant degree. While the focus on Europe and on democracies allows for a certain stability of contextual variables, including countries from Western, Eastern, Northern and Southern Europe also ensures a variety of different cultural and institutional settings are covered (see Figure 3 below for the countries included). My dataset builds on the dataset we collected in the DFG funded project "Inequality and direct democracy in Europe", containing the title, place, date, direct democratic instrument used and results of all national direct democratic votes in the period and area of analysis, with a total of 515 votes (Geißel, 2020). This dataset constitutes the first encompassing collection of data on all the national direct democratic votes in European democracies during a certain period. After extensive research on the content of the proposals, I coded them according to whether they affected the interests of oppressed groups, and if so, which group(s) were affected, and whether the proposals aimed at benefiting (pro-bills) or disadvantaging (contra-bills) the group(s) as defined in Chapter 2. The coding was based on a codebook I developed, building on previous operationalizations of Young's concept (Mancenido-Bolaños, 2020; Pineda, 2020; Tempels et al., 2020; C. C. Williams et al., 2020; Young, 1989). While search engines like www.sudd.ch contain information on votes such as date, title and result, thorough coding required gathering the original

---

[17] I count as democratic all European countries that were considered free according to the Freedom House index in the year of the vote (https://freedomhouse.org/reports/publication-archives, 14.03.24).

texts of direct democratic bills on official sites, comparing them with current laws, researching official information on the proposals sent out by the government in question, and in some cases translating these documents. Below, I list examples of coding; for more details please find the codebook in Appendix A.

Existing research on the topic differs in defining the scope of issues that are relevant for understanding the fate of oppressed groups in direct democracy. While some authors only analyze votes explicitly referring to classic oppressed groups' rights, others look at bills that "affect oppressed groups" in a broader sense, e.g., laws on housing or education. The dissertation sticks to the second tradition – every bill that can be assumed to affect oppressed groups more than other groups in the society is taken into account. The reason for this decision is straightforward: while directly taking away oppressed groups' rights via direct democratic votes is prohibited in some countries under investigation, these groups can still be disadvantaged in other, perhaps more subtle ways. Categories of oppressed groups analyzed here are: LGBTQ+, rights of non-citizens, fees and taxes for non-citizens, discrimination bans, people with disabilities or mental health issues, linguistic minorities, religious minorities, gender, and rule of law/fundamental rights. As a high number of bills affect low SES groups, these bills are divided into the following subcategories: fees and taxes, public transport, education and daycare, social welfare, housing, and healthcare. Finally, I categorized bills affecting political minorities as follows: parliamentary opposition, voting system, and division of power. Chapter 6 and the codebook in Appendix A contain further details on the categories and the clusters they represent. In total, 259 direct democratic votes at national level affected the interests of oppressed groups from 1990 to 2015.

A couple of examples from the codebook illustrate the coding procedure. Bills that were coded as pro-bills, for example, include the introduction of same-sex marriages, the facilitation of naturalization, increasing availability of therapy for people with mental health issues or physical disabilities, the introduction of progressive taxing instead of a flat rate tax, increasing access to public transport, decreasing or abolishing fees for education or daycare (especially for low-income parents), and boosting the rights of opposition parties or strengthening the independence of courts. In contrast, for example bills that discriminate against members of religious minorities or increase fees for education, healthcare, public transport etc. were coded as contra-bills. In some cases, bills affect several oppressed groups or belong to several categories as they include different measures. As a result, these bills are counted several times in the descriptive statistics on the categories and clusters of oppressed groups presented in the next chapter. However, as they only require one vote and a certain, constant number of signatures, I refer to

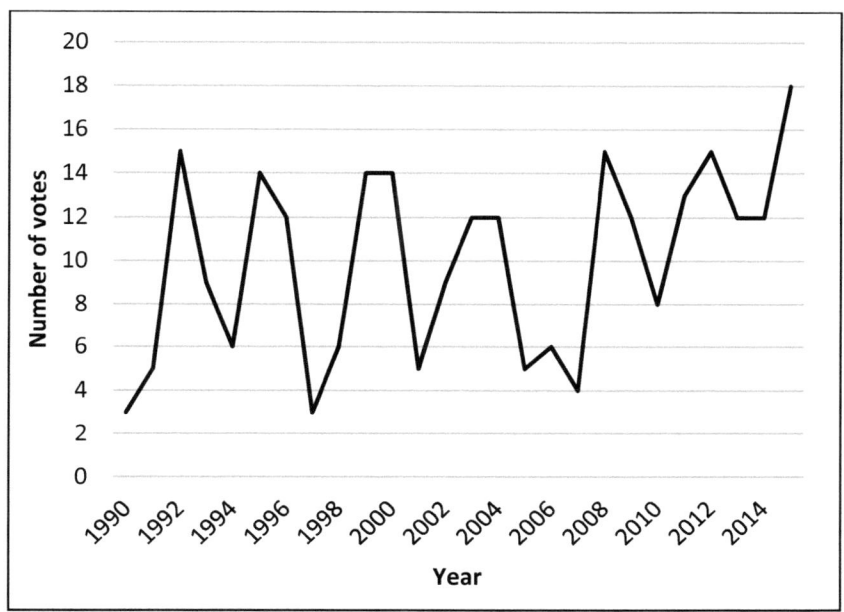

Figure 2: Number of Direct Democratic Votes per Year, 1990-2015.
Source: own dataset

them as one bill and one output in the following bivariate and multivariate statistics.

The timeframe from 1990 to 2015 ensures the inclusion of Eastern and Central Eastern European countries, which introduced direct democratic options in their new constitutions in the early 1990s. In addition, the timeframe is long enough to include a large number of direct democratic votes and to detect possible trends over time, while it also allows for a certain comparability. Figure 2 provides an overview of the number of direct democratic votes affecting oppressed groups per year.

As we can see in Figure 2, there are no longer periods of many or few votes concerning the interests of oppressed groups – years with a high number of bills are often followed by years with much lower numbers. However, we can detect an upward trend between 2007 and 2015. As a result, while the data shows no clear trend towards more or less direct democratic votes affecting oppressed groups, controlling for the effect of time remains vital for the multivariate analyses.

Direct democratic options and their use vary widely between different European countries. In order to provide an overview of the data, Figure 3 shows the number of votes affecting oppressed groups per country.

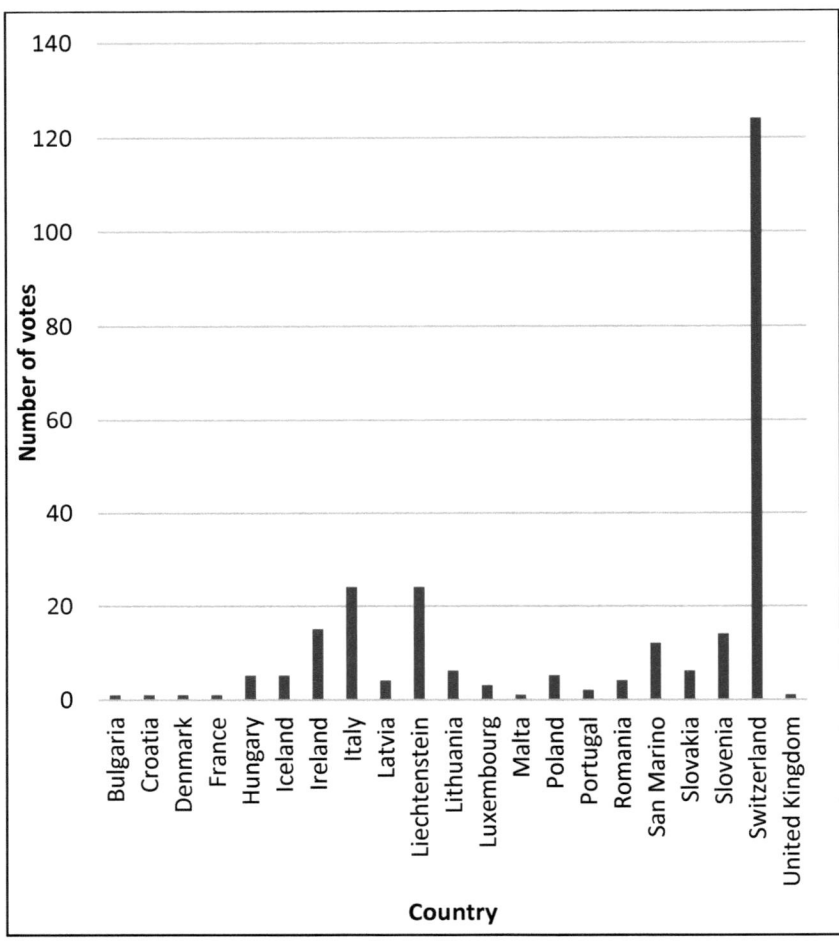

Figure 3: Number of Direct Democratic Votes per Country. Source: own dataset

Not surprisingly, by far the most direct democratic votes affecting the interests of oppressed groups take place in Switzerland. While a number of countries only witnesses one direct democratic vote that is of concern here, Ireland, Italy and Liechtenstein show higher numbers. In geographical terms, votes take place almost everywhere on the continent. Although the constitutions of the Eastern European countries entail direct democratic options, votes on interests of oppressed groups are not particularly common there.

5.2 Methods

The first step in the analyses are descriptive investigations on the number of bills supporting or hindering the interests of oppressed groups differentiated between groups, and the success rates of these pro/contra-bills. In addition, frequencies and means of the explaining variables are calculated depending on whether bills and outputs are pro/contra. The second step involves the bivariate statistics on the correlations between the probability of a direct democratic bill being a pro- instead of a contra-bill, resulting in a pro-output or a contra-output and the various explaining variables, and between the explaining variables themselves. I report Cramér's V for nominal explaining variables and perform bivariate logistic regressions when the explaining variable is quasi-metric. In addition, I perform ttests and anova to test whether means in quasi-metric variables differ in different institutional settings, and report correlation coefficients for correlations between quasi-metric variables. Finally, multivariate multilevel analyses estimate the influence of the explaining variables on the probability of pro-bills at the ballot and of pro- and contra-outputs occurring, respectively.

To test the hypotheses thoroughly, Bayesian multilevel logistic regression analysis is used. In the first models, the dependent variable is the probability that a direct democratic bill relating to the interests of oppressed groups is in support of these interests (a pro-bill). In the following models, the dependent variable is the probability that such a pro-bill is actually adopted at the ballot (pro-output), and the probability that a contra-bill is (contra-output).

The method of choice are Bayesian multilevel crossed-effects logistic models. While the use of logistic models is straightforward given the binary structure of the dependent variables, the following briefly explains the choice of multilevel crossed-effects models and a Bayesian estimation procedure.

First, given the multilevel structure of the data, it makes sense to suspect that there are country-level factors at work here that are not captured by the explaining variables, i.e., there is variation in the probability of a bill containing pro-oppressed group measures as well as in the probability of pro- and contra-outputs, depending on the country of the vote. To account for this variation between countries, one common procedure are multilevel regression analyses. In addition, there might be a time factor at work here because the probability could differ depending on the year in which a vote takes place. Therefore, crossed-effects models are used, in which the intercepts are grouped by country as well as by year. Second, a Bayesian instead of a Maximum Probability framework is used to reduce biased results in models with small numbers of countries and years (Stegmueller, 2013). Figure 4 displays fictional examples of votes clustered into countries and years to clarify the multilevel structure of the data.

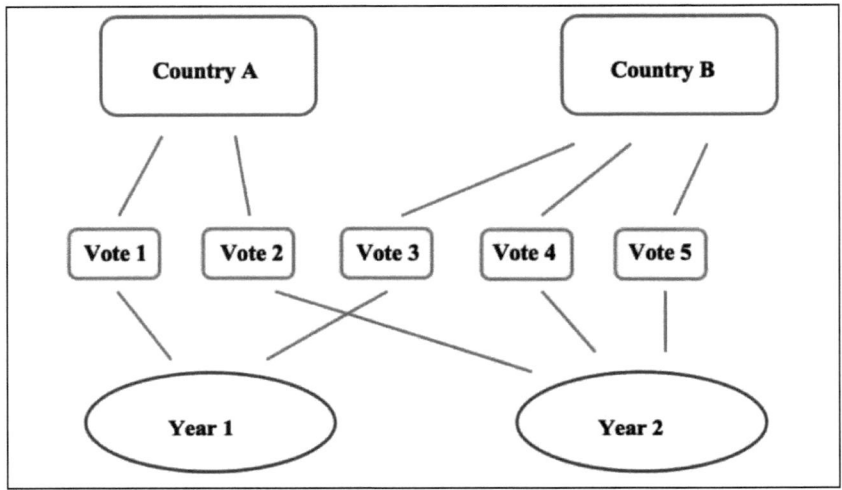

Figure 4: Multilevel Structure of Data. Source: own diagram

In order to facilitate interpretation, I grand-mean center the attitudinal and socio-economic explaining variables for the multivariate analyses. There is an extensive debate in the literature on whether and how to center explaining variables in multilevel analyses (see for example Enders & Tofighi, 2007; Sommet & Morselli, 2017; Wenzelburger et al., 2014). Regarding the whether, I decide to center only those explaining variables that are non-binary, following Wenzelburger et al. (2014). For these variables, it is highly unlikely that they will have a value of 0 – this would mean, for example, that no respondents at all express a negative attitude towards a group, or that nobody reports a university education. Therefore, it enhances interpretation to grand-mean center the variables. However, the means of the dichotomous variables do not tell us very much – a vote can either be initiated top-down or not -, so mean-centering these would complicate interpretations. Regarding the second, as all non-binary variables are level-2 (on the level of countries and years), cluster-mean centering is not an option so I perform grand-mean centering (Enders & Tofighi, 2007). This results in the fixed intercept becoming the log-odds that the dependent variable equals one when all binary explaining variables are 0 and all non-binary ones are set to their means (Sommet & Morselli, 2017).

The first set of explaining variables are the institutional characteristics of the vote. Regarding the direct democratic instrument, bottom-up, top-down and mandatory votes are differentiated. Data on this is included in the dataset collected in the DFG funded project mentioned above. The same holds for data on quora – differentiated between approval quora, turnout quora, and the

"Ständemehr" – and whether the vote result is binding. In addition, a dummy variable on whether the vote takes place in Switzerland is included to account for probable specific characteristics of Swiss votes given its long tradition and extensive use of direct democracy. All of these variables are vote-level variables.

The second set of explaining variables are attitudinal ones. Information on the status of an oppressed group is taken from survey data where attitudes of the constituency towards the group affected by the vote are included (the World Values Survey includes questions asking if there are members of oppressed groups one does not want to have as neighbors, whether men should be advantaged when jobs are scarce, and whether larger income differences are necessary (*World Values Survey: Round Two – Country-Pooled Datafile*, 2014; *World Values Survey: Round Three – Country-Pooled Datafile*, 2014; *World Values Survey: Round Four – Country-Pooled Datafile*, 2014; *World Values Survey: Round Five – Country-Pooled Datafile*, 2014; *World Values Survey: Round Six – Country-Pooled Datafile*, 2014)). The variables are recoded so that they show the mean scores for each country in the wave covering the year of the vote, ranging from 0 to 1. For all cases where one or several of these groups are concerned, the effect of the attitudes towards the group is estimated. In addition, citizens' attitudes about equality in general are included. Data on these are taken from the European Social Survey (asking if it is important that people are treated equally and have equal opportunities (*European Social Survey Round 1 Data (2002). Data File Edition 6.6*, n.d.; *European Social Survey Round 2 Data (2004). Data File Edition 3.6*, n.d.; *European Social Survey Round 3 Data (2006). Data File Edition 3.7*, n.d.; *European Social Survey Round 4 Data (2008). Data File Edition 4.5*, n.d.; *European Social Survey Round 5 Data (2010). Data File Edition 3.4*, n.d.; *European Social Survey Round 6 Data (2012). Data File Edition 2.4*, n.d.; *European Social Survey Round 7 Data (2014). Data File Edition 2.2*, n.d.)). Again, the variable includes the mean scores from 0 to 1. All attitudinal variables are country- and year-specific.

Finally, to identify the influence of the socio-economic context in which a vote takes place, national gross domestic product (GDP) growth per capita in the year of the vote[18] and annual ethnic fractionalization in the country (Drazanova, 2019) are included in the analysis. The former ranges from -1 to 1 and the latter from 0 to 1. The level of education in the constituency is accounted for by using Eurostat data on the share of inhabitants between 15 and 64 years with a tertiary education degree.[19] Again, the variable is recoded to values from 0 to 1. All socio-economic variables are country- and year-specific.

---

18 https://data.worldbank.org/indicator/NY.GDP.PCAP.KD.ZG (14.03.24).
19 https://ec.europa.eu/eurostat/databrowser/view/EDAT_LFSE_03__custom_1694488/default/table?lang=de (14.03.24)

6 Descriptive Results

This chapter contains descriptive results on how many pro- and contra-bills the dataset involves in total as well as for different categories and clusters of oppressed groups. Afterwards, I present the shares of pro- and contra-outputs in total and for the single groups as well as the success rates of pro- versus contra-bills. Focusing on the explaining variables, I compare percentages of pro- and contra-bills and -outputs and success rates between different institutional settings, and mean numbers of attitudes and socio-economic variables when pro- versus contra-bills come to a vote and when they produce pro- and contra-outputs. Finally, I summarize the descriptive findings in light of the hypotheses formulated in Chapter 4.

6.1 Oppressed Groups and Direct Democratic Bills

The descriptive investigation of the dataset starts with an overview of how many of the direct democratic votes in European democracies between 1990 and 2015 at national level contain measures that support or hinder the interests of oppressed groups. As noted above, 259 out of 515 direct democratic bills that make it to the ballot during this timeframe affect oppressed groups in a particular way. For 25 out of these 259 bills, it is not possible to arrive at a straightforward coding based on the information available. Thirteen bills include measures that support oppressed groups as well as measures that disadvantage them. For these bills, it is not possible to make assumptions about the factors that influence whether the bills come to the ballot and are adopted. In addition, separate statistical analyses on thirteen bills would not yield reliable results. Excluding these cases, 221 bills are analyzed – 133 (60.18 %) of the bills contain measures to support oppressed groups (pro-bills), while 88 (39.82 %) contain measures that disadvantage oppressed groups (contra-bills). Pro-bills clearly outweigh contra-bills.

Figure 22 in Appendix B displays how many bills affect certain oppressed groups over time. Rather than certain topics trending in certain periods, Figure 22 shows frequent ups and downs in the numbers of direct democratic votes for each group. Low SES and political groups are those most often affected by votes in almost every year, with regular votes also held on the rights and interests of non-citizens. While direct democratic bills on rights for women are more frequent between 1999 and 2001, the years up to 2015 witness an increase in votes on the rights of members of the LGBTQ+ community.

Can we observe differences in the shares of pro- and contra-bills depending on the group concerned? Table 2 shows the percentages in answer to these questions. As people of low socio-economic status are the group most often affected by a vote, these bills are further differentiated according to the topic they address. Some bills cover more than one category (i.e., affect several groups or topics), which is why the sum of the single categories exceeds the bill total.

Table 2: Oppressed Groups and Direct Democratic Bills in European Democracies 1990-2015

Category	Pro-bills N (%)	Contra-bills N (%)
LGBTQ+	2 (20)	8 (80)
Rights of non-citizens	12 (52.17)	11 (47.83)
Non-citizens: fees & taxes	0	1 (100)
Discrimination ban	2 (66.67)	1 (33.33)
Disability / Mental illness	4 (100)	0
Linguistic minorities	3 (100)	0 (0)
Religious minorities	4 (80)	1 (20)
Gender	7 (77.78)	2 (22.22)
Rule of law / fundamental rights	8 (80)	2 (20)
Total classic oppressed groups	42 (61.76)	26 (38.24)
Low SES: fees & taxes	32 (59.26)	22 (40.74)
Low SES: public transport	5 (100)	0
Low SES: education & daycare	8 (88.89)	1 (11.11)
Low SES: social welfare	23 (69.7)	10 (30.3)
Low SES: housing	5 (50)	5 (50)
Low SES: healthcare	18 (54.55)	15 (45.45)
Total low SES	91 (63.19)	53 (36.81)
Parliamentary opposition	3 (37.5)	5 (62.5)
Voting system	15 (50)	15 (50)
Division of power	19 (73.08)	7 (26.92)
Total politics	37 (57.81)	27 (42.19)
Total	**133 (60.18)**	**88 (39.82)**

Source: own dataset

Let us first take a look at the numbers of bills per category. More than half of the bills entail measures that especially affect low SES groups. Here, fees and taxes are the most common category, followed by policies on social welfare and healthcare. The other bills are almost equally divided between those dealing with political groups (e.g., bills strengthening opposition powers, increasing proportionality of the voting system, or strengthening the division of power (or vice versa)), and those affecting classic oppressed groups such as same-sex couples, non-citizens, people with disabilities or those suffering from mental health issues, linguistic or religious minorities or women. Here, also more general laws are included that aim at protecting oppressed groups, such as bans on discrimination and a guarantee of fundamental rights, both of which often can be found in constitutions. While bills affecting non-citizens and those dealing with the voting system or the division of power are fairly common, the numbers are very low in other categories. Therefore, the shares of pro- compared to contra-bills must be interpreted with caution for these categories.

Second, as noted above, most of the bills that come to a vote are pro-bills – 60.18 % compared to 39.82 % contra-bills. This ratio is similar for all three clusters of categories, ranging from 63.19 % pro-bills for the low SES categories to 57.81 % pro-bills in the political categories. These numbers do not confirm hypothesis H1a, assuming more contra- than pro-bills for low SES groups. While the validity of the ratios in the single categories remains limited due to the low number of cases, some results are nevertheless noteworthy. Bills that deal with topics especially relevant to members of the LGBTQ+ community more often contain measures disadvantaging them than improving their positions. The same holds for bills affecting the parliamentary opposition. These two are the only categories under investigation with this negative ratio. In contrast, direct democratic bills on issues of social welfare (for instance) more often aim at improving the situation of poor people than disadvantaging them (69.7 % vs. 30.3 %). Likewise, more than two thirds of the bills in this category would strengthen the division of power, while numbers are balanced for measures on the proportionality of the voting system.

Overall, for most of the categories, worries about a *Tyranny of the Majority* cannot be confirmed when we look at the bills that come to a direct democratic vote – oppressed groups and their allies seem to be quite successful in putting their interests on the direct democratic agenda. Nevertheless, it might still be the case that pro-bills struggle more to gain a majority of votes at the ballot than contra-bills do. In addition, it is important to note that I only count the numbers of pro- and contra-bills without assessing "to what extent" a measure is pro or contra. The next section entails descriptive statistics on the adopted direct democratic bills affecting oppressed groups (pro- and contra-outputs).

6.2 Oppressed Groups and Direct Democratic Outputs

Out of the 259 bills that come to a direct democratic vote and affect oppressed groups, 94 are successful at the ballot, i.e., gain a majority and pass a possible quorum. Sixteen out of these belong to the 25 bills that cannot be coded in a straightforward way. As a result, 78 adopted bills contain pro- or contra-oppressed group measures. 60.26 % (47) of these include measures that support the interests of the oppressed group(s) concerned (pro-outputs), while 39.74 % (31) contain some form of disadvantage (contra-outputs). Compared to the bill-level, the picture looks slightly better for oppressed groups when it comes to direct democratic outputs – the share of pro-outputs in all outputs is 0.08 % higher compared to the share of pro-bills in all bills. The success rates correspondingly show that the probability of a direct democratic bill being adopted is slightly higher for pro- than for contra-bills, specifically 35.34 % for pro-bills versus 35.23 % for contra-bills. To put this into perspective, out of the 515 direct democratic bills that come to a vote between 1990 and 2015 in total, 37.86 % succeed at the ballot, while 62.14 % fail. This means that bills affecting oppressed groups in general have a slightly below-average probability of success.

Again, an oppressed group is a highly diverse concept. Can we observe differences in the shares of pro- and contra-outputs between groups and topics? Do these differences mirror those at the bill-level, or do they deviate from the bill-level – which would imply that some groups are more likely to succeed at the ballot than others? Table 3 contains the numbers of pro- and contra-outputs, differentiated between single categories and topics. Note that the percentages in brackets are the shares of all adopted bills affecting oppressed groups that are pro- versus those that are contra-bills. The success rates of the respective bills are reported in separate columns.

The first thing to notice from Table 3 is of course that the numbers in each category decrease again when we look only at the bills that gain a majority and pass a possible quorum. As a result, the ratios in the single categories have to be interpreted with even more caution than those of the bills at the ballot. Nevertheless, comparing the success rates reveals some interesting patterns.

First, the share of pro-outputs concerning low SES groups is especially high – almost 70 % of the adopted bills in this cluster benefit such groups. This share is also more than 7 % higher compared to the bill-level. This is mirrored by a roughly 8 % higher success rate of pro- compared to contra-bills in this cluster. In contrast, the share of pro-outputs supporting political groups is slightly lower compared to their share at the ballot (56 % vs. 57.81 %). This is also the only cluster where the success rate for pro-bills is lower compared to the success rate of contra-bills (37.84 % vs. 40.74 %). The ratios

Table 3: Pro- and Contra-Outputs in European Democracies 1990-2015

Category	Pro-outputs N (%)	Contra-outputs N (%)	Success Rate: Pro-bills (%)	Success Rate: Contra-bills (%)
LGBTQ+	2 (40)	3 (60)	100	37.5
Rights of non-citizens	1 (16.67)	5 (83.33)	8.33	45.45
Non-citizens: fees & taxes	0	0	0	0
Discrimination ban	1 (100)	0	50	0
Disability / Mental illness	2 (100)	0	50	0
Linguistic minorities	1 (100)	0	33.33	0
Religious minorities	3 (75)	1 (25)	75	100
Gender	4 (80)	1 (20)	57.14	50
Rule of law / fundamental rights	8 (88.89)	1 (11.11)	100	50
Total classic oppressed groups	22 (66.67)	11 (33.33)	52.38	42.31
Low SES: fees & taxes	8 (47.06)	9 (52.94)	25	40.91
Low SES: public transport	2 (100)	0	40	0
Low SES: education & daycare	2 (100)	0	25	0
Low SES: social welfare	8 (88.89)	1 (11.11)	34.78	10
Low SES: housing	3 (60)	2 (40)	60	40
Low SES: healthcare	7 (77.78)	2 (22.22)	38.89	13.33
Total low SES	30 (69.77)	13 (30.23)	32.97	24.53
Parliamentary opposition	1 (25)	3 (75)	33.33	60
Voting system	5 (55.56)	4 (44.44)	33.33	26.67
Division of power	8 (66.67)	4 (33.33)	42.11	57.14
Total politics	14 (56)	11 (44)	37.84	40.74
Total	**47 (60.26)**	**31 (39.74)**	**35.34**	**35.23**

Source: own dataset

of the cluster of classic oppressed groups have changed into a more positive direction for oppressed groups– 66.67 % are pro-outputs, while 61.76 % are pro-bills. Although the share of pro-outputs is highest for low SES groups, hypothesis H1b, stating that success rates for pro-bills are lower for low SES groups than for other groups, is confirmed nevertheless. This stems from a particularly low probability of bills affecting low SES groups to get adopted in general. However, hypothesis H1c is not confirmed out of the same reason. The success rate of contra-bills affecting low SES groups is lower than both the success rate of contra-bills affecting classic oppressed groups and the success rate of those affecting political groups.

Second, a dive into the single categories offers insights into the origins of the cluster ratios, as well as diverging patterns. Once again, the diversity behind the cluster of classic oppressed groups can be observed: the higher proportion of supportive bills at the output- than at the bill-level mainly stems from the higher success rates of bills benefitting almost all groups and policies in this cluster compared to bills disadvantaging them. In contrast, the share of outputs benefitting religious minorities drops slightly compared to the bills at the ballot. Bills affecting the rights of non-citizens witness the largest drop – from 52.17 % pro-bills to 16.67 % pro-outputs, mirrored by the extremely low success rate of 8.33 % for pro-bills in this category.

Turning to the topics that especially affect low SES groups, it becomes clear that low SES groups benefit in almost every category of bills besides those concerning fees and taxes. Voters do not seem to shy away from granting low SES groups material support, but measures to decrease fees and taxes are less popular than measures to increase them.

Finally, in the categories dealing with aspects of the political system, bills including a strengthening of opposition powers fare specifically worse (25 % pro-outputs vs. 37.5 % pro-bills, or a success rate of 33.33 %). The share of pro-outputs also slightly decreases in the "division of power"-category compared to the ballot (66.67 % vs. 73.08 %; a success rate of 42.11%). However, pro-bills affecting the voting system fare slightly better than contra-bills in the same category (success rates of 33.33 % vs. 26.67 %).

In conclusion, the investigation of the share of pro-outputs partly supports concerns relating to a *Tyranny of the Majority* (not assessing the quality of pro- and contra-measures). Whereas especially women, low SES groups, and general policies strengthening the rule of law and fundamental rights seem to win at the ballot box, this positive picture does not hold for non-citizens and the parliamentary opposition. Table 4 summarizes the ratios at the bill- and output-level and success rates, differentiating between clusters of oppressed groups.

Before analyzing the factors behind these descriptive statistics in bivariate and multilevel regressions, the next subchapter presents the ratios differen-

Table 4: Oppressed Groups and Direct Democracy in European Democracies 1990-2015

Oppressed Groups Affected	Pro-bills (%)	Contra-bills (%)	Pro-outputs (%)	Contra-outputs (%)	Success Rate: Pro-bills (%)	Success Rate: Contra-bills (%)
Classic	61.76	38.24	66.67	33.33	50	32
Low SES	63.19	36.81	69.77	30.23	32.97	24.53
Politics	57.81	42.19	56	44	37.84	40.74
Total	60.18	39.82	60.26	39.74	35.34	35.23

Source: own dataset

tiating between characteristics of direct democratic votes and the means of attitudinal and socio-economic factors for pro- versus contra-bills and -outputs. This serves as a first hint as to whether the data confirm the hypotheses on explaining variables formulated above.

6.3 Explaining Variables

6.3.1 Institutional Explaining Variables, Switzerland

Can we observe differences in direct democratic bills and outputs for oppressed groups between votes with different characteristics? This section presents the ratios of pro- and contra-bills and -outputs and success rates, differentiating between institutional settings. Possibly influential factors could be which direct democratic instrument is used, whether the vote result is binding, whether a quorum is in place that has to be fulfilled, and whether the vote takes place in Switzerland. The first part of the section looks at the institutional factors across all countries. The second part investigates whether there are differences in institutional factors between Switzerland and the other countries examined.

6.3.1.1 Institutional Explaining Variables across all Countries; Votes in Switzerland

The first important vote characteristic is the *direct democratic instrument* employed. As outlined in Chapter 2, I differentiate between top-down, bottom-up and mandatory votes depending on the mechanism of initiation. The ratios of pro- and contra-bills and -outputs presented in Table 5 are a first

Table 5: Direct Democratic Bills and Outputs and Instruments, 1990-2015

	Pro-bills N (%)	Contra-bills N (%)	Pro-outputs N (%)	Contra-outputs N (%)	Success Rate: Pro-bills (%)	Success Rate: Contra-bills (%)
Top-down votes	23 (76.67)	7 (23.33)	8 (72.73)	3 (27.27)	34.78	42.86
Bottom-up votes	80 (55.56)	64 (44.44)	18 (47.37)	20 (52.63)	22.5	31.25
Mandatory votes	30 (63.83)	17 (36.17)	21 (72.41)	8 (27.59)	70	47.06

Source: own dataset

step in testing hypotheses H2a-c, which assume top-down and mandatory votes to be more beneficial for oppressed groups than bottom-up votes. When we first look at the ratios on the bill-level, this assumption seems to hold only in part: whereas the share of pro-bills is considerably higher for top-down compared to bottom-up votes (76.67 % vs. 55.56 %), the difference between bottom-up and mandatory votes (63.83 %) is much smaller. In addition, bottom-up bills are more likely to be pro than contra. Yet, the picture looks different on the output-level. Here, top-down votes still have the highest share of pro-outputs (72.73 %) but compared to the bill-level the share of pro-outputs increases to 72.41 % for mandatory votes. In contrast, the share falls considerably to 47.37 % for the bottom-up votes. Whereas bottom-up bills in general are less likely to succeed, the success rate of the pro-bills is especially low (22.5 %). In contrast, the success rate of bottom-up contra-bills is higher (31.25 %). Top-down contra-bills are also more likely to succeed than pro ones (42.86 % vs. 34.78 %). However, 70 % of the mandatory pro-bills succeed at the ballot compared to 47.06 % of the contra ones.

So, while there are more bottom-up-bills put to a vote that include beneficial measures for oppressed groups, these are less likely to win a majority and pass a possible quorum than their disadvantaging counterparts. This contradicts Kriesi's (2005) assumption of bottom-up votes favoring oppressed groups being more likely to succeed, given that a strong group was a prerequisite for initiating the vote. As a result, the outputs of bottom-up votes more often disadvantage oppressed groups than support their interests, while the outputs of top-down and mandatory votes are more beneficial. Hypotheses H2b and H2c on pro- and contra-outputs therefore seem to hold. The share of pro-bills being lower for bottom-up votes compared to mandatory and top-down ones also lends support to hypothesis H2a. The multivariate analyses will show whether this is confirmed when controlling for other factors.

Table 6: Direct Democratic Bills and Outputs and Bottom-Up-Instruments, 1990-2015

	Pro-bills N (%)	Contra-bills N (%)	Pro-outputs N (%)	Contra-outputs N (%)	Success Rate: Pro-bills (%)	Success Rate: Contra-bills (%)
Initiatives	48 (68.57)	22 (31.43)	5 (45.45)	6 (54.55)	10.42	27.27
Veto Referenda	32 (43.24)	42 (56.76)	13 (48.15)	14 (51.85)	37.5	33.33

Source: own dataset

To dive a little deeper into the bottom-up bills, the next table differentiates between popular initiatives in which citizens gather signatures to bring a bill to a vote that they drafted themselves, and veto referenda, where citizens gather signatures to bring a bill to a vote that has already been adopted by parliament. Can we detect differences between these two kinds of bottom-up votes and their impact on oppressed groups?

Table 6 shows that it is mainly initiatives that contain measures in support of oppressed groups, while veto referenda slightly more often disadvantage them. This corresponds to Kriesi's (2005) finding that initiatives in Switzerland have been used mostly by the left, if we assume that left-leaning parties more frequently propose policies in support of oppressed groups. Yet, for initiatives, pro-bills fare worse at the ballot than contra ones. So, while oppressed groups and their allies seem to use the initiative tool to further their interests, their chances of succeeding are pretty low. In contrast, veto referenda against a parliamentarian contra-bill (coded as pro-bill) succeed more often than those against pro-bills. The higher success rates of veto referenda in general point to the risk aversion of voters, who are more likely to support attempts to preserve the status quo compared to bills trying to change it (see also Kriesi, 2005).

Table 7: Direct Democratic Bills and Outputs, Binding and Not Binding, 1990-2015

	Pro-bills N (%)	Contra-bills N (%)	Pro-outputs N (%)	Contra-outputs N (%)	Success Rate: Pro-bills (%)	Success Rate: Contra-bills (%)
Binding	119 (58.62)	84 (41.38)	42 (59.15)	29 (40.85)	34.45	34.52
Not binding	14 (77.78)	4 (22.22)	5 (71.43)	2 (28.57)	35.71	50

Source: own dataset

Table 8: Direct Democratic Bills and Outputs and Quora, 1990-2015

	Pro-bills N (%)	Contra-bills N (%)	Pro-outputs N (%)	Contra-outputs N (%)	Success Rate: Pro-bills (%)	Success Rate: Contra-bills (%)
Quorum	76 (60.32)	50 (39.68)	20 (52.63)	18 (47.37)	26.32	38
No Quorum	57 (60)	38 (40)	27 (67.5)	13 (32.5)	47.37	31.58

Source: own dataset

A second vote characteristic that might be influential for a vote's output for oppressed groups is *whether the result is binding*, i.e., if parliament has to adopt the bill as formulated in the vote. As Table 7 shows, the ratio of pro-bills and -outputs is far higher when votes are not binding than when they are. While the ratios are positive for oppressed groups in the binding votes as well, the shares of pro-bills and -outputs are substantively smaller than in non-binding votes. However, while the success rates of pro-bills are lower than of contra ones both in binding and non-binding votes, the difference is minimal in votes where the results are binding. Yet, the dataset contains only eighteen bills where the result was not binding. Therefore, it will be interesting to see whether multivariate analyses will reveal the same effects when other contextual factors are taken into account.

The third vote characteristic under examination here is whether there are any *quora* that have to be fulfilled in order for a bill to be adopted. Table 8 presents the ratios of pro- and contra-bills and -outputs differentiated between votes with and without quora in place. The ratios at the bill-level are pretty similar, with the share of pro-bills being a little higher for votes that have to fulfill quora. Again, this changes when we turn to ratios for outputs. Here, the share of pro-outputs drops from 60.32 % to 52.63 % for votes where quora are in place, whereas the share of contra-outputs increases. At the same time, the share of pro-bills increases for votes without quora. Correspondingly, the success rate of pro-bills is much lower than for contra-bills when quora exist (26.32 % vs. 38 %), whereas it is higher for bills that do not have to fulfill a quorum (47.37 % vs. 31.58 %). Confirming hypothesis H3a, quora negatively affect the success rate of pro-bills, but contrary to H3b, a quorum increases the success rate of contra-bills. This implies that quora often work to the disadvantage of oppressed groups; bills supporting their interests seem to struggle more to fulfill quora than bills against their interests. Again, the multivariate analyses will reveal whether these effects persist when controlling for other factors.

The last paragraphs of this section differentiate between different kinds of quora – namely approval quora, turnout quora, and the Swiss Ständemehr,

Table 9: Direct Democratic Bills and Outputs and Approval Quora, 1990-2015

	Pro-bills N (%)	Contra-bills N (%)	Pro-outputs N (%)	Contra-outputs N (%)	Success Rate: Pro-bills (%)	Success Rate: Contra-bills (%)
Approval Quorum	12 (66.67)	6 (33.33)	4 (57.14)	3 (42.86)	33.33	50
No Approval Quorum	121 (59.61)	82 (40.39)	43 (60.56)	28 (39.44)	35.54	34.15

Source: own dataset

Table 10: Direct Democratic Bills and Outputs and Turnout Quora, 1990-2015

	Pro-bills N (%)	Contra-bills N (%)	Pro-outputs N (%)	Contra-outputs N (%)	Success Rate: Pro-bills (%)	Success Rate: Contra-bills (%)
Turnout Quorum	18 (45)	22 (55)	4 (40)	6 (60)	22.22	31.82
No Turnout Quorum	115 (63.54)	66 (36.46)	43 (63.24)	25 (36.76)	37.39	36.36

Source: own dataset

Table 11: Direct Democratic Bills and Outputs and "Ständemehr", 1990-2015

	Pro-bills N (%)	Contra-bills N (%)	Pro-outputs N (%)	Contra-outputs N (%)	Success Rate: Pro-bills (%)	Success Rate: Contra-bills (%)
Ständemehr	47 (68.12)	22 (31.88)	12 (57.14)	9 (42.86)	25.53	40.91
No Ständemehr	86 (56.58)	66 (43.42)	35 (61.4)	22 (38.6)	40.7	33.33

Source: own dataset

according to which the majority of the cantons have to approve in order for a bill to be adopted. This helps identify the type of quorum especially harmful or beneficial for interests of oppressed groups.

Tables 9 to 11 reveal that the success rates of pro-bills are lower than those of contra-bills, regardless of the type of quorum in place. Yet, while a turnout quorum decreases success rates for both pro- and contra-bills, the existence of the Ständemehr especially hinders the former. Whereas the success rate of contra-bills is even higher when a Ständemehr has to be fulfilled, the success rate of pro-bills is considerably lower for bills that have to pass this quorum compared to those that do not face the same requirement (25.53 % vs. 40.7 %). The Ständemehr therefore might be one reason why pro-bills are less likely to succeed in than outside Switzerland (see results below). These results suggest that while oppressed groups might be able to obtain support from a majority of voters, they struggle much more to win a majority in cantons across the whole country. The next section takes a closer look at the characteristics of the Swiss votes. The decreasing success rates for pro- and contra-bills in case of turnout quora imply that if the findings of Aguiar-Conraria and Magalhães (2010) about turnout quora negatively affecting turnout hold, lower turnout does not disadvantage oppressed groups disproportionately. Finally, the higher success rate of contra-bills that have to fulfill an approval quorum compared to those that do not is an interesting pattern. Given results from Marx and Leininger (2022) on lower turnout in case of approval quora, we might assume this to work to the expense of oppressed groups this time. However, due to the low numbers of bills that have to fulfill this quorum, no major conclusions can be drawn.

The last characteristic of interest is whether the vote takes place in the motherland of direct democracy. *Switzerland* is regarded as a special case in research on direct democracy, given the country's long history of popular votes and their important standing in the political decision-making process with few checks on constitutionality (e.g., Stojanović, 2021; Vatter & Danaci, 2010). Table 12 reveals that at the bill-level, there are almost no differences in the ratios of pro- and contra-bills between Swiss votes and those held outside Switzerland. Yet, when we turn to the outputs, it becomes obvious that pro-bills are less likely to succeed in Switzerland than in other countries. Whereas the share of pro-outputs slightly increases compared to the bill-level outside Switzerland, the share drops from 60.38 % at the ballot to 58.82 % for those adopted in Switzerland. To put it differently: in Switzerland, only 31.25 % of pro-bills succeed at the ballot, while 33.33 % of the contra-bills do. Outside Switzerland, pro-bills fare better at the ballot than contra ones (success rates of 39.13 % vs. 36.96 %). These deviating numbers stress the necessity for comparative large-N analyses in research on direct democracy, as findings from Switzerland do not tell us how direct democracy works in general. However, contrary to claims from some scholars of direct democracy that the process works especially well for oppressed groups such as linguistic minorities in Switzerland compared to other countries (Barry, 1975; Bolliger, 2007; Stojanović, 2021), when looking at a larger range of groups, the opponents of such groups seem to benefit more from the country's extensive direct democratic options and tradition.

Table 12: Direct Democratic Bills and Outputs in- and outside Switzerland, 1990-2015

	Pro-bills N (%)	Contra-bills N (%)	Pro-outputs N (%)	Contra-outputs N (%)	Success Rate: Pro-bills (%)	Success Rate: Contra-bills (%)
Switzerland	64 (60.38)	42 (39.62)	20 (58.82)	14 (41.18)	31.25	33.33
Outside Switzerland	69 (60)	46 (40)	27 (61.36)	17 (38.64)	39.13	36.96

Source: own dataset

To sum up, according to descriptive statistics, oppressed groups seem to fare better in direct democratic votes outside Switzerland, in top-down and especially in mandatory votes compared to bottom-up votes, when a vote result is not binding, and when there is no quorum in place. Before investigating differences in constituency attitudes between pro- and contra-bills and -outputs, the following takes a closer look at the institutional factors that might drive the results for Switzerland.

6.3.1.2 Institutional Explaining Variables in Switzerland

A major finding of the above section is the considerably lower success rate of pro-bills in Switzerland compared to those in other countries (31.25 % vs. 39.13 %). Does the Swiss case combine institutional factors that hinder pro-bills as identified in the above? Or are there other factors at work specific to the Swiss votes examined, which would call for the inclusion of Switzerland as a control variable in the regression analyses?

The following compares the success rates for different direct democratic instruments and the existence of a quorum between bills at the ballot in Switzerland and outside the country.[20] If the success rates are similar, the differing overall numbers for Switzerland are probably explained by one of these institutional factors. If the success rates differ, the regression analyses should control additionally for votes taking place in Switzerland as this implies the effects of other country-specific variables.

Table 13 and 14 show that there seem to be factors at work in Swiss votes that go beyond specific direct democratic instruments or the existence of a quorum. Regarding the *instruments*, we see a much higher success rate for bottom-up pro-bills outside Switzerland (29.41 % vs. 17.39 %). Similarly, the success rates for bottom-up contra-bills are lower in Switzerland than in the

---

20   As all of the direct democratic votes in Switzerland are binding, I do not calculate numbers for this characteristic.

Table 13: Direct Democratic Bills and Outputs and Instruments in- and outside Switzerland (CH)

	Pro-bills		Contra-bills		Success Rate: Pro-bills		Success Rate: Contra-bills	
	N CH	N rest	N CH	N rest	% CH	% rest	% CH	% rest
Top-down votes	0	23	0	7	–	34.78	–	42.86
Bottom-up votes	46	34	33	31	17.39	29.41	27.27	35.48
Mandatory votes	18	12	9	8	66.67	75	55.56	37.5

Source: own dataset

Table 14: Direct Democratic Bills and Outputs and Quora in- and outside Switzerland (CH)

	Pro-bills		Contra-bills		Success Rate: Pro-bills		Success Rate: Contra-bills	
	N CH	N rest	N CH	N rest	% CH	% rest	% CH	% rest
Quorum	47	29	22	28	25.53	27.59	40.91	35.71
No Quorum	20	40	17	18	47.06	47.5	25	38.89

Source: own dataset

other countries (27.27 % vs. 35.48 %). For mandatory pro-bills, success rates are lower in Switzerland than outside (66.67 % vs. 75 %), whereas success rates for contra-bills are higher in Switzerland (55.56 % vs. 37.5 %). So, whereas the higher success rate of contra- compared to pro-bills in Swiss votes overall can be found again in bottom-up but not in mandatory votes, the higher success rate of pro- compared to contra-bills outside Switzerland only shows in mandatory votes. Therefore, differences cannot be attributed clearly to specific direct democratic instruments at use. Regarding *quora*, a similar statement can be made: whereas the lower success rate of pro-bills in Switzerland might stem from the higher number of pro-bills there that have to fulfill a quorum (which lowers success rates for pro-bills in and outside Switzerland), the higher success rate of contra-bills outside Switzerland cannot be traced back to different quora regulations. In contrast, although the number of contra-bills that have to fulfill a quorum is higher compared to those that do not have to fulfill one outside Switzerland, the success rate of the former is actually lower than that of the latter (35.71 % vs. 38.89 %). For Switzerland, a clear difference emerges regarding contra-bills: contrary to the success rates of pro-bills, those of contra-bills are much higher when a quorum has to be fulfilled compared to when there is no quorum in place (40.91 % vs. 25 %). These mixed results for institutional variables in and outside Switzerland reveal that there have to be other country-specific factors contributing to the differences in bills and outputs. As a result, Switzerland should be a control variable in the regression analyses to control for factors at work there that are not part of the analyses.

Leaving institutional factors behind, the following section turns to differences in attitudes and socio-economic variables within the constituency when bills concerning oppressed groups come to a vote.

6.3.2 Attitudinal and Socio-Economic Explaining Variables

The first context factors discussed here regarding the constituency where the vote takes place under descriptive analysis are the attitudes of the population regarding certain oppressed groups and equality in general. I assume that more positive attitudes promote the initiation and adoption of pro-bills, whereas more negative feelings result in contra-bills and -outputs – in general and even more pronounced when a bill affects the specific group. Afterwards, I present numbers on the level of education, the GDP growth per capita, and ethnic fractionalization in the respective constituencies. Here, I expect a higher level of education and economic growth to characterize pro-bills and -outputs, while ethnic fractionalization should be higher for pro-bills, but lower for pro- and for contra-outputs. To gain a first impression about whether these variables make a difference to the impact of direct democracy for oppressed groups, Figures 23-32 in Appendix B include the means of the variables in the country and year of the votes on pro- and contra-bills. Details on data sources and variable description can be found in the previous chapter. Tables 38 and 39 in Appendix B contain the numerical means.

For the *variables on single groups*, means refer to all bills voted upon at the time and in the country of measurement. As a result, the variables should tap more into a general tolerance. The variable "negative attitude towards group" includes the above attitudes concerning the group that is actually affected by a bill. Thereby, a more direct relationship between attitudes towards a group and direct democratic bills and outputs for that group can be investigated.

Turning first to the attitudes about whether there are certain groups which one does not want to have as neighbors, a mixed picture emerges. As noted in the previous chapter, the variables were recoded from 0 to 1, with 1 representing a mention of the group as one that is not wanted as neighbors. As a result, the means presented here are the shares of the respondents that mentioned the group in the year and country of the vote (e.g., when a pro-bill comes to a vote, 8.04 % of the respondents claim they do not want to live next to people of a different race, whereas 7.65 % claim the same when a contra-bill is at the ballot). At the bill-level, some means confirm the intuitive assumption that they should be lower for pro- than for contra-bills: fewer people mention that they do not want to have Muslims, members of a different religion or homosexuals as neighbors at the time and place of a vote on bills supporting oppressed groups than on bills disadvantaging them. However, for the other variables, the mean values are higher for pro-bills – wanting no neighbors of a different race, with mental problems or immigrants. When we look at the outputs, this is even more pronounced: the only group that is mentioned less often in the case of pro-outputs compared to contra-outputs are members of a different religion (and, with a small difference, homosexuals). For the other groups, the share of people mentioning them as people they do not want to have as neighbors is actually lower in the case of contra-outputs.

Second, the proxies for attitudes towards women and people of low socio-economic status are investigated. As can be expected, the share of people declaring that jobs should be given to men in times when jobs are scarce is higher for contra- than for pro-bills. However, the share is higher for pro- compared to contra-outputs. With the statement that incomes should be distributed less equally, the surprising picture appears at both levels: at the bill-level, less people express this belief when pro-bills are put to a vote compared to contra-bills. At the output-level, again more people express this belief when a pro-bill gets adopted than when a contra-bill does.

Third, more people hold negative attitudes towards the group concerned when a pro-bill comes to a vote compared to a contra-bill. Similarly, aversion is higher in the case of pro- than in case of contra-outputs. This seems to disconfirm hypotheses H4a-c, assuming that a more negative attitude results in more contra- than pro-bills and increases the chances for contra-outputs while decreasing the chances for pro-outputs.

Fourth, a more general measurement of *attitudes on equality* is the question of whether it is important to treat people equally and grant them equal opportunities. There, the differences between pro- and contra-bills and outputs are rather small, but also slightly more people report this to be important in the case of contra-outputs compared to pro-outputs and contra-bills compared to pro-bills. This hints at the possibility that hypotheses H5b and H5c, assuming a positive effect on pro-outputs and a negative one on contra-outputs, might be disconfirmed in the multivariate analysis.

Finally, socio-economic country-level factors at the time of the vote are analyzed (see Figures 33-35 in Appendix B). Mirroring previous findings on education fostering minority-friendly votes, the share of inhabitants with a degree in tertiary education is higher for pro-bills and -outputs compared to contra ones. This supports hypotheses H6a-c. Likewise, GDP growth per capita is higher for pro-bills and -outputs, lending support to hypotheses H7a-c. Finally, also the level of ethnic fractionalization is slightly higher when pro-bills come to a vote compared to when contra-bills do, and when pro-bills get adopted compared to contra-bills. However, the difference especially for the latter is marginal. This fits hypothesis H8a, assuming a higher share of pro- compared to contra-bills when ethnic fractionalization is high. The result that ethnic fractionalization is lower at the output- compared to the bill-level supports hypotheses H8b and H8c, stating that ethnic fractionalization decreases the chances of any bill to be adopted.

6.4 Summary: Descriptive Results on Hypotheses

This chapter ends with a short overview of what the descriptive results mean in light of the hypotheses formulated in Chapter 4. Besides H1a-c, which require descriptive investigations, the conclusions drawn here are of course only preliminary. Nevertheless, they can give a first hint of what to expect from the bivariate and multivariate analyses. Table 15 on the next page summarizes whether the descriptive findings support or contradict hypotheses.

First, there are actually more pro-bills affecting low SES groups than contra-bills – and the difference is more pronounced for these groups compared to classic oppressed groups and political groups. Yet, the success rate of pro-bills is lower for low SES groups compared to the other groups. However, the success rate of contra-bills is lower for low SES groups as well.

Second, while there are more pro- than contra-bills in bottom-up votes as well, the share of pro-bills is higher in top-down and mandatory votes. Likewise, the share of pro- compared to contra-outputs is higher for top-down and mandatory votes, while it is lower for bottom-up votes. These votes also show the lowest success rate for pro-bills. Whereas top-down votes show a higher success rate for contra- than for pro-bills as well, they still result much more often in pro- than in contra-outputs. Finally, while bottom-up votes are more likely to result in contra- compared to pro-outputs, the success rate of contra-bills is actually lower than it is for top-down and mandatory votes. However, this is a consequence of the lower success rate of bottom-up votes in general. Compared to pro-bills, contra-bills fare better in bottom-up votes.

Third, success rates for pro-bills are considerably higher in votes without quora requirements. Yet surprisingly, success rates for contra-bills are actually lower when no quorum is in place. Quora seem to be an obstacle for bills supporting the interests of oppressed groups in particular, but not for bills disadvantaging these groups. Turnout quora and the Ständemehr are

Table 15: Tests of Hypotheses in Descriptive Analyses

Hypothesis	Result
H1a: more contra-bills for low SES groups	disconfirmed
H1b: low SES groups ↓ pro-outputs	confirmed
H1c: low SES groups ↑ contra-outputs	disconfirmed
H2a: top-down & mandatory votes ↑ pro- bills	supported
H2b: top-down & mandatory bills ↑ pro- outputs	supported
H2c: top-down & mandatory bills ↓ contra- outputs	partly supported
H3a: quora ↓ pro-outputs	supported
H3b: quora ↓ contra-outputs	contradicted
H4a: negative attitude ↓ pro-bills	contradicted
H4b: negative attitude ↓ pro-outputs	contradicted
H4c: negative attitude ↑ contra-outputs	contradicted
H5a: support for equality ↑ pro-bills	contradicted
H5b: support for equality ↑ pro-outputs	contradicted
H5c: support for equality ↓ contra-outputs	contradicted
H6a: education ↑ pro-bills	supported
H6b: education ↑ pro-outputs	supported
H6c: education ↓ contra-outputs	supported
H7a: economic growth ↑ pro-bills	supported
H7b: economic growth ↑ pro-outputs	supported
H7c: economic growth ↓ contra-outputs	supported
H8a: ethnic fractionalization ↑ pro-bills	supported
H8b: ethnic fractionalization ↓ pro-outputs	supported
H8c: ethnic fractionalization ↓ contra-outputs	supported

responsible for lower success rates of pro-bills, whereas approval quora and the Ständemehr account for the higher success rates of contra-bills.

Fourth, negative attitudes towards the group concerned by a vote are in fact more widespread when pro-bills come to a vote than when contra-bills face a ballot. In addition, negative attitudes are at a higher level in the case of pro- versus contra-outputs. These numbers are definitely not what one would expect, so it will be interesting to see if they are supported by the results of the bivariate and multivariate analyses.

Fifth, the support for equal opportunities and equal treatment is slightly lower when pro- instead of contra-bills come to the ballot and in the case of pro-outputs compared to contra-outputs. Chapter 8 will reveal whether this holds in multivariate analyses.

Sixth, when pro-bills are voted upon, the level of university education is higher than when contra-bills are voted upon. It is also higher in cases producing pro-outputs compared to contra-outputs. At first glance, education indeed seems to promote voting in support of oppressed groups.

Seventh, economic growth is higher for pro- than for contra-bills. The same holds for the output-level. Again, descriptive results support the hypotheses, but it remains to be seen whether multivariate analyses will do the same.

Finally, the degree of ethnic fractionalization is slightly higher for pro- than for contra-bills. As it is lower for the output-level in general, this supports the assumption that fractionalization prevents the adoption of bills in general.

This chapter gave an initial overview of the bills, outputs, oppressed groups affected and explaining variables analyzed in this dissertation. The following chapter presents results from bivariate analyses, before moving on to Chapter 8, which contains encompassing investigations based on multivariate, multilevel regression analyses.

7 Bivariate Statistics

Before turning to the multivariate analyses, this chapter presents bivariate statistics. The first section contains measures for the correlations between the explaining variables and whether a bill includes measures in support of or against oppressed groups as dependent variable (pro- or contra-bills). The second section replaces this dependent variable with the probability that these bills are adopted at the ballot (pro- or contra-outputs). Finally, the correlations between the explaining variables are presented. For nominal explaining variables, Cramér's V is reported. For quasi-metric variables, bivariate logistic regressions are performed.

7.1 Explaining Variables and Pro- and Contra-Bills

Table 16 contains the percentages of bills with pro- and contra-oppressed group measures as dependent variable, differentiated between the values of the nominal explaining variables. In addition, Cramér's V measures the correlations of the dependent and these explaining variables. As the dataset contains all the direct democratic votes affecting oppressed groups in European democracies between 1990 and 2015, it represents the full population, rendering measures of statistical significance irrelevant. They are reported in the tables for transparency, but not discussed further.

Looking at the bills that make it to the ballot, whether they are pro or contra correlates only very weakly with the location of the vote in or outside *Switzerland* and with the existence of a *quorum*. However, it correlates with the *direct democratic instrument* used on a moderate level. The percentages imply that this moderate correlation is mainly due to the top-down votes, which far more often include pro-oppressed group measures than bottom-up and mandatory votes. Hypotheses H2a-c assumed the main difference to be between bottom-up votes on the one hand and top-down and mandatory ones on the other. The multivariate analyses in the next chapter will show whether this is indeed the relevant distinction when controlling for other factors. Finally, there is also a moderate correlation between the kind of bills and whether the result of the vote is *binding* for legislation. In votes where the result is not binding, the share of pro-bills is higher than it is in votes with

Table 16: Direct Democratic Bills and Nominal Explaining Variables, Cramér's V

Explaining Variables	Contra-bills (%)	Pro-bills (%)	Cramér's V
Outside Switzerland	40	60	0.0039
In Switzerland	39.62	60.38	
Bottom-up votes	44.44	55.56	
Mandatory votes	36.17	63.83	0.1496*
Top-down votes	23.33	76.67	
Not binding	22.22	77.78	−0.1070
Binding	41.38	58.62	
Quorum	40	60	0.0032
No quorum	39.68	60.32	

*** $p < 0.01$, ** $p < 0.05$, * $p < 0.1$; Source: own dataset

binding results. It will be interesting to see whether this effect of "bindingness" holds in the multivariate analyses, or whether it disappears due to correlations with other explaining variables, as reported in section 4 of this chapter.

Table 17 shows the logistic standard regression coefficients for bivariate logistic regressions between attitudinal and socio-economic variables and the probability of pro- instead of contra-bills. In addition to the general effects of the attitudinal variables, the effect of attitudes towards the group targeted with the bill is also estimated.

For the *attitudinal variables*, it is important to remember that their values contain the share of respondents who reported that they did not want certain groups as their neighbors, jobs should be given to men instead of to women when jobs are scarce, larger income differences are something to aim for, and that equal treatment and opportunities are important. Therefore, regarding the variables on disliked neighbors, it comes as no surprise that the odds of a bill being pro instead of contra are lower when people are more intolerant regarding their neighbors being Muslim, of different religion or homosexual. However, a higher level of intolerance for neighbors of a different race, with mental problems or immigrants increases the probability of a pro-bill.

Turning to the proxies for attitudes towards gender equality and low SES groups, we see negative effects – implying that intolerant attitudes in these categories enhance the probability of contra-bills. When we look at the attitude towards the group concerned, a positive effect emerges, meaning that the probability of a bill supporting this group is actually higher if the constituency holds more negative attitudes towards it. This is highly surprising and contradicts hypothesis H4a. Similarly, the more general question as to whether one regards equal treatment and opportunities as important shows a negative effect, contrary to the assumption in hypothesis H5a.

Table 17: Pro-Bills and Explaining Variables, logistic regression coefficients from single models with standard errors in brackets

Explaining Variable	DV: pro-bill
No neighbors of different race	1.35 (4.43)
No neighbors with mental problems	0.82 (1.57)
No Muslim neighbors	−0.23 (4.49)
No neighbors of different religion	−14.93** (7.64)
No immigrant neighbors	2.24 (3.13)
No homosexual neighbors	−0.23 (1.33)
Jobs for men	−3.17 (3.48)
Larger income differences	−2.62 (3.21)
Negative attitude towards group	4.00* (2.18)
Equal treatment and opportunities	−2.16 (9.45)
Tertiary education degree	5.73** (2.03)
GDP growth/capita	7.75* (4.78)
Ethnic fractionalization	1.45 (1.39)

*** $p < 0.01$, ** $p < 0.05$, * $p < 0.1$; Sources: own dataset, World Values Survey Round 2-6, European Social Survey Round 1-7, Eurostat, Worldbank, Historical Index of Ethnic Fractionalization Dataset

The numbers for the socio-economic variables support the hypotheses. A higher *growth in GDP* per capita and a country being more *ethnically fractionalized* at the time of the vote increase the probability of pro-bills, as assumed in the hypotheses H7a and H8a. The same holds for a higher share of inhabitants with degrees in tertiary *education*, as stated in hypothesis H6a.

7.2 Explaining Variables and Pro-Outputs

After analyzing the factors concerning a bill being pro instead of contra in a bivariate way, the following investigates the bivariate effects on the chances of pro-bills being adopted at the ballot and thereby resulting in pro-outputs. The descriptive results already revealed patterns that differed from those characterizing the bills at the ballot.

Table 18 contains the percentages of successful (pro-outputs) and unsuccessful pro-bills as dependent variable, differentiated between the values of the nominal explaining variables. In addition, Cramér's V measures the correlations between the dependent and these explaining variables.

Table 18: Pro-Outputs and Nominal Explaining Variables, Cramér's V

Explaining Variables	Adopted pro-bills (%)	Not adopted pro-bills (%)	Cramér's V
Outside Switzerland	39.13	60.87	−0.0824
In Switzerland	31.25	68.75	
Bottom-up votes	22.5	77.5	0.4025***
Mandatory votes	70.00	30.00	
Top-down votes	34.78	65.22	
Not binding	35.71	64.29	−0.0027
Binding	35.29	64.71	
Quorum	26.32	73.68	−0.2179**
No quorum	47.37	52.63	

*** $p < 0.01$, ** $p < 0.05$, * $p < 0.1$; Source: own dataset

When we turn to the nominal variables determining pro-outputs, several patterns can be noted. First, there is a weak relationship between the vote taking place in *Switzerland* and pro-outputs. At least on a bivariate level, pro-outputs are less likely in Switzerland than outside it. Second, there is a very strong correlation between the *direct democratic instrument* employed and pro-outputs. The chances of pro-outputs occurring are far higher when it is a mandatory vote, while they are lower for top-down votes and bottom-up ones. The high success rate of mandatory votes probably stems at least in part from the fact that the votes in question are mainly on issues involving constitutional change, containing, for example, broad clauses against discrimination in general. Such issues are general principles with which most people can probably agree and where agreement comes at no cost to voters. Taken together, these numbers support hypothesis H2b, assuming a positive effect of top-down and mandatory votes compared to bottom-up ones on the probability of pro-outputs. Third, as already mentioned, the *"bindingness"* of the vote result displays only a very weak correlation with pro-outputs. Pro-bills are slightly more likely to be adopted when the result is not binding, but the difference is not highly distinguished. Finally, the existence of a *quorum* correlates strongly with the probability of a pro-bill to succeed. As one could expect and as formulated in hypothesis H3a, pro-bills are more likely to be adopted when they do not have to fulfill a quorum.

Table 19 shows the logistic standard regression coefficients for bivariate logistic regressions between attitudinal and socio-economic variables and the probability of a pro-output.

Table 19: Pro-Outputs and Explaining Variables, logistic regression coefficients from single models with standard errors in brackets

Explaining Variable	DV: pro-output
No neighbors of different race	5.52 (6.43)
No neighbors with mental problems	−1.79 (2.33)
No Muslim neighbors	8.48 (7.46)
No neighbors of different religion	−8.02 (16.37)
No immigrant neighbors	2.60 (4.14)
No homosexual neighbors	0.45 (1.88)
Jobs for men	0.01 (4.55)
Larger income differences	4.17 (4.36)
Negative attitude towards group	5.14 (3.93)
Equal treatment and opportunities	−12.70 (11.60)
Tertiary education degree	−2.16 (2.52)
GDP growth/capita	3.14 (4.86)
Ethnic fractionalization	−3.95** (1.91)

*** $p < 0.01$, ** $p < 0.05$, * $p < 0.1$; Sources: own dataset, World Values Survey Round 2-6, European Social Survey Round 1-7, Eurostat, Worldbank, Historical Index of Ethnic Fractionalization Dataset

The results of the bivariate regressions with the *attitudinal* and socio-economic variables and the probability of pro-outputs are mixed as well. Although for most of the regressions, the dependent variable does not distinguish between the groups concerned, what seems to be a random distribution of negative and positive effects still comes as a surprise. Regarding the "neighbor"-variables, one would expect the chances of a pro-output to be higher when fewer people are intolerant towards their neighbors. Indeed, this negative effect shows for not wanting neighbors with mental problems or of a different religion. Yet, a higher tolerance towards neighbors of a different race, Muslims, immigrants and homosexuals actually decreases the probability of pro-outputs. Additionally, the more people regard larger income differences as necessary, the more likely are pro-outputs, as they are the more people think jobs should be given to men when jobs are scarce. The same holds for negative attitudes towards the group targeted with the bill – these increase the chances of pro-outputs, contradicting the negative effect assumed in hypothesis H4b. The more general measure of attitudes towards equality, naming equal treatment and opportunities as important, also reduces the chances of pro-outputs, disconfirming hypothesis H5b. Summing up, the bivariate results for the attitudinal variables offer no clear picture.

In the last part of this section, we turn to socio-economic variables and their effects on pro-outputs. Here, we see that a higher share of inhabitants with a *tertiary degree* and a higher *ethnic fractionalization* decrease the probability of pro-outputs, disconfirming hypothesis H6b while supporting hypothesis H8b. The first finding in particular comes as a surprise, as past theoretical and empirical work implied tolerance towards oppressed groups rises with education level (Vatter et al., 2014). The effect of *GDP growth* per capita is in the positive direction expected in hypothesis H7b. The next section investigates the bivariate factors affecting whether contra-bills are successful.

7.3 Explaining Variables and Contra-Outputs

The following presents the results of bivariate analyses of the explaining variables and the probability that a bill containing contra-oppressed group measures is adopted (contra-outputs). Do these factors contrast those for pro-outputs, or are other mechanisms at work here?

Table 20 contains the percentages of successful (contra-outputs) and unsuccessful contra-bills as dependent variable, differentiated between the values of the nominal explaining variables. In addition, Cramér's V measures the correlations between the dependent and these explaining variables.

Cramér's V indicates a moderate correlation between the *direct democratic instrument* in use and the probability of contra-outputs. While these are

Table 20: Contra-Outputs and Nominal Explaining Variables, Cramér's V

Explaining Variables	Adopted contra-bills (%)	Not adopted contra-bills (%)	Cramér's V
Outside Switzerland	36.96	63.04	−0.0379
In Switzerland	33.33	66.67	
Bottom-up votes	31.25	68.75	
Mandatory votes	47.06	52.94	0.1376
Top-down votes	42.86	57.14	
Not binding	50	50	−0.0675
Binding	34.52	65.48	
Quorum	38	62	0.0666
No quorum	31.58	68.42	

Source: own dataset

Table 21: Contra-Outputs and Explaining Variables, logistic regression coefficients from single models with standard errors in brackets

Explaining Variable	DV: contra-output
No neighbors of different race	0.05 (6.63)
No neighbors with mental problems	8.51* (6.76)
No Muslim neighbors	−5.92 (7.11)
No neighbors of different religion	−4.69 (7.91)
No immigrant neighbors	−3.57 (5.37)
No homosexual neighbors	0.32 (2.11)
Jobs for men	−4.18 (6.12)
Larger income differences	−9.61 (6.57)
Negative attitude towards group	−4.90 (4.48)
Equal treatment and opportunities	18.52 (17.23)
Tertiary education degree	−1.77 (3.31)
GDP growth/capita	−24.88*** (9.24)
Ethnic fractionalization	−1.93 (2.27)

*** $p < 0.01$, ** $p < 0.05$, * $p < 0.1$; Sources: own dataset, World Values Survey Round 2-6, European Social Survey Round 1-7, Eurostat, Worldbank, Historical Index of Ethnic Fractionalization Dataset

most common in mandatory votes, contra-bills are more likely to fail than to win across all instruments. This seems to disconfirm hypothesis H2c, assuming a positive effect mainly from bottom-up votes. There is also a very weak correlation with the vote taking place in *Switzerland*, where contra-outputs are less common. For the other variables, correlations are weak as well. Therefore, it seems that these institutional variables are more relevant for the fate of pro-bills. The higher chances for contra-outputs when *quora* are in place compared to when they are not contradicts hypothesis H3b.

Table 21 contains the logistic standard regression coefficients for bi-variate logistic regressions between attitudinal and socio-economic variables and the probability of contra-outputs.

Explaining contra-outputs, Table 21 yields a number of interesting findings. First, focusing on *attitudes*, almost all of the "neighbor"-variables show negative effects, meaning that higher intolerance actually decreases the chances of contra-outputs. This also holds for the more specific measure of a negative attitude towards the group affected by the vote, thereby disconfirming hypothesis H4c, and whether men should be prioritized before women when jobs are scarce. The only effects in the assumed direction are the positive effects of higher intolerance for neighbors of a different race and homosexuals. However, a preference for larger income differences makes contra-outputs less likely, while positive attitudes towards equal treatment and opportunities in general increase their chances, disconfirming hypothesis H5c.

Second, there is a negative effect for *GDP growth* per capita. In economically challenging times, contra-bills obviously have better chances of being adopted, as assumed in hypothesis H7c. The effects of the other socio-economic variables imply negative effects for the share of inhabitants with *tertiary degrees* and *ethnic fractionalization* on the probability of contra-outputs. These findings lend support to hypotheses H6c and H8c. Summing up, no clear conclusions can be drawn on the similarities and differences for factors determining pro- versus contra-outputs. While the directions of some effects are similar, others are different. The last section on bivariate results deals with correlations between the diverse explaining variables.

7.4 Correlations between Explaining Variables

To dive a little deeper into the relationships between the explaining variables, this section deals with correlations between these variables. It starts with institutional variables, proceeds with attitudinal ones and finishes with socio-economic variables. Appendix B contains Tables 40-48 with results of the analyses.

For the correlations between the vote taking place in Switzerland and other explaining variables, we see in Table 40 that this is highly correlated with the direct democratic instrument and with the vote being binding. This is because all Swiss direct democratic votes are binding and top-down votes do not exist there. There is also a strong correlation with the existence of a quorum, which is more common in Switzerland. The results for all the attitudinal variables show that Swiss respondents on average are more tolerant than people outside Switzerland taken together (Table 41). The share of people with tertiary degrees is higher in Switzerland, whereas the growth in GDP per capita is lower. Ethnic fractionalization is above average. These results suggest that the effects found in the bivariate analyses presented above are very likely to change once Switzerland is included as a control in the analyses in the next chapter.

Table 42 shows that there are strong correlations between the direct democratic instrument and whether the vote result is binding and must fulfill a quorum. All the votes that are not binding are in fact top-down ones. These are also more likely to not have to fulfill a quorum, while more mandatory votes must pass one. Again, this suggests that the effects of the other institutional variables might differ from the bivariate effects mentioned above once the direct democratic instrument is controlled for. The differences in attitudinal and socio-economic variables are not really telling (Table 43). Nevertheless, it seems as if the constituency shows less tolerant attitudes in top-down votes. Moreover, for bottom-up votes, the mean ethnic fractionalization is highest, while education is highest in case of mandatory votes.

Whether a vote result is binding correlates only weakly with the existence of a quorum (Table 44). In addition, numbers for not binding votes are so small that the differences in the means for the attitudinal and socio-economic variables are not really telling (Table 45). Yet, it seems that in the case of not binding votes, the constituency is less tolerant, while also less ethnically fractionalized. Only the growth of GDP and the share of inhabitants with tertiary degrees are a bit higher for the time and place of these votes.

The correlations between the attitudinal and socio-economic variables offer some interesting findings (see Tables 46-48). First, and as was to be expected, intolerant attitudes correlate strongly positive with one another. This holds for whether an individual does not want several groups as neighbors, but also (to a lesser degree) for whether jobs should be given to men rather than to women and whether larger income differences are desirable. This finding supports taking these variables as proxies for attitudes towards gender equality and low SES groups. Second, the level of tolerance in a society in general increases with the level of education, as supposed by Christmann and Danaci (2012). Third, higher growth in GDP per capita comes with less tolerance towards all of the groups included here. Finally, higher ethnic fractionalization is positively correlated with tolerance towards most of the groups, with the exception of members of a different religion or Muslims.

7.5 Summary: Bivariate Results on Hypotheses

Table 22 summarizes the results of the bivariate analyses in light of the hypotheses formulated in Chapter 4. Compared to the description of distributions and mean values in the previous chapter, the correlations and bivariate regressions calculated here subject the hypotheses to more thorough tests. In addition, it is now possible to make statements about effects on pro- and contra-outputs in contrast to merely comparing the mean values of variables in cases of one or the other output. Table 22 does not include results on hypotheses 1a-c, as they rest on descriptive statistics.

First, the direct democratic instrument used indeed correlates moderately with a bill being pro instead of contra, and mandatory and top-down votes witness a higher share of pro-bills than bottom-up votes do. The instruments also correlate strongly and significantly with a pro-bill being adopted – this

Table 22: Tests of Hypotheses in Bivariate Analyses

Hypothesis	Result
H2a: top-down & mandatory votes ↑ pro- bills	confirmed
H2b: top-down & mandatory bills ↑ pro- outputs	confirmed
H2c: top-down & mandatory bills ↓ contra- outputs	disconfirmed
H3a: quora ↓ pro-outputs	confirmed
H3b: quora ↓ contra-outputs	disconfirmed
H4a: negative attitude ↓ pro-bills	disconfirmed
H4b: negative attitude ↓ pro-outputs	disconfirmed
H4c: negative attitude ↑ contra-outputs	disconfirmed
H5a: support for equality ↑ pro-bills	disconfirmed
H5b: support for equality ↑ pro-outputs	disconfirmed
H5c: support for equality ↓ contra-outputs	disconfirmed
H6a: education ↑ pro-bills	confirmed
H6b: education ↑ pro-outputs	disconfirmed
H6c: education ↓ contra-outputs	confirmed
H7a: economic growth ↑ pro-bills	confirmed
H7b: economic growth ↑ pro-outputs	confirmed
H7c: economic growth ↓ contra-outputs	confirmed
H8a: ethnic fractionalization ↑ pro-bills	confirmed
H8b: ethnic fractionalization ↓ pro-outputs	confirmed
H8c: ethnic fractionalization ↓ contra-outputs	confirmed

result is mainly caused by the high share of adopted bills in mandatory votes in general. Yet again, the share of pro-outputs is also higher in top-down votes compared to bottom-up votes. Finally, there is a moderate correlation between the direct democratic instrument and whether a contra-bill is adopted. However, the share of contra-outputs is higher in mandatory and top-down votes than it is in bottom-up votes.

Second, whether a quorum is in place correlates strongly with the share of adopted pro-bills, with a higher share of bills being adopted when there are no quora requirements. There is only a weak correlation with the share of adopted contra-bills, but contrary to expectations, more contra-bills get adopted when quora have to be fulfilled.

Third, a more negative attitude towards the group affected by a vote actually raises the probability of a pro- rather than a contra-bill. The same holds for the probability of a pro-output: higher levels of a negative attitude towards the group increase chances for pro-outputs as well. In contrast, a more negative attitude decreases the probability of a contra-output. Each of these effects goes against the expectations formulated in the hypotheses.

Fourth, more respondents claiming that equal treatment and opportunities are important decreases the chances of a pro- instead of a contra-bill coming to the ballot. It also decreases the probability that a pro-bill is adopted and therefore produces a pro-output, while it increases chances of a contra-output. Again, all these results run contrary to expectations. It will be interesting to see whether they hold in the multivariate multilevel analyses.

Fifth, a higher level of university education indeed boosts the probability that a bill is pro instead of contra. Yet, contrary to expectations, it cuts the probability of a pro-output. Confirming H6c, it also decreases the probability of a contra-output.

Sixth, the bivariate analyses confirm all hypotheses on economic growth: higher growth increases the probability of pro-bills and pro-outputs, while it decreases the probability of contra-outputs.

Finally, at least in the bivariate results, ethnic fractionalization also has the effects expected of it: higher fractionalization enhances the probability of a pro-bill, but it reduces both the probability of a pro-output and that of a contra-output.

In this chapter, I investigated how different explaining variables correlate with and influence whether a direct democratic bill that affects an oppressed group supports or disadvantages that group, whether a pro-bill is successful at the ballot, and whether a contra-bill is. Correlations between the explaining variables gave a first hint as to which effects might change in the multivariate analyses. The next chapter contains the results of these multivariate regression analyses, which also control for possible variance between the countries and years covered in my dataset.

8 Multivariate Statistics

This chapter entails the core of my analyses – multivariate logistic regressions determining the key factors for bills with pro- and contra-oppressed group measures to come to and win at the direct democratic ballot. Its structure is similar to the previous chapter, in presenting first the results for the probability of bills with pro-oppressed group measures at the ballot as dependent variable (pro-bills), second the probability of bills with pro-oppressed group measures to win (pro-outputs), and then finally, the probability of bills with contra-oppressed group measures succeeding (contra-outputs). Do factors work in opposite directions for pro- compared to contra-outputs? Or are there factors that contribute similarly to both kinds of outputs, thereby explaining the success of a bill more generally?

Unfortunately, data availability prevents calculation of a full model including all explaining variables at the same time – this would result in analyzing only one country. Data on the institutional factors and whether the vote takes place in Switzerland is available for all votes, so these variables are stepwise included and afterwards kept in all models. Thereby, their substantial effects, as observed in the bivariate statistics, are always accounted for. Data on support for equality is available for 95 votes in thirteen countries, data on education for 163 votes in 19 countries, data on economic growth for 212 votes in 21 countries, and data on ethnic fractionalization is available for 186 votes in fifteen countries. Data on negative attitudes towards the group affected by the vote is only available for 27 votes. As a result, models including this variable would not yield very reliable results and are therefore dropped in the following. In some of the models, the inclusion of an additional variable and the reduction of cases caused by that lead to changes in the directions of the effects of other variables. If not otherwise noted, additional analyses reveal that this is only caused by the smaller sample size and not due to correlations between variables. Finally, most of the effects are rather small and/or show large standard deviations, with the credible interval often including zero. As my dataset represents a full sample of all votes affecting oppressed groups in this period, this does not limit the explanatory power of the results. However, it is important to bear in mind that future research might find deviating effects for other countries or time spans. Because the dataset represents a full sample, I do not report levels of significance.

8.1 The Probability of Pro-Bills

The first part of the multivariate analyses investigates which institutional, attitudinal and socio-economic factors increase or decrease the probability of pro-bills at the ballot instead of contra ones.

The results shown in Tables 23-25 support some of the hypotheses while contradicting others: the analysis of all votes in Model 5 (Table 24) supports hypothesis H2a, assuming a negative effect of bottom-up votes on pro-bills compared to top-down and mandatory votes. A prospering economy increases the probability of bills supporting oppressed groups, as was suspected in hypothesis H7a (Model 8). Likewise, a higher share of inhabitants who graduated from university raises the probability of pro-bills as assumed in hypothesis H6a (Model 7), and higher ethnic fractionalization increases the probability of pro-bills as well as assumed in hypothesis H8a (Model 9). Yet,

Table 23: The Probability of Pro-Bills I, Bayesian multilevel logistic regressions

Dependent Variable: Pro-Bill = 1 Bayesian multilevel logistic regressions	Model 1 Mean (sd)	Model 2 Mean (sd)	Model 3 Mean (sd)	Model 4 Mean (sd)
(Intercept)	0.50 (0.28)	0.20 (0.30)	−0.06 (1.09)	−0.18 (1.12)
Mandatory (Reference = Bottom-up)		0.44 (0.40)	0.51 (0.41)	0.43 (0.38)
Top-down (Reference = Bottom-up)		1.20 (0.55)	1.43 (0.80)	1.45 (0.85)
Binding			0.21 (1.06)	0.25 (1.04)
Quorum				0.15 (0.34)
Num. obs.	221	221	221	221
Num. Groups: Country	21	21	21	21
Num. Groups: Year	26	26	26	26
Var: Country (Intercept)	0.27	0.15	0.30	0.15
Var: Year (Intercept)	0.42	0.44	0.49	0.42
ICC Country	0.08			
ICC Year	0.11			

Source: own dataset

Table 24: The Probability of Pro-Bills II, Bayesian multilevel logistic regressions

Dependent Variable: Pro-Bill = 1 Bayesian multilevel logistic regressions	Model 5 Mean (sd)	Model 6 Mean (sd)	Model 7 Mean (sd)
(Intercept)	0.01 (1.24)	−2.84 (2.70)	0.23 (1.42)
Mandatory (Reference = Bottom-up)	0.43 (0.41)	0.90 (0.74)	0.56 (0.52)
Top-down (Reference = Bottom-up)	1.43 (0.92)	3.30 (2.24)	1.41 (1.09)
Binding	0.06 (1.16)	2.57 (2.41)	0.09 (1.31)
Quorum	0.22 (0.43)	0.80 (0.73)	0.12 (0.48)
Switzerland	0.22 (0.90)	1.50 (1.00)	0.09 (0.84)
Equal treatment		−26.07 (15.53)	
Education			9.65 (4.58)
Num. obs.	221	95	163
Num. Groups: Country	21	13	19
Num. Groups: Year	26	14	23
Var: Country (Intercept)	0.67	0.48	0.46
Var: Year (Intercept)	0.55	8.99	1.67

Sources: own dataset, European Social Survey Round 1-7, Eurostat

contradicting hypothesis H5a, higher support among the constituency for treating people equally decreases the probability of pro-bills (Model 6). The next sections will discuss these findings in more detail.

Table 25: The Probability of Pro-Bills III, Bayesian multilevel logistic regressions

Dependent Variable: Pro-Bill = 1 Bayesian multilevel logistic regressions	Model 8 Mean (sd)	Model 9 Mean (sd)
(Intercept)	−0.14 (0.94)	−0.33 (1.39)
Mandatory (Reference = Bottom-up)	0.26 (0.46)	0.64 (0.48)
Top-down (Reference = Bottom-up)	1.56 (0.72)	0.80 (1.00)
Binding	0.13 (1.05)	0.01 (1.24)
Quorum	0.41 (0.41)	0.43 (0.42)
Switzerland	0.34 (0.79)	0.57 (0.61)
GDP growth/capita	9.82 (5.01)	
Ethnic fractionalization		0.55 (2.69)
Num. obs.	212	186
Num. Groups: Country	21	15
Num. Groups: Year	26	26
Var: Country (Intercept)	0.99	0.14
Var: Year (Intercept)	0.32	1.02

Sources: own dataset, Worldbank, Historical Index of Ethnic Fractionalization Dataset

8.1.1 Variation between Countries and Years

The intra class correlations (ICCs) in Model 1 point to low, but detectable variation between countries as well as between years, supporting the choice to use a crossed-effect model. Of the overall variation in bills being pro or contra, 8 % stems from variation between countries, while 11 % stems from variation between years. Time trends seem to be more important than regional trends for whether a bill contains pro- or contra-oppressed group measures. As indicated by the mean estimate, a bill is more likely to contain pro- than contra-oppressed group measures.

8.1.2 Institutional Explaining Variables, Switzerland

Models 2-5 show that compared to *bottom-up votes*, the probability of pro-bills is much higher in mandatory or top-down votes. The inclusion of additional variables does not affect these effects in a substantial way. In the full sample, the effects are particularly strong for top-down votes. In addition, if a vote result is *binding* and when *quora* exist that have to be fulfilled, bills are more likely to be pro-oppressed group as well (Model 5). Higher stakes and hurdles do not seem to hinder oppressed groups in bringing their interests to the ballot, while they decrease the probability of contra-bills. Finally, bills in *Switzerland* are also more likely to contain pro-oppressed group measures than bills in other countries. Figure 5 details the mean coefficients and credible intervals for Model 5.

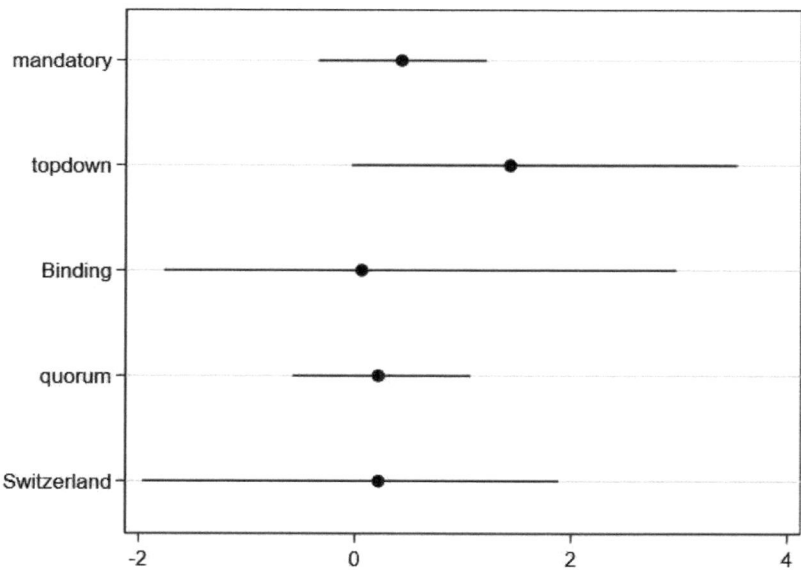

Figure 5: Institutional Factors, Switzerland and Pro-Bills, Model 5 (mean coefficients, credible intervals)

8.1.3 Attitudinal Explaining Variable

Model 6 shows that more *support for equal treatment and opportunity* in general actually substantially decreases the probability of pro-bills (see Figure 6). Compared to contra-bills, pro-bills are far less likely to be found at the ballot when a constituency finds equality more important.

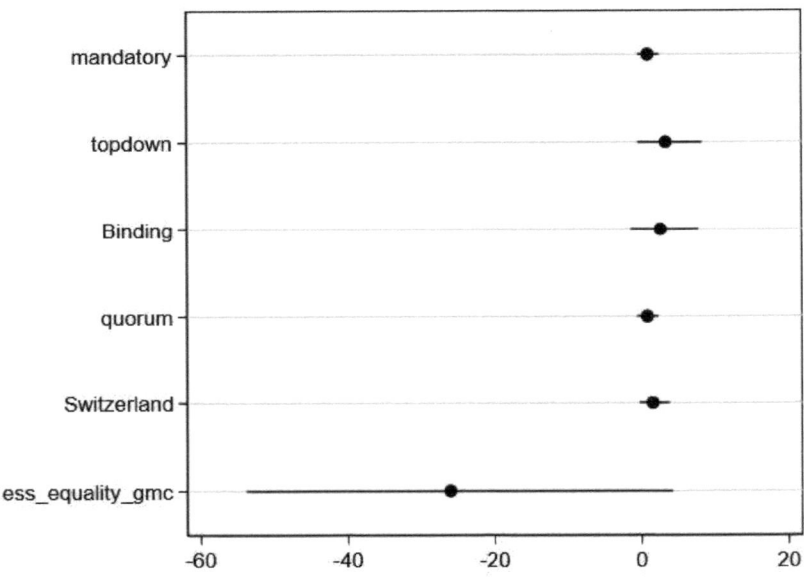

Figure 6: Equality and Pro-Bills, Model 6 (mean coefficients, credible intervals)

8.1.4 Socio-Economic Explaining Variables

According to Model 7, a higher share of people with a *tertiary degree* increases the probability of a bill containing pro-oppressed group measures (Figure 7), as does higher *economic growth* (Model 8, Figure 8). Finally, higher *ethnic fractionalization* makes pro-bills more likely as well, as shown in Model 9 (Figure 9). Summing up the effects of socio-economic variables, the probability of pro-bills is higher when the constituency is more educated, more ethnically fractionalized, and when the economy is prospering.

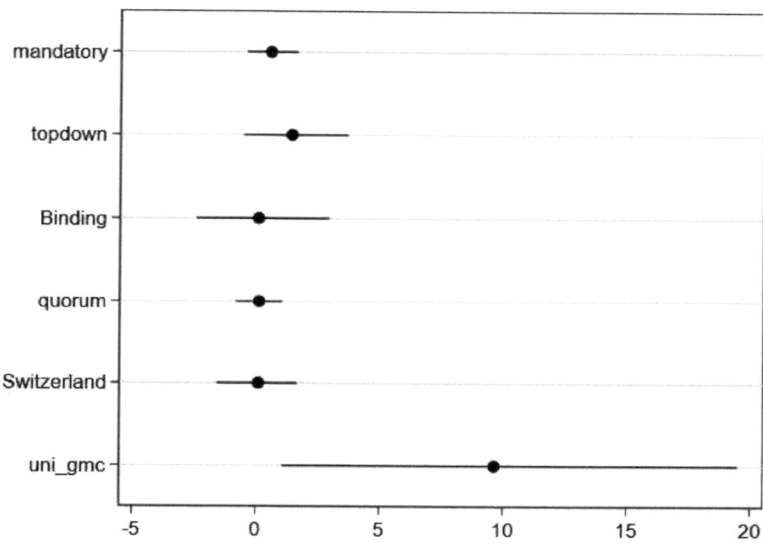

Figure 7: Education and Pro-Bills, Model 7 (mean coefficients, credible intervals)

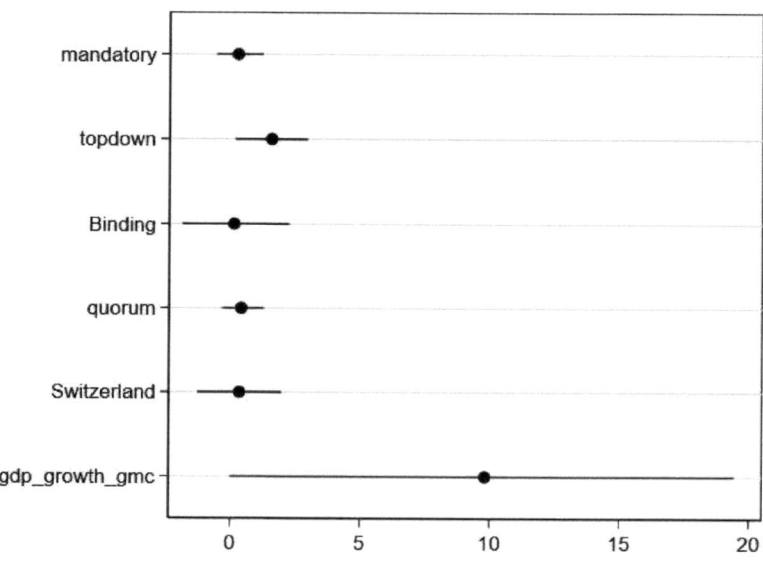

Figure 8: GDP Growth and Pro-Bills, Model 8 (mean coefficients, credible intervals)

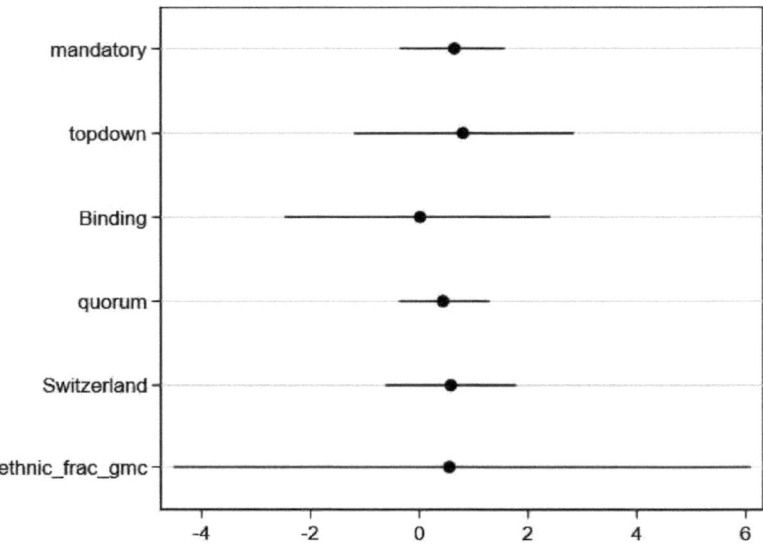

Figure 9: Ethnic Fractionalization and Pro-Bills, Model 9 (mean coefficients, credible intervals)

Summing up, the first part of the analysis, dealing with factors that influence the probability of pro-bills, supports hypothesis H2a, H6a, H7a and H8a on direct democratic instruments, the level of tertiary education, economic growth and ethnic fractionalization. In contrast, it contradicts hypothesis H5a on general support for equality.

However, in terms of the actual output of direct democratic votes, it is crucial to analyze the factors that lead a bill with pro-oppressed group measures to succeed at the ballot (pro-outputs). Can we detect the same effects as at bill-level? Or do some factors foster pro-oppressed group measures being brought to the ballot, but work to their disadvantage in the actual vote? The next section will answer these questions.

8.2 The Probability of Pro-Outputs

The second part of the multilevel analyses investigates the influence of institutional, attitudinal and socio-economic variables on the probability that the pro-bills from above are adopted at the ballot – which involves winning a majority of votes and also passing a possible quorum.

The results shown in Tables 26-28 confirm and disconfirm three hypotheses, respectively. Hypothesis H3a, assuming a negative influence of the existence of a quorum on pro-outputs, and hypothesis H2b on the positive influence of mandatory and top-down votes compared to bottom-up votes are confirmed when controlling for all institutional variables and Switzerland (Model 5). In contrast, hypothesis H5b, assuming a positive influence of a constituency that supports equal treatment and opportunities, is disconfirmed – the more people support equal treatment and opportunities, the less probable it actually is for a pro-bill to be adopted (Model 6). The hypotheses on the influence of the socio-economic variables are partly confirmed. In contrast to the positive impact assumed in hypothesis H6b, higher education decreases chances for pro-outputs (Model 7). The same holds for higher economic growth (Model 8), which was assumed to enhance chances as well in hypothesis H7b. Finally, and according to expectations in hypothesis H8b, higher ethnic fractionalization decreases the chances of pro-outputs (Model 9). The next sections discuss the findings in more detail.

Table 26: The Probability of Pro-Outputs I, Bayesian multilevel logistic regressions

Dependent Variable: Pro-Output = 1 Bayesian multilevel logistic regressions	Model 1 Mean (sd)	Model 2 Mean (sd)	Model 3 Mean (sd)	Model 4 Mean (sd)
(Intercept)	−0.56 (0.54)	−1.21 (0.44)	−1.13 (1.67)	1.19 (2.94)
Mandatory (Reference = Bottom-up)		2.32 (0.58)	2.40 (0.60)	7.05 (3.39)
Top-down (Reference = Bottom-up)		0.49 (0.64)	0.18 (1.07)	−0.12 (1.26)
Binding			−0.00 (1.74)	−0.60 (2.72)
Quorum				−6.20 (3.49)
Num. obs.	133	133	133	133
Num. Groups: Country	19	19	19	19
Num. Groups: Year	26	26	26	26
Var: Country (Intercept)	2.86	0.97	3.67	36.46
Var: Year (Intercept)	0.15	0.22	0.27	0.23
ICC Country	0.47			
ICC Year	0.04			

Source: own dataset

Table 27: The Probability of Pro-Outputs II, Bayesian multilevel logistic regressions

Dependent Variable: Pro-Output = 1 Bayesian multilevel logistic regressions	Model 5 Mean (sd)	Model 6 Mean (sd)	Model 7 Mean (sd)
(Intercept)	−0.71 (2.19)	49.46 (20.97)	6.05 (2.94)
Mandatory (Reference = Bottom-up)	5.42 (1.62)	22.92 (9.42)	7.30 (1.91)
Top-down (Reference = Bottom-up)	0.26 (1.38)	−45.74 (10.20)	−5.96 (2.53)
Binding	0.67 (2.45)	−37.79 (25.34)	−4.31 (2.74)
Quorum	−4.56 (1.55)	−22.64 (9.70)	−6.56 (1.86)
Switzerland	−0.32 (3.30)	−1.08 (11.32)	−2.60 (2.94)
Equal treatment		-6.61 (30.95)	
Education			−9.55 (5.32)
Num. obs.	133	65	101
Num. Groups: Country	19	11	16
Num. Groups: Year	26	13	20
Var: Country (Intercept)	26.58	1916.42	46.95
Var: Year (Intercept)	0.09	0.31	0.32

Sources: own dataset, European Social Survey Round 1-7, Eurostat

Table 28: The Probability of Pro-Outputs III, Bayesian multilevel logistic regressions

Dependent Variable: Pro-Output = 1 Bayesian multilevel logistic regressions	Model 8 Mean (sd)	Model 9 Mean (sd)
(Intercept)	0.31 (2.87)	18.78 (12.73)
Mandatory (Reference = Bottom-up)	5.32 (2.31)	5.97 (2.07)
Top-down (Reference = Bottom-up)	−0.90 (0.94)	−24.54 (13.01)
Binding	1.21 (3.21)	−18.79 (13.73)
Quorum	−4.63 (2.44)	−5.21 (1.97)
Switzerland	−2.16 (1.97)	2.41 (2.47)
GDP growth/capita	−12.81 (6.83)	
Ethnic fractionalization		−13.19 (6.51)
Num. obs.	130	108
Num. Groups: Country	19	13
Num. Groups: Year	26	25
Var: Country (Intercept)	25.36	39.54
Var: Year (Intercept)	0.23	0.12

Sources: own dataset, Worldbank, Historical Index of Ethnic Fractionalization Dataset

8.2.1 Variation between Countries and Years

As we can see from the ICCs in Model 1, much of the variation in the probability of a pro-bill being adopted stems from differences between countries – 47 % – while 4 % of the variation stems from differences between years. In contrast to the bill-level, where a pro-bill is voted upon is far more decisive for its output than when the vote takes place. 133 pro-bills are put to a vote in 19 countries, covering the whole timespan from 1990 to 2015. The intercept indicates that fewer bills are adopted than fail.

8.2.2 Institutional Explaining Variables, Switzerland

Direct democratic instruments show a similar pattern when it comes to whether pro-bills are successful at the ballot compared to whether they come to a vote. Mandatory votes increase pro-bills' chances of success compared to bottom-up votes in Models 2-5. Top-down votes exert a positive influence in almost all of these models as well, with the exception of Model 4. Similarly, once the vote taking place in Switzerland is controlled for in Model 5, pro-outputs are more likely when a vote result is *binding*. However, pro-outputs are less likely in *Switzerland* compared to other countries. The same holds for the existence of a *quorum*, which lowers the probability of pro-outputs substantially (Models 4 and 5). Figure 10 visualizes the results of Model 5.

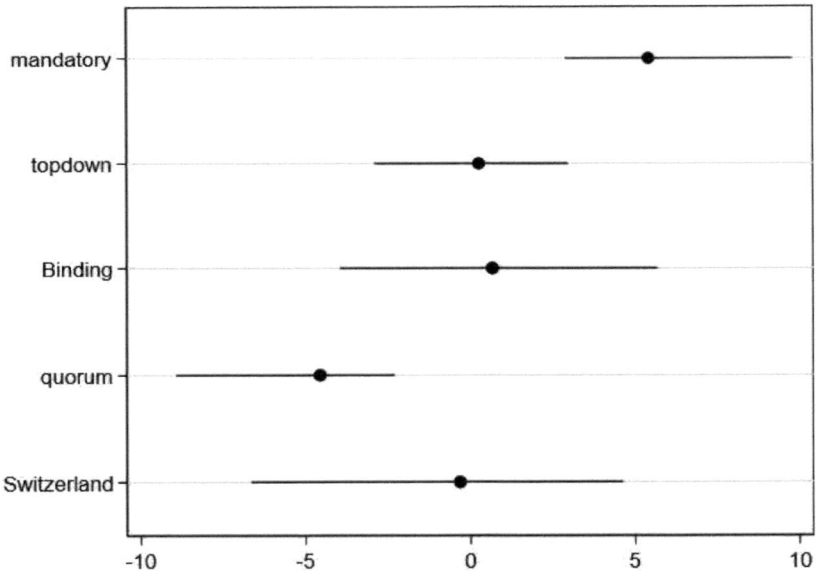

Figure 10: Institutional Factors, Switzerland and Pro-Outputs, Model 5 (mean coefficients, credible intervals)

8.2.3 Attitudinal Explaining Variable

Model 6 shows that *support for equal treatment and opportunities* in a constituency has a negative impact on the chances of pro-outputs (Figure 11). Contrary to H5b, the probability of a pro-bill being adopted is actually lower when the constituency regards equality as important.

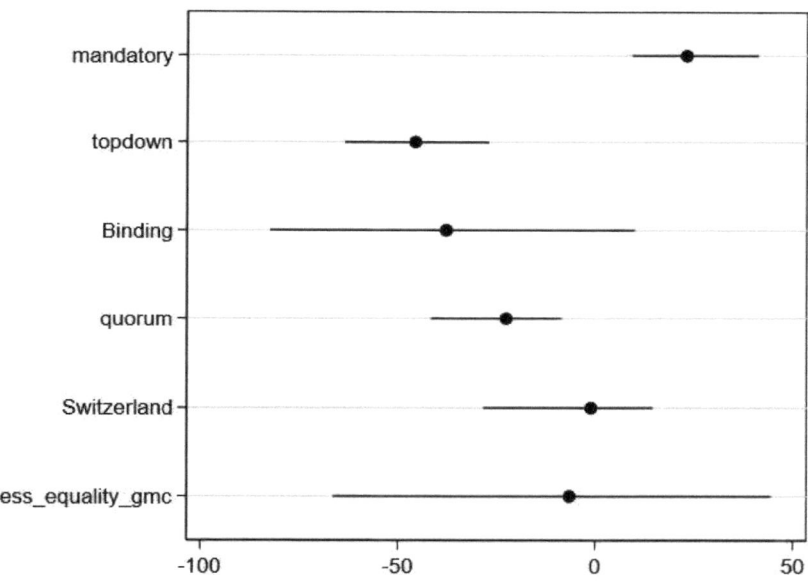

Figure 11: Equality and Pro-Outputs, Model 6 (mean coefficients, credible intervals)

8.2.4 Socio-Economic Explaining Variables

Model 7 shows a negative effect for the share of people with *tertiary education degrees* on the probability of pro-outputs: the more people have a degree, the less likely a pro-bill is to win (Figure 12). Higher *growth in GDP* per capita decreases the probability of pro-outputs according to Model 8 (Figure 13). Finally, Model 9 shows a negative effect for the *ethnic fractionalization* in the country and year of the vote on the probability of pro-outputs (Figure 14).

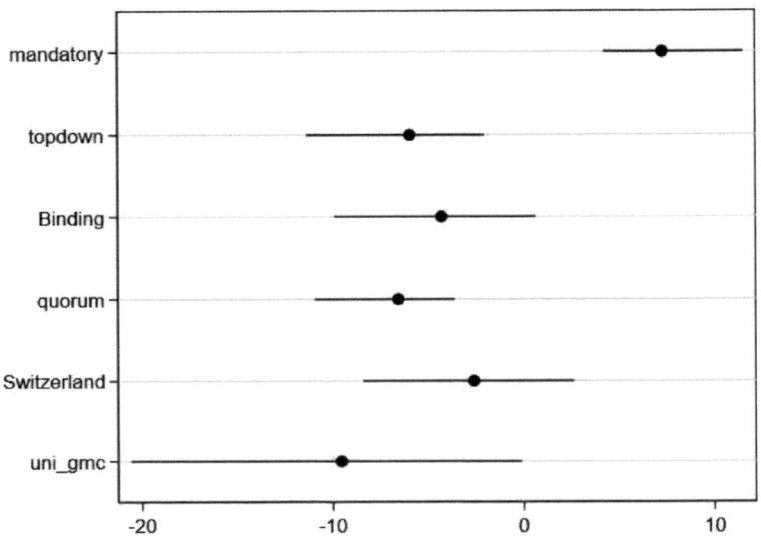

Figure 12: Education and Pro-Outputs, Model 7 (mean coefficients, credible intervals)

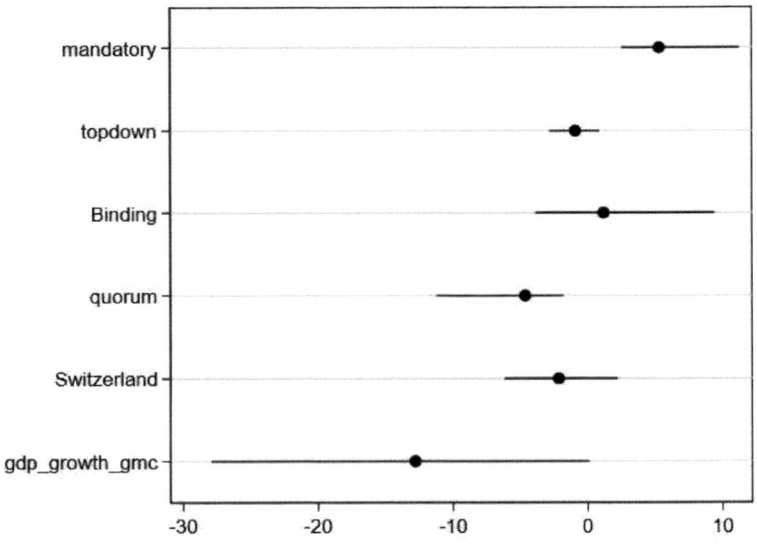

Figure 13: GDP Growth and Pro-Outputs, Model 8 (mean coefficients, credible intervals)

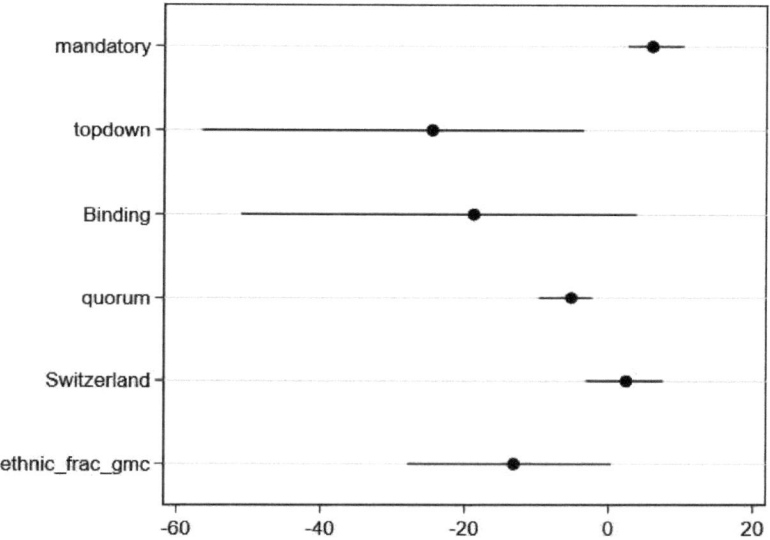

Figure 14: Ethnic Fractionalization and Pro-Outputs, Model 9 (mean coefficients, credible intervals)

Summing up, the second part of the analysis (dealing with the factors influencing pro-outputs) confirms hypotheses H2b, H3a, and H8b on direct democratic instruments, quora, and ethnic fractionalization. Hypotheses H5b, H6b, and H7b on the level of support for equal treatment and equal opportunities, tertiary education and economic growth are disconfirmed.

The findings that oppressed groups are most successful in mandatory or top-down, binding votes without quora and in countries where there is less support for equality in general as well as lower levels of university education, economic growth and ethnic fractionalization are crucial for understanding the circumstances in which oppressed groups are able to put forward their interests through direct democratic votes. However, when it comes to the danger of a *Tyranny of the Majority* developing, the success factors for contra-bills are of essence. The next section will analyze whether institutional, attitudinal, and socio-economic factors work in the opposite way to pro-outputs, or whether they function similarly, suggesting they are general factors relating to the success of a bill at the ballot.

8.3 The Probability of Contra-Outputs

The third and final part of the multilevel analysis investigates the influence of institutional, attitudinal, and socio-economic factors on the probability of contra-bills' adoption via a direct democratic ballot.

The results shown in Tables 29-31 indicate mechanisms similar to the pro-outputs – most of the factors analyzed here seem to influence the success rates of direct democratic bills generally, regardless whether these bills support or undermine the interests of oppressed groups. The negative effect of economic growth suggested in hypothesis H7c and the negative effect of ethnic fractionalization (hypothesis H8c) are confirmed (Model 8, Model 9). These variables show similar effects as for pro-outputs. However, the level of education now increases the probability of a contra-output, disconfirming hypothesis H6c (Model 7). The expected negative effect of quora (hypothesis

Table 29: The Probability of Contra-Outputs I, Bayesian multilevel logistic regressions

Dependent Variable: Contra-Output = 1 Bayesian multilevel logistic regressions	Model 1 Mean (sd)	Model 2 Mean (sd)	Model 3 Mean (sd)	Model 4 Mean (sd)
(Intercept)	−0.94 (1.20)	−0.84 (0.66)	0.69 (3.17)	−0.36 (2.76)
Mandatory (Reference = Bottom-up)		0.81 (0.73)	0.99 (0.79)	0.72 (0.77)
Top-down (Reference = Bottom-up)		−0.16 (1.31)	−1.05 (1.98)	−0.30 (1.62)
Binding			−1.98 (3.66)	−0.73 (2.44)
Quorum				0.46 (0.80)
Num. obs.	88	88	88	88
Num. Groups: Country	12	12	12	12
Num. Groups: Year	24	24	24	24
Var: Country (Intercept)	6.74	3.33	6.99	3.58
Var: Year (Intercept)	0.62	0.29	0.29	0.91
ICC Country	0.67			
ICC Year	0.16			

Source: own dataset

Table 30: The Probability of Contra-Outputs II, Bayesian multilevel logistic regressions

Dependent Variable: Contra-Output = 1 Bayesian multilevel logistic regressions	Model 5 Mean (sd)	Model 6 Mean (sd)	Model 7 Mean (sd)
(Intercept)	−0.39 (2.21)	−42.10 (27.24)	−3.82 (6.45)
Mandatory (Reference = Bottom-up)	0.44 (0.65)	1.98 (1.90)	1.12 (1.55)
Top-down (Reference = Bottom-up)	0.10 (1.46)	41.87 (26.03)	1.05 (3.91)
Binding	−0.52 (2.12)	38.54 (27.02)	1.55 (5.64)
Quorum	0.17 (0.65)	1.29 (1.66)	0.16 (1.34)
Switzerland	0.09 (0.93)	−1.81 (4.32)	1.23 (2.89)
Equal treatment		79.82 (42.27)	
Education			2.71 (14.79)
Num. obs.	88	30	62
Num. Groups: Country	12	7	10
Num. Groups: Year	24	11	21
Var: Country (Intercept)	2.21	34.53	21.02
Var: Year (Intercept)	0.13	1.76	19.44

Sources: own dataset, European Social Survey Round 1-7, Eurostat

H3b) is not confirmed as well (Model 5). Similarly, the negative effect of support for equal treatment and opportunities assumed in hypothesis H5c, and hypothesis H2c, assuming a positive effect on the probability of contra-outputs for bottom-up votes compared to mandatory and top-down votes, are disconfirmed (Model 6, Model 5). The next sections discuss these findings in more detail.

Table 31: The Probability of Contra-Outputs III, Bayesian multilevel logistic regressions

Dependent Variable: Contra-Output = 1 Bayesian multilevel logistic regressions	Model 8 Mean (sd)	Model 9 Mean (sd)
(Intercept)	−5.78 (3.68)	−6.15 (5.84)
Mandatory (Reference = Bottom-up)	0.95 (1.04)	1.17 (1.36)
Top-down (Reference = Bottom-up)	0.24 (1.84)	−0.82 (2.41)
Binding	3.26 (3.45)	1.71 (4.90)
Quorum	0.82 (0.74)	1.37 (1.30)
Switzerland	0.45 (3.22)	3.37 (6.51)
GDP growth/capita	−34.60 (17.87)	
Ethnic fractionalization		−10.16 (12.85)
Num. obs.	82	78
Num. Groups: Country	12	10
Num. Groups: Year	24	23
Var: Country (Intercept)	10.70	39.30
Var: Year (Intercept)	2.91	3.69

Sources: own dataset, Worldbank, Historical Index of Ethnic Fractionalization Dataset

8.3.1 Variation between Countries and Years

According to the ICCs reported in Model 1, compared to pro-outputs, even more of the variation in contra-outputs is explained by variation between countries and also slightly more variation is explained by differences between years. Indeed, 67 % stemming from variation between countries and 16 % from variation between years are remarkable shares and clearly justify a crossed-effect, multilevel approach. Especially the location of a vote seems to be very important for whether a contra-bill is adopted at the ballot. 88 contra-bills come to a vote in 12 countries and in almost every year of the analyzed period. As for the pro-bills, contra-bills are less likely to succeed than they are to fail.

8.3.2 Institutional Explaining Variables, Switzerland

The results for the *direct democratic instruments* mirror those for pro-outputs – mandatory votes boost the probability that contra-bills will succeed compared to bottom-up votes, as mandatory votes increase the probability of pro-outputs (Models 2 to 5). The same holds for top-down votes when controlling for votes taking place in Switzerland in Model 5. The existence of a *quorum* increases the probability of contra-outputs, contrary to the negative effect for pro-outputs (Model 5). It seems that quora make it harder for oppressed groups to improve their status through direct democratic votes, and that quora also do not protect them from negative consequences. Turning to the control variable, Model 5 shows that the vote taking place in *Switzerland* now slightly increases its chances of success. Similarly, in contrast to pro-outputs, the vote result being *binding* reduces the probability of a contra-bill's adoption (Models 3 to 5). That a vote has unavoidable consequences seems to prevent voters from (further) discriminating against oppressed groups. Figure 15 summarizes the results of Model 5.

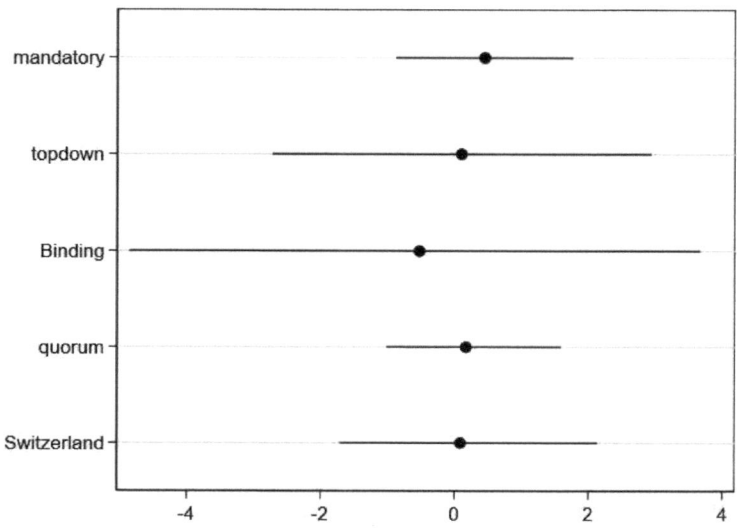

Figure 15: Institutional Factors, Switzerland and Contra-Outputs, Model 5 (mean coefficients, credible intervals)

8.3.3 Attitudinal Explaining Variable

Model 6 shows a positive effect for *support for equal treatment and opportunities* on contra-outputs, which seems counterintuitive (Figure 16). Mirroring the surprising findings for the probabilities of pro-bills and pro-outputs, the more people claim equal treatment and opportunities important, the more probable a contra-bill is to be adopted at the ballot. In contrast to Model 5, a vote taking place in Switzerland now exerts a negative effect on the probability of a contra-output. Additional analysis reveals that this is due to the inclusion of the equality variable and is therefore a result from the level of support for equal treatment correlating with whether a vote takes place in Switzerland in this sample.

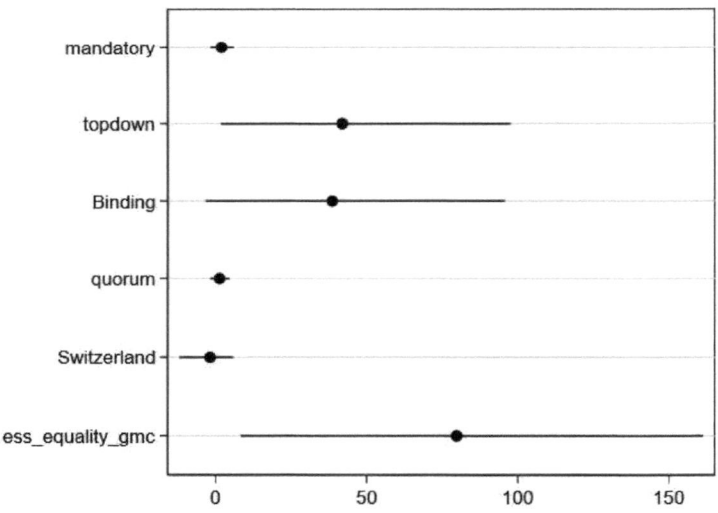

Figure 16: Equality and Contra-Outputs, Model 6 (mean coefficients, credible intervals)

8.3.4 Socio-Economic Explaining Variables

According to Model 7, a higher share of people with *tertiary education degrees* increases the probability of contra-outputs – contrary to pro-outputs, which are less likely with more academically educated inhabitants (Figure 17). Compared to Model 5, a vote result being binding has a positive effect on the probability of contra-outputs in Model 7. Additional analysis reveals

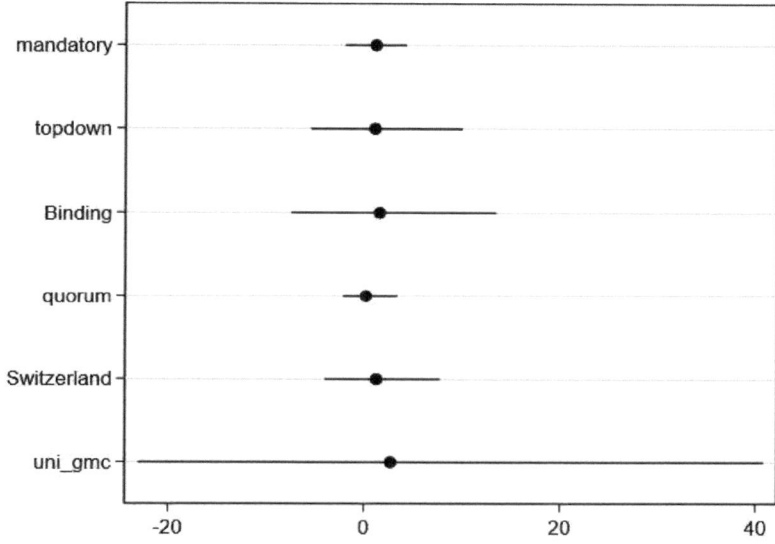

Figure 17: Education and Contra-Outputs, Model 7 (mean coefficients, credible intervals)

that this is due to the inclusion of the education variable. The level of academic education therefore correlates with whether vote results are binding in this sample. Model 8 shows that higher *economic growth* negatively affects the probability of contra-outputs (Figure 18). Finally, we see a negative effect of the level of *ethnic fractionalization* on the probability of contra-outputs in Model 9 (Figure 19). Additional analysis shows that the positive effect of a vote result being binding compared to the negative one in Model 5 stems from the inclusion of the fractionalization variable, so both variables correlate in this sample. Both economic growth and ethnic fractionalization also exert negative effects on the probability of pro-outputs – they hinder the adoption of any bill that affects oppressed groups, regardless of its implications.

Summing up, the third part of the analysis, investigating factors affecting contra-outputs, confirms hypotheses H7c and H8c on the effects of economic growth and ethnic fractionalization. However, it disconfirms hypothesis H2c on direct democratic instruments, hypothesis H3b on quora, hypothesis H5c on support for equal treatment and opportunities as well as hypothesis H6c on the level of education.

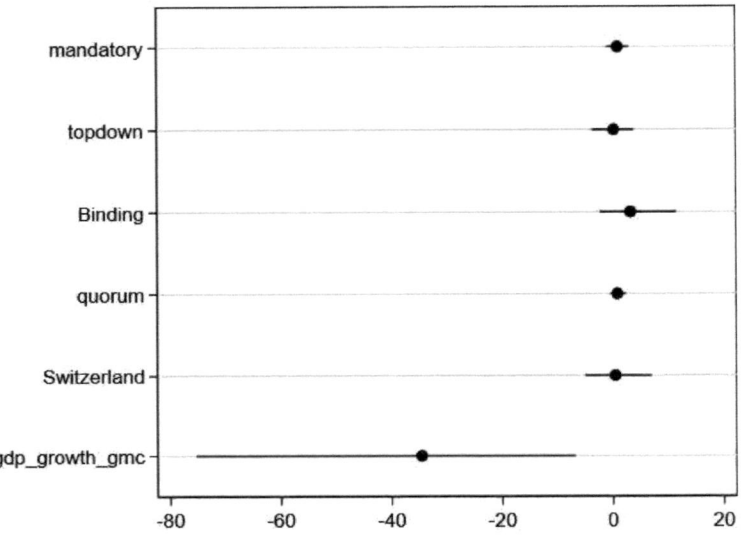

Figure 18: GDP Growth and Contra-Outputs, Model 8 (mean coefficients, credible intervals)

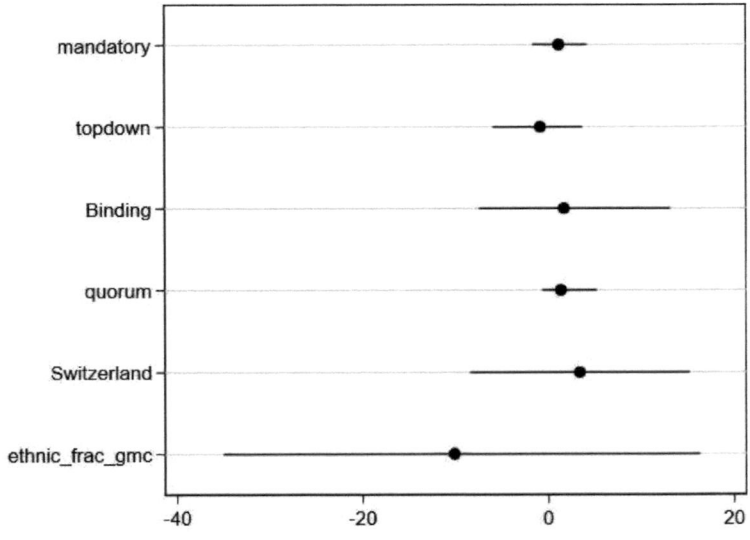

Figure 19: Ethnic Fractionalization and Contra-Outputs, Model 9 (mean coefficients, credible intervals)

8.4 Diagnostics

I carried out a number of tests to check whether performing logistic regressions fits the data I am analyzing. First, logistic regressions assume a linear relationship between the logarithmic chance of success and every explaining variable (Kohler & Kreuter, 2012). Figures plotting the relationship between my dependent variables and the quasi-metric explaining variables sometimes reveal the s-shaped form required for logistic regressions. However, sometimes they also reveal (multiple) u-shaped forms. Yet, including additional variables in the multivariate regressions and accounting for variation based on country and year mitigates the relationships, so logistic regressions can be performed.

Second, analyzing the values of leverage and discrepancy in the single models reveals that the dataset does not include single observations that heavily influence the relationships analyzed here and which therefore should have been excluded from analysis.

8.5 Summary: What Determines the Fate of Oppressed Groups in Direct Democracy?

This chapter analyzed the institutional, attitudinal and socio-economic factors that affect pro-bills, pro-outputs and contra-outputs in Bayesian multilevel crossed-effect logistic regressions.

First, compared to contra-bills, pro-bills are more likely in mandatory and top-down compared to bottom-up votes, when the vote result is binding, when a quorum has to be fulfilled, and when the vote takes place in Switzerland. In addition, more inhabitants with tertiary education degrees, higher economic growth and higher ethnic fractionalization make pro-bills more likely. In contrast, higher support for equality in the constituency decreases the probability of a pro-bill.

Second, a number of factors determines whether a direct democratic bill that affects an oppressed group is adopted, regardless whether it is pro or contra. Compared to bottom-up votes, mandatory and top-down votes make pro- and contra-outputs more likely. Higher economic growth and ethnic fractionalization decrease the chances of adoption for both kinds of bills.

Third, the four factors where the content of a bill seems to make a difference are whether the vote result is binding, whether it has to fulfill a quorum, whether it takes place in Switzerland, and the level of tertiary education. While pro-outputs are more likely when the result of a vote has to be translated into law, contra-outputs are less likely in this case. That a vote result is binding does not seem to prevent voters from passing a bill if this bill entails measures to support oppressed groups. However, voters seem to have second thoughts about voting for a bill that contains measures to disadvantage oppressed groups if the vote result is binding. This finding calls for making the results of direct democratic votes binding. While there are theoretical fears about this leading to a *Tyranny of the Majority*, my empirical results suggest the opposite.

For quora, it is the other way around – pro-outputs are less likely when there is a quorum in place, while contra-outputs are slightly more likely. Again, a bill's content makes a difference in terms of the impact of quora, rather than a quorum decreasing the probability of adoption in general. In theory, quora are often assumed to protect oppressed groups from a *Tyranny of the Majority*. Yet, my findings suggest that they only make it harder for these groups to succeed at the ballot, while at the same time not preventing discriminating outputs.

Votes taking place in Switzerland show similar effects like those where the vote result is not binding – compared to votes outside Switzerland, pro-outputs are less likely in Swiss votes, whereas contra-outputs are more likely there. Swiss voters, with their long experience in direct democracy, seem to be less willing to support oppressed groups compared to voters in other countries.

Finally, and contrary to expectations about higher educated people voting more in support of oppressed groups, pro-outputs are actually less likely where the level of academic degrees is higher, while contra-outputs are more likely. Where academic education is widespread, people seem to shy away from voting in support of oppressed groups. The next chapter puts these findings in a theoretical and empirical context.

9 Discussion

This chapter puts the results presented in the last three chapters in the context of theoretical considerations and former empirical findings. In addition, I present the results of some additional analyses, exploring a few of the most counter-intuitive patterns revealed in the multivariate regressions. For the surprising results where additional analyses are beyond the scope of this dissertation, I develop theoretical and methodological arguments that might explain these findings. Finally, I outline what we can learn from applying the concept of oppressed groups in research on direct democracy.

Summing up, especially binding vote results, the absence of quora, votes outside Switzerland and low levels of tertiary education promote pro-outputs while decreasing the probability of contra-outputs. As a result, binding votes and no quora seem to be the most promising institutional designs to support oppressed groups in direct democratic votes. However, a couple of factors seem to increase the probability of direct democratic bills succeeding at the ballot in general, regardless of the content of the bill. These are mandatory and top-down compared to bottom-up votes, as well as lower levels of economic growth and ethnic fractionalization.

9.1 Overview: Hypotheses and Results

Table 32 summarizes which hypotheses were confirmed and which were disconfirmed in the descriptive and multivariate analyses.

The next paragraphs contain discussions of the results along the lines of the sets of hypotheses, given the theoretical and empirical foundations of these hypotheses. In some cases, additional analyses test whether possible explanations are supported by the data.

Table 32: Tests of Hypotheses in Descriptive (H1), Bivariate (H4) and Multilevel Logistic Analyses

Hypothesis	Result
H1a: more contra-bills for low SES groups	disconfirmed
H1b: low SES groups ↓ pro-outputs	confirmed
H1c: low SES groups ↑ contra-outputs	disconfirmed
H2a: top-down & mandatory votes ↑ pro- bills	confirmed
H2b: top-down & mandatory bills ↑ pro- outputs	confirmed
H2c: top-down & mandatory bills ↓ contra- outputs	disconfirmed
H3a: quora ↓ pro-outputs	confirmed
H3b: quora ↓ contra-outputs	disconfirmed
H4a: negative attitude ↓ pro-bills	disconfirmed
H4b: negative attitude ↓ pro-outputs	disconfirmed
H4c: negative attitude ↑ contra-outputs	disconfirmed
H5a: support for equality ↑ pro-bills	disconfirmed
H5b: support for equality ↑ pro-outputs	disconfirmed
H5c: support for equality ↓ contra-outputs	disconfirmed
H6a: education ↑ pro-bills	confirmed
H6b: education ↑ pro-outputs	disconfirmed
H6c: education ↓ contra-outputs	disconfirmed
H7a: economic growth ↑ pro-bills	confirmed
H7b: economic growth ↑ pro-outputs	disconfirmed
H7c: economic growth ↓ contra-outputs	confirmed
H8a: ethnic fractionalization ↑ pro-bills	confirmed
H8b: ethnic fractionalization ↓ pro-outputs	confirmed
H8c: ethnic fractionalization ↓ contra-outputs	confirmed

9.2 Hypotheses 1a-c: Low SES Groups

For theoretical and empirical reasons, low SES groups were assumed to be at a particular disadvantage in direct democratic votes. As outlined in Chapters 2 and 4, they lack the resources to promote bills supporting their interests as they cannot finance large campaigns, often do not possess staff and networks to collect large numbers of signatures, lack access to the media, and members of the group tend to vote less often than better off groups do. In addition, many people of low socio-economic status are non-citizens, which inhibits them from casting a direct democratic vote at the national level (Parkinson, 2020; Schäfer & Schoen, 2013). Pro-bills for low SES groups often involve costs to better off inhabitants, providing an additional incentive to campaign against these bills. Those same reasons that might make it difficult for pro-bills supporting low SES groups to come to the ballot and pass might also work to increase the chances for contra-bills and -outputs: low SES groups lack resources to confront campaigns against their interests and lack the mobilization at the ballot that their opponents tend to possess.

Yet, the descriptive results in this dissertation offer a mixed picture. There are actually *more pro- than contra-bills* at the ballot that affect low SES groups between 1990 and 2015 in European democracies. Low SES groups even outperform other groups when we only consider the bills at the ballot – 63.19 % (91) of the bills being pro-bills in this cluster represents the highest share of pro-bills, compared to 61.76 % (42) pro-bills for classic oppressed groups and 57.81 % (37) pro-bills for political groups. It seems that low SES groups are indeed able to bring their topics to a vote. This result hints at resources and networks some social scientists do not believe them to have (e.g., Parkinson, 2020), while backing the hopes placed on direct democracy as a tool for empowerment by others (e.g., Lacey, 2021; Leemann, 2015; Serdült & Welp, 2012; Stojanović, 2021). As parliamentary policies are often biased towards the preferences of higher social classes (e.g., Elsässer et al., 2021), direct democracy might constitute a remedy to this malaise of representative democracy. Low SES groups probably also benefit from the enthusiasm that (especially left-leaning) parties show in the direct democratic arena; parties which might gain electorally from pushing for bills that support these groups (see for example Kriesi, 2005).

In contrast, hypothesis 1b is confirmed in my data – *pro-bills indeed have the lowest success rate* when direct democracy affects low SES groups compared to all other groups. Whereas the success rates for pro-bills are 37.84 % (14 out of 37) for political groups and even 52.38 % (22 out of 42) for classic oppressed groups, pro-bills supporting the interests of low SES groups only succeed in 32.97 % of all instances in which they come to a vote (30 out of 91). So, while low SES groups and their allies seem to be able to collect enough signatures or encourage parliament or government to put their interests to a vote, only in about a third of cases do they actually win this vote – compared to a slightly higher success rate of 37.86 % of all direct democratic bills between 1990 and 2015. This fits the assumption of better off people not being willing to share their privileges, successfully campaigning against the interests of low SES groups, and turning out in higher numbers, thereby blocking measures that would increase socio-economic equality.

Two things might explain this difference between bill- and the output-level. First, better off people might be willing to provide a signature in order to bring a bill supporting low SES groups to a vote, given that this is a relatively cheap thing to do. However, they might refrain from supporting these groups in the actual vote, when they have to decide whether they are actually willing to pay the costs of the bill. Second, and on a more institutional note, it takes far fewer signatures to bring a bill to a vote than it takes votes in order for the bill to pass. Possible disadvantages of low SES groups therefore are much more likely to show at the output- than at the bill-level. This finding also makes an important theoretical point in reinforcing the argument that, although group size matters in direct democratic votes, it does not guarantee success. When a large group lacks the resources to win a vote and turns out in low numbers, success at the ballot may nevertheless evade it despite the group's seeming numerical advantage. Finally, the comparatively low number of pro-outputs fits the overall agenda of economic liberalization in many European countries since the 1990s. These populations are seemingly willing to share legal benefits with classic oppressed groups and increase the power of politically oppressed groups, but their willingness to support low SES groups (and pay to do so) is much lower. This corresponds to previous research on lower tax rates and state expenditure in Swiss cantons with more direct democratic options (Feld & Kirchgässner, 2000) and on the negative effect of direct democracy on redistribution in Switzerland and Germany (Feld et al., 2010; Töller & Vollmer, 2013). In addition, the results hint at the disadvantages low SES groups face at the ballot due to lower participation rates as well as due to less willingness to grant benefits to people perceived as less deserving of them, e.g., the unemployed or the poor (Ennser-Jedenastik, 2021; Schäfer & Schoen, 2013). However, the findings question the potential of direct democratic votes to empower low SES groups beyond agenda-setting (e.g., Leemann, 2015; Serdült & Welp, 2012). While the indirect effects of unsuccessful pro-bills might still lead to improvements for low SES groups, for such groups these improvements are less likely to happen through the ballot box than they are for classic oppressed and political groups.

Following the line of H1b and the confirming results, one would expect H1c to be confirmed as well – i.e., the *success rate for contra-bills* should be higher for low SES groups compared to other groups. This, however, is not true according to my data. The success rate of 24.53 % (13 out of 53) for those contra-bills affecting the interests of low SES groups is actually *lower than for political groups*, with 40.74 % (11 out of 27) of these contra-bills winning at the ballot, and *especially low compared to the success rate of contra-bills affecting classic oppressed groups* (42.31 %, 11 out of 26). It seems that, in comparison, opponents of the interests of low SES groups are more successful in preventing bills supporting these interests to win than they are in pushing through bills containing measures against these interests. This might also reflect a status quo bias of voters who do not want to increase benefits to low SES groups, but also do not want them to decrease. The higher resources and turnout of opponents of low SES groups mentioned by Parkinson (2020) and Schäfer and Schoen (2013) do not automatically result in the success of bills targeting low SES groups. In addition, the fact that the success rate of contra-bills is lower than for pro-bills means that the probability for low SES groups to improve their situation via direct democratic votes is higher than their probability to be disadvantaged in these votes.

9.3 Explaining Variables: Institutional Effects

9.3.1 Hypotheses 2a-c: Direct Democratic Instruments

Turning now to the results of the multilevel analyses, H2a assuming *top-down and mandatory bills to be more likely to be pro-bills* than bottom-up bills is indeed what we find in the data. In particular, a bill being initiated top-down instead of bottom-up increases the probability of it being a pro- instead of a contra-bill. Yet, the positive effect of bills being mandatory instead of bottom-up is persistent across all models as well. As a result, while bottom-up votes seem to be used more frequently to prevent improvement or even provoke deterioration in the situation of oppressed groups, these other direct democratic instruments seem to offer more opportunities for enhancing their circumstances. This corresponds to previous findings on mandatory and top-down bills fostering equality, bottom-up votes hindering minority protection, and suggesting that political elites are more tolerant than the general electorate (Christmann & Danaci, 2012; Gamble, 1997; Geißel et al., 2019a; Vatter & Danaci, 2010). However, it disconfirms theoretical assumptions about bottom-up votes being more supportive of oppressed groups and offering them channels of influence (Eder & Magin, 2008; Vatter, 2007). As mandatory bills often contain constitutional changes, for example introducing anti-discrimination legislation, a positive effect could be expected. The positive impact of top-down bills is more noteworthy, as this effect is of considerable size even though the timespan and countries of analysis experienced left- as well as right-wing governments and parliamentary majorities.

When it comes to which kind of direct democratic instruments increase the *probability of a pro-bill to win*, thereby resulting in a pro-output, confirming hypothesis H2b I find that *top-down and mandatory votes indeed increase the probability of a pro-output* compared to bottom-up votes. This fits with previous findings regarding bottom-up votes hindering minority protection compared to mandatory votes in Switzerland and the U.S., and top-down and mandatory votes fostering equality-outputs in European democracies, while again calling into question the role of bottom-up votes as instruments for influence for oppressed groups (Eder & Magin, 2008; Gamble, 1997; Geißel et al., 2019a; Vatter, 2007; Vatter & Danaci, 2010). The reasoning behind the positive effect of mandatory votes might be similar to that outlined above – mandatory bills often contain broad clauses against discrimination, where resistance is marginal. In case of a top-down pro-bill, voters might be more willing to support a bill drafted by elected representatives than one drafted by a (sometimes small) group of their fellow citizens. This should particularly apply in times when support for the government is high.

Finally, H2c is disconfirmed, since compared to bottom-up votes, *top-down and mandatory votes are actually more likely to result in contra-outputs*. Mandatory and top-down votes seem to be more likely to succeed than bottom-up votes in general, regardless of whether they support or disadvantage oppressed groups. Their positive effect on contra-outputs therefore does not completely disconfirm earlier findings by Gamble (1997) and Vatter and Danaci (2010). As Geißel et al. (2019a) investigate direct democratic outputs more broadly under the aspect of equality, their contrasting results are interesting, but might be due to this different focus. In general, the assumption mentioned above might apply again, that voters are more willing to support bills drafted by representatives than those drafted by other citizens.

To sum up, there is no perfect direct democratic instrument for oppressed groups – top-down and mandatory votes seem to be the most beneficial instruments since they increase the probability of pro-bills and -outputs. However, they also increase the probability of contra-outputs. In order to protect oppressed groups from harmful direct democratic outputs, bottom-up bills seem to be the best instrument as they are in general less likely to be adopted.

9.3.2 Hypotheses 3a and b: Quora

The reasoning behind H3a and b was simple – quora increase the hurdles for a direct democratic bill to be adopted, so their existence should reduce the probability of pro- as well as contra-outputs. This is also why they are frequently mentioned as a way to protect oppressed groups in direct democracy (Eder & Magin, 2008; Guasti & Bustikova, 2020). Yet, the multilevel analyses reveal a different reality – the *existence of a quorum actually increases chances of a contra-output* slightly. In contrast, the *probability of a pro-output is reduced* as expected.

This finding seems completely counter-intuitive at first – why should a bill be more likely to succeed when it needs more people to vote for it? One possible explanation is the following: a quorum might serve as a potential mechanism for mobilizing opponents of oppressed groups. In the case of a vote on a pro-bill, these people abstain from the vote in order to let it fail. In the case of a contra-bill at the ballot, a quorum works as an additional mobilization mechanism for the opponents of the affected oppressed group, so they turn out in higher numbers. Research on direct democratic votes about same-sex marriage bans in the U.S. supports this assumption – opponents of same-sex marriage are mobilized to turn out in disproportionate numbers (Simon et al., 2018). Knowing that a quorum must be fulfilled, proponents of a contra-bill might increase their efforts to mobilize voters in order for the bill to pass. This reasoning depends on the existence of a large number of people who support the contra-bill but who, if not mobilized would abstain, since they do not care enough about the cause to turn out without this mobilization. Now, if no additional measures are taken to mobilize these people because there is no quorum in place, the contra-bill might fail at the ballot, because only its opponents turn out to vote. However, if higher mobilization efforts lead to the bill's supporters casting a vote, it might be adopted. If we follow this line of argument, two mechanisms might explain the negative effect of quora on pro-outputs. First, quora might not represent an incentive to increase mobilization efforts among supporters of pro-bills, as maybe these people are more likely to turn out in general, regardless of whether a quorum has to be fulfilled. Second, when a quorum is in place, a large number of the pro-bill's opponents might abstain from the vote in order to let it fail. Summing up, this would suggest that mechanisms of (de-)mobilization by quora work differently for supporters of oppressed groups than for their opponents.

Previous findings from Switzerland suggest that especially those voters with right-wing/conservative attitudes turn out in higher numbers in votes where turnout is higher (Lutz, 2007). As there is no consensus in the literature about the correlation between quora and turnout (e.g. Aguiar-Conraria & Magalhães, 2010; Marx & Leininger, 2022; Thomeczek, 2021), I perform a bivariate linear regression analysis with the level of turnout as dependent variable and the existence of a quorum as independent variable. The results reveal that a quorum has a significantly negative effect on the level of turnout in direct democratic votes affecting oppressed groups, mirroring findings on German votes by Thomeczek (2021) and Marx and Leininger (2022). In general, quora seem to demobilize voters from turning out, either because they assume that the bill will not pass the quorum anyway and thus that their participation is useless, or because opponents of a bill abstain to let it fail. Yet, the positive effect of quora on the probability of contra-outputs and the negative effect on the probability of pro-outputs suggests that they do serve to mobilize certain people, specifically, the opponents of oppressed groups.

The importance of this becomes even more obvious when looking at which bills actually fail because they do not fulfill quora requirements. In total, roughly 19 % of unsuccessful pro-bills fail because of a quorum (16 out of 85), while for unsuccessful contra-bills the figure is 22.41 % (13 out of

58). Based on these numbers, one would indeed assume quora to work as a mechanism of protection for oppressed groups more often. Contrary to the assumptions mentioned above, oppressed groups are in fact able to "win by abstention" in a higher share of votes against their interests than their opponents are. The exception here is Switzerland, where only two pro-bills fail due to a quorum and not a single contra-bill fails for this reason. Winning by abstention is obviously not a successful strategy there.

This brings us back to what we can conclude from the finding that more contra-bills fail due to a quorum, while a quorum exerts a positive impact on the probability of contra-outputs in the multivariate analyses. If we expect quora to work only in the way described in the beginning of the last paragraph, the percentages would suggest that the existence of a quorum has a negative effect on the probability of contra-outputs that is even more pronounced than its negative effect on the probability of pro-outputs. But the fact that they actually increase the probability of contra-outputs, even as they prevent a quarter of contra-outputs because turnout is too low, implies that outside of Switzerland, quora requirements serve as a central mechanism of mobilization for opponents of oppressed groups. Yes, the 13 contra-bills that failed due to a quorum might have been successful without a quorum requirement. However, results from the multivariate analyses suggest that a number of contra-outputs would have been prevented from happening if their supporters had not been motivated to participate because they wanted to push turnout over the level required by the quorum. Therefore, the existence of quora has the exact opposite impact for oppressed groups from what is often assumed in the literature – preventing pro-bills from succeeding while increasing chances for contra-outputs.

9.3.3 Explorative Analyses: Binding Vote Results and Switzerland

I included two variables in the analyses for which I did not have assumptions based on theory or previous research – whether a vote result is binding and whether a vote takes place in Switzerland versus elsewhere. Nevertheless, I will discuss the findings on these variables' effects here, as they contribute to the possibility of designing direct democratic votes to benefit oppressed groups and comparative literature on direct democracy.

First, *binding vote results increase the probability of bills being in support of oppressed groups* rather than against their interests. This might be because binding votes provide an additional incentive for supporters of oppressed groups to bring a bill to the ballot and/or because their opponents shy away from promoting a disadvantaging bill if the impact of the bill would be imminent. A *pro-bill is furthermore more likely to be adopted* if the vote result is binding, whereas a *contra-bill is less likely to be adopted* in this case. That the effect for pro-outputs only is positive when Switzerland is controlled for stems from the fact that bills in general are less likely to be adopted in Switzerland compared to other countries (discussed below) and that all vote results have to be implemented there. The causal mechanism behind the effects on the output-level might be similar to the one mentioned above for the bill-level: binding vote results might encourage supporters of oppressed groups to turn out, while simultaneously inhibiting discriminatory voting behavior. As a result, binding direct democratic votes are not only valuable from the perspective of participatory democratic theory by giving voters immediate decision-making power. They also serve the interests of oppressed groups. In contrast, the argument of non-binding votes serving to protect oppressed groups, since these votes place a parliamentary check prior to a bill's implementation, does not seem to hold. While I do not have data on the enactment of non-binding contra-outputs, the fact that these contra-outputs occur more often in non-binding votes should not be dismissed with the argument that "parliament will probably put an end to them anyway". Not implementing a bill adopted in a direct democratic vote comes with electoral costs that many parties are not willing to pay, which is why Setälä, for example, considers legally non-binding votes to be "de facto binding" (Setälä, 1999, p. 338). Being transparent about the consequences of a vote by making vote results binding seems to be the better strategy to promote the interests of oppressed groups.

Second, how do oppressed groups fare in the motherland of modern direct democracy, Switzerland? If a vote takes place in *Switzerland*, it is *more likely to be on a pro-bill* than when held outside the country. Oppressed groups and their allies seem to be able to benefit from the long tradition of direct democracy in Switzerland – they might also have more experience in bringing their issues to a vote. With *pro-outputs being less likely* in Switzerland, theoretical and empirical arguments about Swiss direct democracy promoting the interests of oppressed groups and supporting their integration do not seem to hold (Kriesi, 2005; Moeckli, 2018; Stojanović, 2021). The finding that *contra-outputs are more likely* in Switzerland than in other countries reinforces this impression – whereas opponents of oppressed groups seem to be able to use their experience, resources and networks to benefit from the established direct democratic options in Switzerland, supporters of oppressed groups seem to be at a disadvantage there. However, outside Switzerland, oppressed groups fare much better in direct democratic votes, since pro-outputs are more likely and contra-outputs are less likely to happen there.

143

9.4 Explaining Variables: Attitudinal Effects

9.4.1 Hypotheses 4a-c: Negative Attitudes

Based on research from Switzerland and the theory of social identity, H4a-c assume that attitudes among the electorate towards the group affected by a bill have an influence on direct democratic bills and outputs. Although data is only available for 27 votes, bivariate analyses disconfirm all of the three hypotheses on this. First, *more negative attitudes actually increase the probability of pro-bills* at the ballot. Second, more negative attitudes also *increase the probability of pro-outputs*. Third, more negative attitudes *decrease the probability of contra-outputs*. Of course, with only 27 votes under analysis here, these could be spurious results. Nevertheless, it is surprising that they all point in the opposite direction from what you would expect. This contradicts theoretical assumptions based on the theory of social identity and empirical findings about discrimination against outgroups in direct democratic votes in Switzerland, while ingroups fare substantially better (Vatter, 2007; Vatter et al., 2014; Vatter & Danaci, 2010). Therefore, let us assume just for a moment that the results in this dissertation actually represent a pattern. What might be an explanation for that? For H4a, it might be that in a country with a large negative sentiment towards an oppressed group, direct democratic efforts to improve that group's position are a way of shedding light on its interests, which are unlikely to be on the parliamentary agenda. For H4b and H4c, it might be a combination of low turnout and extremely motivated supporters of oppressed groups. If turnout in a direct democratic vote is very low (as it tends to be in a number of votes) and unequal, voters and survey respondents just do not mirror each other. If people with a negative attitude towards the group affected by a bill are more likely to abstain while the group's supporters are motivated to cast a vote in its interest, a negative attitude observed in a survey might actually result in direct democratic outputs in favor of the oppressed group.

9.4.2 Hypotheses 5a-c: Support for Equality

People who think everyone should have equal opportunities and should be treated equally should be more likely to support bills favoring oppressed groups and less likely to support bills disadvantaging them. However, this assumption does not hold in the multilevel analysis – *higher support for equal treatment actually decreases the probability of pro-bills* (H5a) *and their chances to succeed* (H5b). Similarly, it *increases the probability of con-*

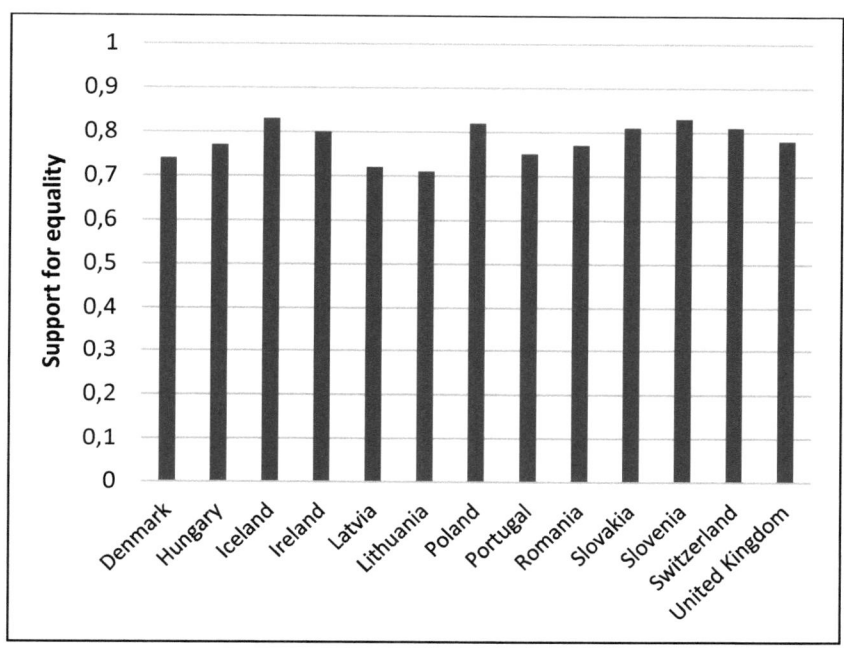

Figure 20: Support for Equal Treatment and Opportunities per Country.
Sources: own dataset, European Social Survey Round 1-7

tra-outputs (H5c). So, all of these results seem to contradict empirical findings of oppressed groups faring better in countries and states with a more liberal population (Bochsler & Hug, 2015; Christmann, 2012; Gerber & Hug, 2002; Lewis, 2013; Milic et al., 2014). A possible explanation for these findings might be the one from above – turnout might be low and voters might then not be a random subset of a country's population. Another possibility might be that people are not able to vote according to their attitudes. Yet, taking a closer look at the data suggests something different: in reality, the attitudinal variable here does not measure an attitude decisive for voting behavior in direct democratic votes affecting oppressed groups. The variable's variation between countries and years is so small and the mean values are so high that, following this, almost every bill at the ballot should be a pro-bill and every output a pro-output. Figures 20 and 21 illustrate this point by displaying the mean values of the support for equal opportunities and equal treatment variable (ranging from 0 to 1) for every country and year in the dataset.

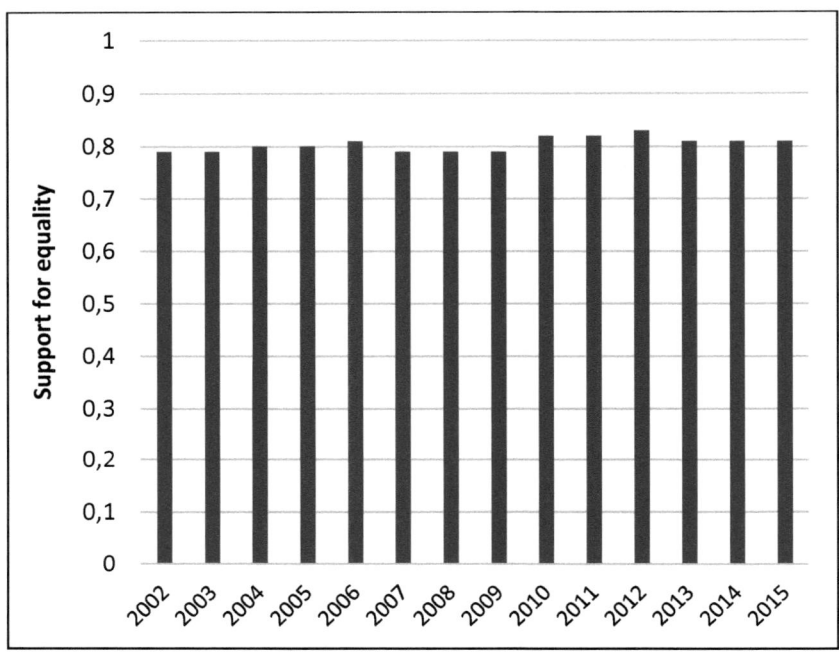

Figure 21: Support for Equal Treatment and Opportunities per Year.
Sources: own dataset, European Social Survey Round 1-7

As both Figures show, support for equal treatment and opportunities barely varies between countries and years. For countries, it stretches from 0.71 in Lithuania to 0.83 in Slovenia and Iceland. For years, it goes from 0.79 in 2002, 2003, 2007, 2008 and 2009 to 0.83 in 2012. Overall, these are pretty high values for a variable ranging from 0 to 1. It seems that almost everyone claims to find equal treatment and opportunities very important. It is indeed very hard to imagine someone claiming that people should not be given equal opportunities. However, this does not translate into equality enhancing voting behavior at the direct democratic ballot in all cases. Therefore, future research should measure the effect of other attitudinal variables that correlate more closely with voting behavior.

9.5 Explaining Variables: Socio-Economic Effects

9.5.1 Hypotheses 6a-c: Education

Based on findings from Switzerland on education and voting behavior, and more general findings on support for far-right parties among lower educated people, H6a-c assume an overall positive impact for education level on the record of direct democracy for oppressed groups (Christmann & Danaci, 2012; Gidron & Hall, 2017; Inglehart & Norris, 2017; Vatter et al., 2014). The multivariate analyses confirm two of these hypotheses, while the third is disconfirmed. As expected, *higher levels of university education in the constituency increase the probability of pro- compared to contra-bills* (H6a). In a more highly educated society, direct democratic bills supporting oppressed groups have a higher probability of being drafted and making it to the ballot. A higher share of inhabitants educated at university increases the chances of members of oppressed groups also attending universities, thereby increasing skills, establishing networks, and accessing the financial resources necessary to bring a bill to the vote. In addition, if higher educated people are more tolerant, it should be easier for oppressed groups in higher educated societies to find allies for their cause, providing resources, access to networks, and signatures for bottom-up votes. As mentioned in Chapter 7, my bivariate analyses indeed find negative attitudes towards oppressed groups to be less common in countries with a higher share of university graduates.

However, according to the multivariate analyses, higher levels of tertiary education do not seem to promote pro-outputs (H6b). In contrast, the *probability of a pro-bill being adopted at the ballot is lower* in countries where more people report a university education. This finding is puzzling – shouldn't a higher number of educated people, who are said to be more tolerant and display less discriminatory voting behavior, make it easier for a bill supporting oppressed groups to win a majority of votes? Especially given the findings about a higher share of pro-bills at the ballot in these countries? Yet, while higher educated people seem to be willing to support the initiation of a pro-bill, they seem to be less willing to vote for bills that would actually improve the situation of oppressed groups in concrete ways. There are at least two possible explanations for this pattern.

First, the differences between the bill- and the output-level might be caused by the lower number of signatures necessary to initiate a vote compared to the number of votes a bill needs to be adopted. Therefore, in a country with a high share of university educated people, there might be more people willing to provide signatures and resources in order to bring a pro-bill to a vote compared to countries with lower levels of education. However, the number and resources of these people might not be sufficient for the pro-bill to actually win a majority of votes. Yet, while this might explain why a higher number of pro-bills does not necessarily correlate with a higher number of pro-outputs, it cannot explain why pro-outputs are even less likely to occur in countries with higher levels of education compared to other countries. This brings us to the second explanation.

Second, the lower probability of pro-outputs in countries with more inhabitants who attended university might be due to pro-bills affecting groups of low socio-economic status. The literature cited above refers to a higher tolerance and less discriminatory behavior from higher educated people towards classic oppressed groups like non-citizens or members of the LGBTQ+ community, on whom previous research focused and who belong to my cluster of classic oppressed groups. However, many bills in my dataset mainly affect low SES groups. Due to intersectionality, these bills of course probably also affect some categories of classic oppressed groups. Yet, they mostly include material interests without mentioning a specific oppressed group. Tolerance might therefore be less decisive for voting decisions compared to decisions about granting rights or material benefits to specific groups, e.g., people with disabilities. This explains why the causal mechanism assumed for education and direct democratic outputs for classic oppressed groups might not hold for low SES groups. But why should it be reversed for direct democratic outputs affecting these groups? The reason behind this might be a correlation between education and income. People who attended university on average have higher incomes than those who did not attend. They are therefore less likely to belong to a low SES group themselves and thereby to benefit from a pro-bill in this cluster. On the contrary, they might have to pay for such a bill – or at least be afraid of losing some of their privileges to people who some of them might think of as less deserving. This probably does not apply to all university educated people, which leaves room for some of them using their resources to bring pro-bills of all clusters to the ballot, confirming H6a. Yet, it might be an explanation for why pro-outputs are less likely in countries with higher levels of education. This fits results from a recent analysis of British panel data, where achieving a university degree led to less authoritarian values and racial prejudices, but increased right-wing economic attitudes (Scott, 2022).[21] In a similar vein, a bigger group size of low SES groups in countries lower on university degrees could mean that more people vote in support of these groups as they themselves would benefit from pro-outputs. To investigate whether levels of education correlate differently with pro-outputs depending on the group concerned, I repeat the multilevel Bayesian model (Table 27, Model 7) excluding bills affecting low SES groups. Table 33 shows the results.

---

21 Items measuring right-wing economic attitudes are for example "government should redistribute income from the better off to those who are less well off" and "private schools should be abolished" (Scott, 2022, p. 7, supplementary data).

Table 33: Education and the Probability of Pro-Outputs without low SES bills, Bayesian multilevel logistic regressions

Dependent Variable: Pro-Output without low SES= 1 Bayesian multilevel logistic regressions	Model 1
	Mean (sd)
(Intercept)	8.62 (6.95)
Mandatory (Reference = Bottom-up)	13.09 (4.20)
Top-down (Reference = Bottom-up)	−6.04 (4.67)
Binding	−10.31 (5.79)
Quorum	−3.82 (2.85)
Switzerland	−4.78 (4.60)
Education	−51.22 (18.21)
Num. obs.	48
Num. Groups: Country	13
Num. Groups: Year	17
Var: Country (Intercept)	1.99
Var: Year (Intercept)	35.65

Sources: own dataset, Eurostat

Table 33 reveals that higher education does not have a different effect on the probability of pro-outputs if I exclude bills that affect low SES groups. Bills supporting the interests of classic oppressed groups and political groups are less likely to succeed at the ballot if the level of tertiary education is higher as well. The explanation that the overall result only stems from higher educated people voting against the interests of low SES groups does not hold. We have to keep in mind that the model calculated above only includes 48 votes. Nevertheless, votes affecting low SES groups are not alone responsible for the negative effect of higher levels of education on the probability of pro-outputs.[22]

---

22 Analyses of the bills that affect low SES groups alone also result in a negative effect of education on the probability of pro-outputs.

Similarly, and again contradicting findings on education reducing discriminatory voting behavior (Vatter et al., 2014) and decreasing support for far-right parties (Gidron & Hall, 2017; Inglehart & Norris, 2017), the analyses also disconfirm hypothesis H6c and reveal that *higher levels of education actually increase the probability of contra-outputs*. As mentioned above for the pro-outputs, one can think of several reasons why direct democratic outputs might be more harmful when the level of academic degrees is higher for bills affecting low SES groups. However, it is difficult to think of reasons why a higher share of people who graduated university should also result in more contra-outputs for classic oppressed and political groups. Future research might investigate possible causal mechanisms behind this in case studies.

Summing up, while higher levels of tertiary education foster pro-bills at the ballot, they also reduce the chances for pro-outputs and increase those for contra-outputs. The higher probability of pro-bills confirms earlier research on higher educated people showing less discriminatory voting behavior (Vatter et al., 2014), lower educated people being more likely to support far-right parties (Gidron & Hall, 2017; Inglehart & Norris, 2017), and my bivariate analyses on higher levels of tolerance in countries with a higher share of university graduates. However, higher educated voters seem to discriminate by denying support at the ballot for direct democratic bills that favor oppressed groups and also lending support to bills disadvantaging oppressed groups. Right-wing economic attitudes only explain this result in parts, as higher tertiary education also reduces the probability of the adoption of pro-bills that support classic oppressed groups and political groups. Future research can investigate possible causal mechanisms further and develop explanations for these surprising patterns.

9.5.2 Hypotheses 7a-c: Economic Growth

Results for the effects of economic growth on the probability of pro-bills, pro-outputs and contra-outputs are partly similar to the results on the effects of education. First, H7a, which assumes a *higher probability for pro-bills in times of higher economic growth* is confirmed in the analyses. It seems that people are more willing to initiate direct democratic votes in support of oppressed groups in times of economic prosperity. This fits previous findings on lower support for extremist parties in times of economic growth in Europe (Rao et al., 2018).

Similarly, the *probability of contra-outputs is lower* when the economy grows more. This confirms H7c. Putting it differently, contra-outputs are more likely in times of less economic growth or even economic decline. This fits the assumption that people are less willing to give when they possess less or fear that their wealth is about to shrink. It also corresponds to previous research stating higher support for populism among people with declining income and lower levels of perceived social status (Gidron & Hall, 2017; Inglehart & Norris, 2017). Taken together, these results suggest that oppressed groups are relatively safe in times of economic growth, but less so in more difficult periods. In these times, mechanisms of protection are especially relevant to prevent discrimination in direct democratic votes and the allies of oppressed groups should be especially alert.

However, lower support for contra-bills does not mean that pro-bills perform better at the ballot during higher economic growth. Contradicting H7b, economic growth actually *decreases the chances of bills supporting oppressed groups*. While this seems counter-intuitive at first – should not there be greater willingness to share rights and benefits in times of economic prosperity? – the reasoning mentioned above for higher levels of education might come into play here as well. Higher economic growth often correlates with a higher number of wealthy people, who might believe they contribute more to growth and do not want to provide welfare for groups they perceive as less deserving. The ability of high SES groups to block initiatives in support of oppressed groups by financing large campaigns against these bills has already been recognized by Gerber (1999). This reasoning should again apply mainly to bills affecting low SES groups. Therefore, I analyze whether economic growth has a positive effect on the probability of pro-outputs for classic oppressed groups and political groups. Table 34 provides the results.

In Table 34 we detect a similar pattern to the analyses on the effect of education. Growth in GDP per capita has a negative effect on pro-outputs for classic oppressed groups and for political groups. However, additional analyses reveal that the effect is actually positive if only pro-outputs for low SES groups are taken into account. During times when the economy is prospering, voters seem to be willing to grant material benefits to low SES groups, but they seem less willing to benefit classic oppressed and political groups compared to times of economic struggle. A possible explanation might be that in those countries where economic growth was highest during the timeframe under analysis, voters might be more conservative and therefore less willing to grant rights to oppressed groups. Future research is required to investigate the causal mechanisms behind these findings further.

Summing up, oppressed groups are better off in faster growing economies when it comes to bringing their interests to the ballot box and preventing contra-outputs. These benefits – agenda-setting and a greater capacity for self-preservation – support the conclusion that overall, direct democratic votes are better for oppressed groups if held in times of economic growth and oppressed groups at least need additional protection in times of economic decline. However, when classic oppressed and political groups are able to get a pro-bill to a vote in economically challenging times, they actually fare better than in votes held in periods of greater prosperity.

Table 34: GDP Growth and the Probability of Pro-Outputs without low SES bills, Bayesian multilevel logistic regressions

Dependent Variable: Pro-Output without low SES= 1 Bayesian multilevel logistic regressions	Model 1
	Mean (sd)
(Intercept)	−1.11 (3.26)
Mandatory (Reference = Bottom-up)	4.28 (1.86)
Top-down (Reference = Bottom-up)	−1.40 (1.66)
Binding	1.11 (3.17)
Quorum	−3.16 (1.68)
Switzerland	−1.96 (1.92)
GDP growth/capita	−11.60 (8.51)
Num. obs.	63
Num. Groups: Country	14
Num. Groups: Year	22
Var: Country (Intercept)	9.20
Var: Year (Intercept)	1.26

Sources: own dataset, Worldbank

9.5.3 Hypotheses 8a-c: Ethnic Fractionalization

Finally, direct democratic votes do not seem to fulfill the hopes placed in them of stabilizing countries with high ethnic fractionalization (Landemore, 2020; Stojanović, 2021) – although contra-outputs are less common in these countries, so are pro-outputs. First, confirming H8a, *higher ethnic fractionalization increases the probability that a bill at the ballot supports oppressed groups* instead of disadvantaging them. The assumption behind H8a was that higher ethnic fractionalization means the existence of more groups that are able to initiate pro-bills in their favor. This seems to be exactly what is happening – groups succeed in putting their interests on the political agenda via direct democratic votes.

Second, however, *pro-bills face higher obstacles at the ballot in fractionalized countries*, confirming H8b. One explanation for this might be that it is probably harder to mobilize a majority for a bill in countries with more groups. Tensions between these groups might also reduce the probability that one group will support the interests of another. In addition, the finding of a lower probability for pro-outputs in ethnically fractionalized countries fits previous research about lower welfare spending in these countries (Alesina & Glaeser, 2004; Gisselquist, 2014; Mollerstrom, 2015).

Third, there is also one positive effect for oppressed groups living in fractionalized countries – *contra-outputs are less likely* there as well, confirming H8c. Here, the fact that it is harder to mobilize a majority in support of a bill in fractionalized societies might come in useful. Therefore, similar to countries with a high level of economic growth, oppressed groups are better protected from harmful bills in countries with high ethnic diversity.

9.6 Summary: What Works Best for Oppressed Groups in Direct Democracy?

Before I turn to discussing the use of the concept of oppressed groups in light of my empirical findings, this section summarizes the conditions that favor pro- rather than contra-bills at the ballot and encourage the success of pro-bills and the defeat of contra-bills. Given ongoing calls for extending direct democratic options and the risks that doing so might entail for oppressed groups, translating my findings into suggestions for the use of direct democracy represents one of this thesis' major contributions.

First, to boost the chances of bills that contain measures to improve the situation of oppressed groups (rather than disadvantaging them further) being brought to a vote, my findings suggest expanding the options for mandatory and top-down votes and institutionalizing binding votes. In addition, countries with a high level of university education, a high level of economic growth or a high level of ethnic fractionalization constitute the contexts most likely to be favorable for oppressed groups. However, lower support for equality among the population and a negative attitude towards the group affected by the bill do not seem to be an obstacle. Whereas higher numbers of pro-bills do not in themselves guarantee success at the ballot, simply bringing oppressed groups' interests to a vote and thereby onto the public agenda can help promote those interests and may therefore be viewed as a positive strategy. In contrast, contra-bills can foster stereotypes and turn public sentiment against oppressed groups even when the bills do not result in contra-outputs, so to safeguard those groups' interests it is crucial to stop these bills from appearing at the ballot.

Second, in terms of increasing the probability of pro-outputs, mandatory and top-down votes again have the best record. However, pro-bills supporting the interests of low SES groups are less likely to succeed than bills affecting classic oppressed or political groups. To maximize the chances of pro-outputs, there should also be no quorum and the vote result should be binding. Regarding the context in which a vote takes place, a negative attitude towards the affected group is again no hindrance, while support for equality does not help pro-bills to succeed. Surprisingly, pro-bills fare better in countries with lower levels of university education or lower levels of economic growth, while the probability of pro-outputs also rises if ethnic fractionalization is low.

Finally, contra-outputs represent the worst *Tyranny of the Majority*, so conditions to prevent them are therefore of the utmost importance. According to my analyses, bottom-up votes, votes without quora, and those with binding vote results are the most promising for achieving this goal. In addition, votes outside Switzerland are less likely to result in contra-outputs. A negative attitude towards the group affected by a vote does not actually increase the chance of a contra-bill winning, unlike higher support for equality does (but note the low variation of this variable). Contra-outputs are less likely where university education is low or economic growth is high, while ethnic fractionalization also makes them less probable.

Four factors stand out as promoting pro-outputs while preventing contra-outputs – and the fact that two of them are institutional ones makes it relatively easy to implement my suggestions: the absence of quora and the implementation of binding vote results. In contrast, votes outside Switzerland being more beneficial and those in countries with lower levels of university degrees does not result in clear-cut recommendations. Results on the effect of quora came as a surprise, as it has been suggested that quora protect oppressed groups (Eder & Magin, 2008). Yet, at least according to my data, in reality, they protect the opponents of oppressed groups because they reduce pro-bills' chances of success while increasing the probability that a contra-bill is adopted. The call for binding vote results, however, supports participatory claims about increasing the influence of voters. It also enables greater transparency about the implications of a vote. Again, one could argue that non-binding vote results can protect oppressed groups. Yet, my findings suggest the contrary. Therefore, when direct democratic options are extended, it should be mainly without regulations on quora and with a guarantee of vote results being translated into law.

Before turning to the discussion of the use of the concept of oppressed groups in direct democracy, there is a general methodological point that might explain why some hypotheses were disconfirmed that I want to briefly examine. As mentioned above, I merely calculate the numbers of pro- and contra-bills and -outputs and do not differentiate according to the intensity of a proposed measure. In a fictional example, a pro-bill containing the introduction of universal healthcare would count as much as a pro-bill lowering the fees for doctor appointments by a couple of cents. This lack of nuance means that some hypotheses might be confirmed that would be disconfirmed if the bill's intensity was taken into account. For example, although quora might increase the chances of contra-outputs in general they might still be effective in preventing the adoption of particularly harsh contra-bills. This potentially limits the conclusions one can draw from those results confirming hypotheses, and it is important to bear this limitation in mind. Yet despite this, I believe that my results nonetheless offer valuable insights as they reveal how often bills supporting or opposing oppressed groups are brought to the ballot and succeed, and the factors that influence the success of a pro- or contra-bill, broadly speaking.

9.7 The Concept of Oppressed Groups in Direct Democracy

Applying the concept of oppressed groups in the analysis of direct democratic bills and outputs proved to be a fruitful strategy that allowed me to investigate a wide array of bills targeting a variety of different groups. Using Young's concept enabled analysis of the implications of direct democracy for groups that are classically referred to as minorities, such as members of the LGBTQ+ community or non-citizens, as well as low SES groups and political groups.

But, given the results described, which groups can be considered oppressed in direct democratic votes? Specifically, which of the group characteristics listed in Chapter 2 are influential for a group's fate in direct democracy?

A group that is at a disadvantage in direct democratic votes are people of low socio-economic status. While they are able to bring bills supporting their interests to the ballot, the chances for pro-outputs are lower for these bills compared to others. This means that for low SES groups, lacking resources severely limits their chances at the ballot. As a result, they are rarely able to improve their situation via direct democratic votes. This contributes to their ongoing oppression as described by Young (1990). Therefore, while my analyses do not provide insights into whether parliamentary decision-making or direct democratic votes are more beneficial to low SES groups, the latter clearly do not offer a remedy for oppression.

Following Young (1990), low SES groups experience oppression through exploitation, marginalization, powerlessness and cultural imperialism – even in their everyday life. According to my analyses, direct democratic votes perpetuate some of these forms of oppression. A first face of everyday oppression, referring to Young's work, is low SES groups experience of exploitation as "social processes [...] bring about a transfer of energies from one group to another to produce unequal distributions, and in the way in which social institutions enable a few to accumulate while they constrain many more." (Young, 1990, p. 53). Second, they are marginalized as they are "people the system of labor cannot or will not use. [...] A whole category of people is expelled from useful participation in social life and thus potentially subjected to severe material deprivation and even extermination." (ibid.). The lower probability of pro-outputs in direct democratic votes for low SES groups in my analyses is an example of how useful participation is made difficult for marginalized people. Given the capacities it takes to participate successfully in politics (Brady et al., 1995), Young's second remark on marginality in capitalism comes to mind: "even when material deprivation is somewhat mitigated by the welfare state, marginalization is unjust because it blocks the opportunity to exercise capacities in socially defined and recognized ways." (Young, 1990, p. 54). Third, low SES groups also experience powerlessness, as defined by Young as "inhibition in the development of one's capacities, lack of decisionmaking power in one's working life, and exposure to disrespectful treatment because of the status one occupies." (ibid., 58). Finally, this can result in cultural imperialism, as low SES groups "experience how the dominant meanings of a society render the particular perspective of one's own group invisible at the same time as they stereotype one's group and mark it out as the Other." (ibid., 58-59). Low SES groups are often portrayed as being lazy and thereby undeserving, presumably resulting in unwillingness to share resources with them via direct democratic votes.

Low SES groups being at a disadvantage at the direct democratic ballot points to the importance of one group characteristic discussed in Chapter 2 – resources. Resources indeed seem to be an important prerequisite in order to win a vote and produce a pro-output. Without resources, supporters of the group cannot campaign for its interests, win over influential allies, gain access to the media, and ultimately vote in high numbers. Obstacles also appear in the form of bureaucratic hurdles – bills have to be formulated using legal wording, and the different stages of initiating a vote have to be known and completed successfully. Whereas the high share of pro-bills supporting low SES groups at the ballot suggests that these groups are able to mobilize resources to master the pre-vote steps, campaigning and turnout seem to work to their disadvantage in the vote itself.

The cultural imperialism experienced by low SES groups described above hints at another group characteristic that affects a group's success in direct democracy – the group being perceived as an outgroup instead of an ingroup by large parts of society. Unfortunately, it was not possible to test this thoroughly, as data was unavailable for most of the votes. Yet, non-citizens, who represent a legal outgroup, do face disadvantages especially at the output-level of direct democracy. In contrast, members of the LGBTQ+ community can nowadays be described as an ingroup in many European countries. However, a much higher share of contra- compared to pro-bills and more outputs disadvantaging than supporting this group points to difficulties they encounter in direct democracy, potentially mirroring persistent conservative attitudes in some countries under investigation. These first hints call for the gathering and analysis of more data on attitudes towards the groups affected by direct democratic votes, as well as for a more detailed investigation of the fate of groups lacking political rights such as non-citizens.

For the characteristic of group size, findings are ambivalent. Low SES groups, which often represent significant parts of the population, have lower chances of success at the ballot. In contrast, many bills and outputs support the interests of women as a large group. Similarly, relatively small groups such as linguistic minorities and people with disabilities often benefit from direct democratic votes. This suggests that resources and attitudes towards groups are more important than the actual group size – questioning again the notion of a *Tyranny of the Majority*.

Finally, not every group defined as oppressed turned out to truly be so in direct democratic votes. On the contrary, for most of the groups, pro-bills outnumber contra-bills and success rates for pro-bills are higher than success rates for contra-bills. Members of the LGBTQ+ community and the parliamentary opposition are the only groups at a disadvantage at bill- as well as output-level. Low SES groups face disadvantages regarding pro-outputs, while the picture is mixed for women and religious minorities. As mentioned above, members of linguistic minorities and people with disabilities mostly benefit from direct democratic votes.

Summing up, Young's concept of oppressed groups is useful for comprehensively analyzing the implications of direct democracy for a wide array of social groups. My results, especially on low SES groups, underline the importance of taking these groups into account when analyzing the implications of direct democratic votes, instead of focusing on a narrower understanding of minorities. The results of my analyses, however, call for a differentiated application of the concept. Oppressed groups come in a variety of forms, and not all of them suffer in direct democracy. Here, resources available to a group and community attitudes towards it are decisive. This puts low SES groups and non-citizens at a particular disadvantage in many countries. For other groups, attitudes differ between countries and from year to year, and resources are distributed in different ways. Therefore, it is important that a concept of oppressed groups in direct democracy allows for flexibility so it can be adapted in different contexts.

10 Conclusions

> "I know only one way to prevent men from degrading themselves: it is to grant to no one, with omnipotence, the sovereign power to debase them."
>
> Tocqueville, *Democracy in America* (2012, p. 423)

Direct democratic votes have become increasingly popular worldwide during the last decades, yet skepticism about granting people the right to decide directly on policies, which carries the risk of discriminating against oppressed groups remains widespread. With empirical insights scarce thus far and offering mixed results, political parties as well as political theorists are fiercely debating the potential advantages of direct democracy, as well as its drawbacks. This dissertation addresses this research gap by being the first study that quantitatively and cross-nationally analyzes how oppressed groups fare in direct democratic votes. To this end, I analyze all direct democratic votes held at national level in European democracies between 1990 and 2015. In addition, the dissertation touches new conceptual ground by applying the concept of oppressed groups by Iris M. Young for the first time in research on direct democracy (Young, 1990). My results shed light on the fate of oppressed groups in direct democracy and the circumstances that can benefit them. Thereby, the dissertation offers an important contribution to the current political and scholarly debate. Do direct democratic votes result in a *Tyranny of the Majority*[23] in the sense of endangering oppressed groups, or can direct democracy be of use to these groups in their pursuit of their interests?

In the following, I summarize the main contributions of this dissertation and provide answers to my research questions. Additionally, I discuss the limitations of my approach and suggest avenues for future research on oppressed groups and direct democracy.

10.1 Oppressed Groups can Benefit from Direct Democracy

The first research question addressed in this dissertation is

Do direct democratic bills and outputs support or disadvantage the interests of oppressed groups (pro-bills/-outputs or contra-bills/-outputs)?

---

[23] For a discussion on the term Tyranny of the Majority, see Chapter 2.3.1.

10.1.1 Addressing the Gap: A Quantitative, Comparative Analysis of Oppressed Groups in Direct Democracy

This study represents the first cross-national analysis of direct democratic votes over a timespan of 25 years, enabling a quantitative assessment of the implications of direct democracy for a variety of groups. By providing empirical evidence on one of the major criticisms of direct democracy, it thereby contributes to the ongoing debate in academia as well as in society generally about whether to extend direct democratic options.

On the one hand, scholars in the tradition of participatory democratic theory stress the importance of involving as many people as possible in decisions on political issues affecting them. To these scholars, this embodies the definition of democracy as rule by the people (e.g., Pateman, 1970). In addition, they hope that extending direct democratic options might be a remedy for the current problems in representative democracies, such as dissatisfied and inactive citizens (e.g., Bowler et al., 2017; Dalton, 2004). On the other hand, sceptics stress the potential dangers of majoritarian popular decision-making on political issues, especially the possibility of oppressed groups being outvoted permanently and thereby discriminated against. The absence of representative mechanisms to protect these groups is feared to endanger their rights as well as to manifest structures of poverty (e.g., Bell, 1978; Bellamy, 2018; Eule, 1990; Gamble, 1997; Haskell, 2001; Lacey, 2021; Lewis, 2013). Depending on their political ideology and electoral strategies, political actors use these arguments to either promote or warn against direct democracy. For many years, demands for more direct democratic options in European democracies – especially from parties on the left of the political spectrum – grew evermore insistent; now, however, we are currently witnessing these same parties exercising greater caution.[24] At the same time, right-wing populist parties now regularly demand and employ direct democratic options, thereby increasing fears of discrimination (e.g., Batory & Svensson, 2019).

Empirical insights on whether recent direct democratic votes can fulfill the hopes placed in them or instead confirm their criticisms aimed at them have revealed mixed results thus far, mainly depending on the operationalization, timespan, and the groups, votes, countries, or regions under analysis. Regarding the implications of direct democracy for oppressed groups, previous research suggests it can lead both to benefits as well as the risk of discrimination in Switzerland, depending on the group concerned, while direct democratic mechanisms resulting in discrimination is more common in the U.S. (Lewis, 2013; Vatter & Danaci, 2010). However, results from the

---

24 E.g., the German Greens: https://cms.gruene.de/uploads/documents/Wahlprogramm_Englisch_DIE_GRUENEN_Bundestagswahl_2021.pdf (29.02.24).

U.S. cannot be compared easily due to differing research designs, and quantitative analyses on direct democratic outputs from other countries besides Switzerland are missing completely. Instead, all existing studies either focus on single countries or even regions within countries, or only analyze one specific vote.

This dissertation addresses this research gap by analyzing all the direct democratic votes on the national level in European democracies between 1990 and 2015. In addition, applying the concept of oppressed groups by Iris M. Young deviates from the focus of previous research on minorities, a term that is often poorly defined and differently specified. According to Young, oppressed groups are those that face exploitation, marginalization, powerlessness, cultural imperialism and/or violence (Young, 1990).[25] This includes for example linguistic and religious minorities, members of the LGBTQ+ community, women, people with a history of migration, working-class and poor people, and those with mental or physical disabilities (Mancenido-Bolaños, 2020; Pineda, 2020; Tempels et al., 2020; C. C. Williams et al., 2020; Young, 1989). Using this concept instead of the more popular term "minorities" enables me to study the impacts of direct democratic votes on a variety of groups that are especially likely to be discriminated against, but who do not necessarily represent a numerical minority. Additionally, the criterion of oppression excludes rather powerful minorities. I focus on three clusters of groups: the first includes bills affecting so-called classic oppressed groups, i.e., non-citizens, members of the LGBTQ+ community, women, linguistic and religious minorities, people with mental health issues and those with physical disabilities, as well as more general bills containing fundamental rights or banning discrimination. The second cluster includes bills that especially affect people of low socio-economic status (low SES groups) in areas such as housing, healthcare, social welfare, schooling etc. The final cluster contains bills affecting the interests of disadvantaged political groups, i.e., the rights of the parliamentary opposition, the proportionality of the voting system, and the division of power.

I differentiate between two stages of the direct democratic process, which are central to my analyses: the bill- and the output-level. The bill-level includes all direct democratic bills that come to a national vote. The output-level includes all bills that are adopted at the ballot, i.e., that gain a majority of votes and pass a potential quorum. Pro-bills are bills that aim at supporting the interests of oppressed groups, while contra-bills aim at disadvantageing these groups. Pro-outputs are adopted pro-bills, whereas contra-outputs are adopted contra-bills. This approach offers an encompassing overview of both which bills make it to the ballot and which bills succeed there. Previous research either focused solely on the outputs of direct democratic votes in

---

25 Chapter 2.1 outlines the concept of oppressed groups in more detail.

specific regions or countries or analyzed lawmaking on civil rights in countries with more or less direct democratic options in general, regardless of whether this lawmaking had anything to do with direct democracy. Claims about the effects of direct democracy therefore were based on less than solid ground.

10.1.2 Results: Pro-Bills and -Outputs Outnumber Contra-Bills and -Outputs

My descriptive analyses show that more direct democratic bills support oppressed groups than disadvantage them: of 221 bills affecting the interests of oppressed groups, 133 are pro-bills compared to 88 contra-bills. Oppressed groups and their allies are therefore able to bring their issues to the ballot. While their opponents also succeed in initiating direct democratic votes, pro-bills outweigh contra ones. This eases academic and societal concerns that direct democracy always results in a *Tyranny of the Majority* at the ballot box. In contrast, direct democracy offers an opportunity for oppressed groups to put their topics on the agenda. This backs the hopes of scholars who believe that for oppressed groups, direct democracy represents a tool for empowerment and agenda-setting (e.g., Lacey, 2021; Leemann, 2015; Serdült & Welp, 2012; Stojanović, 2021).

Turning to the outputs, more pro-bills than contra-bills gain a majority of votes and pass a possible quorum – of 78 successful bills affecting oppressed groups, 47 are pro-outputs compared to 31 contra-outputs. This again suggests that direct democracy does not correspond to a *Tyranny of the Majority*. However, pro-bills and contra-bills succeed at similar rates. While 35.23 % of contra-bills are adopted, 35.34 % of pro-bills are. This finding points to the possibility of oppressed groups to be disadvantaged in direct democratic votes, lending some support to the critics of such instruments (e.g., Gamble, 1997; Lewis, 2013; Merkel & Ritzi, 2017). Section 10.3 below offers insights into which groups face particular obstacles and why this might be the case. Table 35 summarizes the descriptive findings on pro- and contra-bills and -outputs and the success rates for all oppressed groups taken together.

Table 35: Direct Democratic Bills, Outputs and Success Rates in European Democracies 1990-2015

	Pro-bills	Contra-bills	Pro-outputs	Contra-outputs	Success Rate: Pro-bills	Success Rate: Contra-bills
N	133	88	47	31		
%	60.18	39.82	60.26	39.74	35.34	35.23

Source: own dataset

10.1.3 Limitations and Avenues for Future Research

In analyzing all national-level direct democratic votes in European countries over a timespan of 25 years and applying the concept of oppressed groups for the first time, this dissertation has a broad agenda. Nevertheless, there are some methodological as well as theoretical limitations that should be noted. Together with my results, they lay the groundwork for future research on the implications of direct democracy for oppressed groups.

First, the focus on the bill- and output-level prevents analysis of the stages before and after the ballot, i.e., who initiated the vote, how the campaign was organized, what was discussed in the media and how it portrayed oppressed groups, which bills got withdrawn from a vote because parliament had already adopted them or a court ruled them unconstitutional etc. Similarly, there is no analysis of what happened after the vote – whether bills were actually implemented and how, what consequences this had for oppressed groups, whether unsuccessful bills influenced legislation or public sentiment anyway, and so on. A review by Lupia and Matsusaka (2004) suggests both an indirect effect for unsuccessful direct democratic bills and hesitancy in implementing successful ones.

Second, the coding procedure did not allow measurement of the quality of a pro- or contra-bill. Therefore, we do not know whether the more drastic pro- or contra-bills that come to the ballot are more successful than moderate ones. We also do not know whether the explaining variables work differently depending on how consequential a bill is.

Addressing the first limitation, case studies might help to investigate what happens before and after a direct democratic vote. Here, especially close votes could be an interesting subject for analysis. What characterizes the network of initiators of the vote? Which coalitions prove to be successful for oppressed groups? How is the campaign organized? Which stereotypes are employed and how does this resonate in the media? Further quantitative research could investigate the differences between bills that make it to the ballot and bills that are adopted beforehand by parliament. Is a pro-bill or a contra-bill more likely to find parliamentary support? Which types of initiators are most likely to convince parliament to adopt their proposal? Are there instances in which initiators continue to the ballot instead of withdrawing their bill when parliament signals support? Another interesting comparison would be that between direct democratic bills that are implemented exactly as formulated, those which are implemented differently, and those which are not implemented at all. Are pro- or contra-outputs more likely to be denied implementation? Does it depend on the closeness of the vote, or who initiated it? Are there differences between bills affecting different oppressed groups? Finally, case studies might reveal the actual mid- to long-term consequences of implemented bills for oppressed groups. These might also deviate substantively from the original content of the bill as coded in this dissertation. For example, a bill lowering fees for healthcare might result in deteriorating healthcare and strengthen a system of private healthcare with higher standards of care for those who can afford it. Even though such a bill would be coded as a pro-output here, it would actually worsen the situation for low SES groups in the long run. These analyses of the stages before and after the bill- and output-level are important if we are to arrive at an encompassing understanding of the full implications of direct democracy for oppressed groups.

Addressing the second limitation, differentiating between bills according to the quality of their impact would be enlightening, but is challenging to achieve in practice. However, case studies might be an option here, too. By tracing the journey of a bill proposing a rather small change compared to a bill proposing more radical measures, future research might identify differences in their campaigns, success level, and possible implementation. For example, are bills proposing same-sex unions more successful compared to bills proposing same-sex marriage? This would enable a more detailed evaluation of the direct democratic bills and outputs affecting the interests of oppressed groups.

In addition, further research could analyze pro- and contra-bills and -outputs on other continents using similar methods in order to reveal patterns that travel globally versus more regional ones. U.S. states provide some famous examples of direct democratic votes favoring resourceful actors and threatening oppressed groups (e.g., Gamble, 1997; Lewis, 2013; Simon et al., 2018). While political science in the U.S. has analyzed some of these, other parts of the world have been largely neglected. One of the countries where direct democratic votes are most frequent is Uruguay, however, analyses on the consequences of these votes for oppressed groups are lacking (Krämling et al., 2022). On the one hand, analyzing pro- and contra-bills and -outputs should become easier with direct democracy thriving worldwide. On the other hand, it requires substantial research on bill proposals to reliably code their content. Therefore, scholars stemming from the regions under investigation, who are familiar with the context of these direct democratic votes and fluent in the language of the proposals, should carry out this research. This would not only broaden our understanding of direct democracy, but also address the Western-centric centrism in research on the topic.

My application of the concept of oppressed groups and my data collection and descriptive results on bills and outputs in European democracies between 1990 and 2015 provide the foundations for all these future undertakings. The following section focuses on my second contribution, namely identifying factors that support or hinder the interests of oppressed groups at the ballot.

10.2 Binding Votes and Absence of Quora Benefit Oppressed Groups

After revealing the record of oppressed groups in direct democratic votes in Europe between 1990 and 2015, identifying relevant variables for the emergence of bills at the ballot and their success is important to gain insights into how direct democracy works and which settings should be promoted. Therefore, another research question of interest is

What explains whether supportive rather than disadvantaging bills come to a vote (pro- instead of contra-bills)? What explains supportive and disadvantaging outputs (pro- and contra-outputs), respectively?

10.2.1 Addressing the Gap: Multilevel Logistic Regressions

In order to gain an encompassing understanding of why pro- instead of contra-bills reach the ballot and which factors affect the probability of pro- or contra-outputs, multivariate analyses are necessary. Whereas some studies to date have analyzed the impact of the direct democratic instrument on outputs for oppressed groups, investigation of other institutional, attitudinal, or socio-economic explaining variables is mostly missing. However, this investigation is key not only to deepen our understanding of influential factors in direct democracy, but also to identify the most promising settings for promoting the interests of oppressed groups in direct democratic votes.

As outlined in Chapter 5.2, I calculate Bayesian multilevel crossed-effects logistic models in order to account for variation between countries and years as well as for a comparatively low number of both. Institutional explaining variables of interest are the direct democratic instrument employed, whether vote results are binding, and the existence of a quorum. In addition, I control for a vote taking place in Switzerland. Attitudinal explaining variables are the importance of equal treatment and equal opportunities, and negative attitudes towards the group affected by a vote. As noted in Chapter 9.4, due to the low variation in support for equality, results for this variable have low explanatory power. In addition, limited data availability prevents a multivariate analysis including attitudes towards the affected group. Finally, socio-economic explaining variables include the level of GDP per capita growth in the country and year of the vote, the level of tertiary education, and the level of ethnic fractionalization.

10.2.2 Results: Institutional Variables are Key

Different variables are influential in different ways in terms of whether a bill at the ballot is pro or contra oppressed groups, whether a pro-bill gains a majority and passes a possible quorum, and whether a contra-bill succeeds. While limitations in data availability prevent reliable conclusions for the influence of attitudes, the analyses of institutional and socio-economic explaining variables offer interesting insights. Chapter 9 includes more detailed discussions of the findings as well as additional analyses. The following summarizes the main points.

The probability of pro- instead of contra-bills at the ballot is higher in mandatory and top-down votes compared to bottom-up votes. This corresponds to previous findings while contradicting theoretical hopes of bottom-up votes offering alternative channels of influence for oppressed groups (Christmann & Danaci, 2012; Eder & Magin, 2008; Gamble, 1997; Geißel et al., 2019a; Vatter, 2007; Vatter & Danaci, 2010). Pro-bills are also more likely in binding votes. In addition, they are more likely in countries and times of higher tertiary education, higher economic growth, and higher levels of ethnic fractionalization. These results mirror earlier findings on the effect of education by Vatter et al. (2014), the results of my bivariate analyses on the correlation between education and tolerance, and research on lower support for extremist or populist parties in times of economic growth (Gidron & Hall, 2017; Inglehart & Norris, 2017; Rao et al., 2018).

The chances for pro-bills to succeed are highest in mandatory and top-down votes (corresponding to findings from Vatter & Danaci, 2010), votes without quora requirements, and those with binding vote results. In contrast to theoretical expectations and the results on pro-bills, pro-outputs are more likely in countries and years of lower tertiary education and lower economic growth, contradicting findings from Vatter et al. (2014) on education and research on more extremist voting behavior in economically challenging times (Gidron & Hall, 2017; Inglehart & Norris, 2017; Rao et al., 2018). Additional analyses reveal that the negative effect of education is not due to votes on the interests of low SES groups alone (contradicting assumptions that the effect is only due to well-educated and wealthy voters being less willing to share their benefits), but also holds for bills affecting classic oppressed groups and political groups. Regarding economic growth, the negative effect actually only holds for pro-outputs affecting classic oppressed and political groups, while higher growth increases the probability of a pro-output for bills affecting low SES groups. Lower levels of ethnic fractionalization increase the chances of pro-outputs, thereby mitigating hopes that pro-outputs might stabilize highly fractionalized countries (Landemore, 2020; Stojanović, 2021).

In order to avoid contra-outputs, identifying conditions under which they are least likely to occur is key. My analyses suggest that the best institutional settings in this regard are bottom-up votes, votes without quora requirements, and those with binding vote results. Especially the first two findings come as a surprise, as Gamble (1997) and Vatter and Danaci (2010) identified bottom-up votes as particularly dangerous for oppressed groups, and quora are theoretically regarded as a mechanism of protection in direct democracy (Eder & Magin, 2008). Now confirming previous assumptions, contra-outputs are less likely when economic growth is higher (Gidron & Hall, 2017; Inglehart & Norris, 2017; Rao et al., 2018). A possible explanation could be that voters might have a stronger status quo bias in times of economic growth. Again contradicting previous assumptions, contra-outputs are more likely when the level of tertiary education is higher (Vatter et al., 2014). Interestingly, high levels of ethnic fractionalization reduce the chances for contra-outputs. Table 36 provides an overview of the different effects of the explaining variables depending on the dependent variable of interest. Note that top-down and mandatory votes, low levels of economic growth and of ethnic fractionalization increase the probability of bills affecting oppressed groups to be adopted in general, regardless of whether it is a bill supporting or disadvantaging the interests of the group.

Summing up, two institutional settings in particular result in higher numbers of pro- compared to contra-bills, higher chances for pro-outputs, and lower probabilities for contra-outputs. According to my analyses, binding vote results promote all of these. In addition, the absence of quora requirements is crucial at the output-level. Especially the results on the latter come as a surprise, as it has been assumed previously that quora protect oppressed groups in direct democratic votes by requiring a larger segment of the electorate to vote, thereby potentially also requiring turnout from oppressed groups and their allies (e.g., Eder & Magin, 2008). My analyses suggest that in reality, quora function instead as a mobilization mechanism for the opponents of oppressed groups, who might put in increased efforts during a campaign to fulfill the quorum. This corresponds to research from Simon et al. (2018), who found that opponents of same-sex marriage turned out disproportionately often in votes on same-sex marriage bans in U.S. states. In

Table 36: Effects on the Probabilities of Pro-Bills, Pro-Outputs and Contra-Outputs

Explaining variables	Dependent variables		
	Probability Pro-bill	Probability Pro-output	Probability Contra-output
Mandatory vote instead of bottom-up	+	+	+
Top-down vote instead of bottom-up	+	+	+
Quora	(not tested)	−	+
Binding vote results	+	+	−
Tertiary education	+	−	+
Economic growth	+	−	−
Ethnic fractionalization	+	−	−

+ = positive effect, − = negative effect; Sources: own dataset, Eurostat, Worldbank, Historical Index of Ethnic Fractionalization Dataset

addition, binding vote results seem to motivate oppressed groups and their supporters to bring their interests to a vote and turn out at the ballot. In contrast, their opponents seem to shy away from discriminatory voting behavior when parliament is obliged to adopt a bill if it passes the vote. Therefore, to promote the interests of oppressed groups via direct democracy while also protecting them from harmful outputs, binding vote results should be implemented and quora requirements abolished.

10.2.3 Limitations and Avenues for Future Research

The limitations listed in 10.1.3 also apply to my multilevel analyses. In addition, lack of data becomes even more pronounced here, as it inhibits the analysis of some variables. However, the results revealed in the multilevel analyses can also serve as a point of departure for future research. In the following, I outline three ideas for future undertakings.

First, future research could reveal the causal mechanisms behind the more unexpected results of my quantitative analyses by investigating case studies on the most outstanding votes. For example, looking in more detail at occasions where pro-bills failed even though the level of tertiary education was very high might reveal relevant factors that are hidden in quantitative analysis. Is it the case that pro-bills are more critically discussed when the level of university education is high? Another case study could be on the loss of a pro-bill at the ballot in times of strong economic growth. What is it that makes voters vote against the interests of oppressed groups even though the economy is prospering? The results of both undertakings could help identify measures to increase the chances of success for oppressed groups in highly educated and prospering constituencies.

Second, another avenue for future research lies in investigating the motivations and experiences of oppressed groups in the context of direct democratic votes. Interviews with group members, both at leadership and grassroots level, could reveal their experiences in organizing votes to pursue their interests or counter campaigns against votes aimed at disadvantaging them. Researchers might also participate in campaigns to observe directly the strategies and hindrances in the field. However, it would also be interesting to interview group members who decided against using the direct democratic vein and ask what prevents them from doing so. In this way, one might identify any significant obstacles that should be removed to make direct democracy as accessible as possible for oppressed groups. Finally, an investigation of turnout of the oppressed groups affected by a vote might offer interesting insights into what drives oppressed groups to the ballot and the role their turnout plays in producing direct democratic outputs supporting their interests.

Third, additional data might be gathered on how people perceive different oppressed groups. This would enable a thorough testing of the social identity theory. In a perfect world for quantitative research, surveys on direct democratic votes would offer individual level data, so one could identify relevant factors for decisions in direct democratic votes at the level of the voter. Here, insights on the effects of attitudes on voting behavior might help to mitigate the harming influence of attitudes or restrict the range of topics for direct democratic votes to prevent discriminating votes driven by negative attitudes or stereotypes.

The final contribution of this dissertation is the more differentiated view it provides for which oppressed groups benefit from and which are disadvantaged by direct democratic votes. Applying the concept of oppressed groups in research on direct democracy for the first time enables this detailed analysis. In addition, the results gathered here deepen our understanding of which group characteristics are important for their fate in direct democracy, and thereby help to refine a concept of oppressed groups in direct democracy. The following section focuses on these topics.

10.3 It Depends on the Resources and Attitudes

One of the key advantages in applying the concept of oppressed groups in the analysis of direct democratic bills and outputs lies in the variety of groups the concept encompasses. This allows identification of which groups do face obstacles at the ballot, and which groups might benefit from direct democratic processes. Therefore, the last research question of interest is

Can we observe differences in bills and outputs depending on which oppressed group is affected by the vote? Based on this, what constitutes the concept of oppressed groups in direct democracy?

10.3.1 Addressing the Gap: A Differentiated Analysis of Direct Democratic Votes

In order to evaluate comprehensively the record of direct democracy, it is important to analyze its implications for a wide variety of groups. Yet, previous research mostly focused on specific groups such as same-sex couples or linguistic minorities (e.g., Simon et al., 2018; Stojanović, 2021). Results from analyses covering a wider array of groups already hinted at differentiated implications, but besides an assumed influence of attitudes, explanations for such differences remained mostly absent (e.g., Gamble, 1997; Lewis, 2013; Vatter & Danaci, 2010). Additionally, whereas case studies and theoretical considerations suggested low SES groups as being especially vulnerable in direct democracy (Schäfer & Schoen, 2013), those were usually excluded from analyses of direct democracy's implications for minorities.

However, a thorough understanding of the implications of direct democracy for oppressed groups requires an encompassing analysis of votes affecting a broad array of groups as well as a differentiated approach to identify those groups which face the biggest hurdles at the ballot. This deepens our understanding of how direct democracy works and enables considerations of steps and measures to protect vulnerable groups or even to increase the probability that they might benefit from direct democratic processes.

10.3.2 Results: Different Implications for Different Groups

Differences between groups appear in descriptive analyses at the bill- as well as at the output-level. For example, there are eight contra-bills affecting members of the LGBTQ+ community, whereas only two bills support this group. This mirrors findings from case studies by Di Bari (2021). In contrast, seven bills promote gender equality, while only two bills aim at restricting it. For low SES groups, 91 pro-bills are brought to the ballot compared to 53 contra-bills. Low SES groups seem to be able to put their issues on the direct democratic agenda even though they are short on important resources like money and networks. This might counteract the unequal responsiveness these groups face from parliaments (Elsässer et al., 2021). However, the success rate of pro-bills affecting low SES groups is lower than the success rate for other oppressed groups – 32.97 % for low SES groups vs. 37.84 % for political and 50 % for classic oppressed groups. This corresponds to previous research on the negative effects of direct democracy on redistribution and the disadvantages low SES groups face at the ballot (Ennser-Jedenastik, 2021; Feld et al., 2010; Parkinson, 2020; Schäfer & Schoen, 2013; Töller & Vollmer, 2013). Chapters 2 and 9 include further discussions on the important role of resources in direct democracy. Whereas low SES groups are less likely to improve their situation through direct democratic outputs, at least the success rate for contra-bills affecting these groups is lower than for other groups as well. Only 24.53 % of the contra-bills for low SES groups succeed, while 40.74 % do so for political groups and even 42.31 % do so for classic oppressed groups. The lack of socio-economic resources seems to prevent low SES groups from benefitting from direct democratic votes, but it does not result in them being disadvantaged even further compared to other oppressed groups. In general, voters seem to prefer the status quo when interests of low SES groups are touched upon, not willing to grant benefits, but also not willing to restrict benefits to them.

Numerically, outputs are low for other groups, making differences hard to evaluate. Taken together, classic oppressed groups seem to fare relatively well compared to low SES groups in terms of pro-outputs, and political groups fall somewhere in between. In terms of contra-outputs, political groups are the only ones for whom contra-bills succeed more often than pro-bills do, pointing to the importance of political resources at the ballot. The success rate is highest for contra-bills affecting classic oppressed groups, as it is for pro-bills affecting these groups. As a result, direct democratic votes are very consequential for classic oppressed groups, with the consequences running both ways – pro-bills supporting their interests succeed quite often, but so do contra-bills disadvantaging them. Table 37 depicts bills and outputs for specific oppressed groups.

What is revealed by the record of direct democratic votes when Iris M. Young's concept of oppressed groups is applied? My findings show that not all these groups can be considered oppressed in direct democracy as well, since categories such as women, religious and linguistic minorities, and people with disabilities or mental health issues are often able to benefit from direct democracy. Such groups manage to bring their interests to the ballot and often succeed in winning the vote in their favor. However, bills and outputs disadvantaging members of the LGBTQ+ community outnumber

Table 37: Different Oppressed Groups and Direct Democracy in European Democracies 1990-2015

Oppressed Groups Affected	Pro-bills (%)	Contra-bills (%)	Pro-outputs (%)	Contra-outputs (%)	Success Rate: Pro-bills (%)	Success Rate: Contra-bills (%)
LGBTQ+	20	80	40	60	100	37.5
Non-Citizens	50	50	16.67	83.33	8.33	41.67
Disability/ Mental illness	100	0	100	0	50	0
Linguistic minorities	100	0	100	0	33.33	0
Religious minorities	80	20	75	25	75	100
Gender	77.78	22.22	80	20	57.14	50
Low SES	63.19	36.81	69.77	30.23	32.97	24.53
Politics	57.81	42.19	56	44	37.84	40.74
Total	60.18	39.82	60.26	39.74	35.34	35.23

Source: own dataset

those benefitting them, low SES groups are less likely to achieve pro-outputs, and non-citizens are at a disadvantage at the output-level as well. In addition, contra-bills affecting political groups more often succeed than pro-bills. As a result, the application of the concept of oppressed groups in the context of direct democracy suggests emphasis is needed on the role of resources, political rights and attitudes towards the group affected by a vote. Groups with few resources, rights and/or that are perceived as an outgroup by large parts of society are at a disadvantage in direct democratic votes. In contrast, groups with access to resources and/or those perceived as ingroups can benefit from direct democratic tools, even though they might experience oppression in other arenas. This refined concept allows adaptation for different contexts, as different groups possess diverse amounts of resources and have varying standings depending on the country and year under investigation.

10.3.3 Limitations and Avenues for Future Research

As with the descriptive overall analysis and the multilevel analyses mentioned above, the differentiated descriptive analysis of bills and outputs for specific groups also has some limitations. At the same time, it paves the way for future research on the topic.

First, although the timespan and range of countries is relatively large, numbers on pro- and contra-outputs and -bills for single categories of oppressed groups are still quite low for conducting multilevel analyses. As a result, those findings should be viewed with some caution. This also affects the application of the concept of oppressed groups. Numbers for bills affecting low SES groups are comparatively high, so we can conclude with some certainty that these groups are disadvantaged in direct democratic pro-outputs. However, numbers for specific classic oppressed groups are comparatively low. Therefore, while these numbers suggest that non-citizens can be considered oppressed in direct democracy, whereas for example linguistic minorities cannot, more data is needed to confirm this.

Second, the findings presented here show the record of direct democracy for oppressed groups, but they do not compare this record to that for representative decision-making. As a result, we do not know whether direct democratic votes perform better or worse than parliaments regarding the interests of oppressed groups. There are some theoretical and empirical arguments as to why direct democracy should be better or worse than representative democracy, but it is hard to provide a thorough test. For example, Bochsler and Hug (2015) analyze the effect of direct democratic options on civil rights legislation. Yet, we do not know whether such legislation really is different because of these options, or whether other factors are influential. Vatter and Danaci (2010) investigate whether direct democratic decisions influenced parliamentary action to protect minorities or extend their rights in Switzerland. However, outside Switzerland this presumably depends on the ideological stance of the current government as well as its popularity. Therefore, even if we found more pro-outputs in direct democratic than in parliamentary votes, this would not necessarily mean that direct democracy is *per se* better for oppressed groups than representative democracy, instead the result might just stem from the reign of a government that opposes the interests of oppressed groups. While this government might win elections based on other policies, an electorate that is more supportive of oppressed groups might show in direct democratic votes on specific topics affecting them. My analyses provide the first hints with regard to some groups. For example, the disadvantage faced by low SES groups at the direct democratic ballot mirrors the unequal responsiveness of parliaments towards them (e.g., Elsässer et al., 2021). However, the finding that low SES groups are able to bring pro-bills supporting their interests to a vote hints at these groups possibly benefitting from direct democracy in a more indirect way.

These limitations can be challenged in future research on the implications of direct democracy for (different) oppressed groups. I outline ideas for doing so in the following.

Addressing the first limitation, future research might engage in analyzing data from an even longer time period to increase the number of votes in the single categories of oppressed groups as well as of those stemming from outside the Swiss context. Another strategy to reach this goal might be the analysis of subnational direct democratic votes, which might also reveal different mechanisms at work on this level. I initially planned to carry out such an analysis in this dissertation and therefore collected data on all subnational votes in European democracies from 1990 to 2015. However, I found that of 810 votes affecting oppressed groups, 785 took place in Switzerland. As a result, I refrained from this endeavor as the comparative value of the analyses would be rather small. Fortunately, direct democracy continues to flourish in Europe, so data on national votes from more recent years is becoming available. As the numbers of votes in my analyses are rather limited once you look at specific groups or include more explaining variables, adding more votes would give my results a more solid basis (or challenge them, depending on the findings).

Addressing the second limitation, future research could explore new ways to compare the record of direct democratic votes on the interests of oppressed groups with the record of parliamentary votes. This would enable recommendations on whether direct democratic decisions should substitute representative ones. Most probably, circumstances would be revealed under which each of the two arenas is most promising or threatening for oppressed groups, thereby informing decisions on what to institutionalize in different situations. Unfortunately, as mentioned above, this is a challenging issue to evaluate. One opportunity would be to focus on veto referenda and investigate whether they change parliamentary decisions for the better or the worse for oppressed groups. This would still depend on a number of other factors such as the government currently ruling, requirements to initiate a veto referendum and pass a bill, the popularity of the government and so on. However, it could be a starting point for evaluating and comparing the arenas. Another option could be case studies – e.g., what hints at a pro-output happening only due to direct democratic options? Although interdependencies should be taken into account as well, a comparison between direct democratic and representative lawmaking might enable recommendations on whether to extend one form of decision-making at the expense of the other.

Future research can build on this thesis, address its limitations, and explore the fate of oppressed groups in direct democracy in more depth. For all these future undertakings, my thesis contributes an important point of departure. First, its application of the concept of oppressed groups provides new conceptual ground for investigating the impacts of direct democracy for people who might be in particular danger of being disadvantaged in majoritarian votes. The conceptual part also engages with Iris M. Young's work and transfers her ideas to a new area. Second, the efforts I undertook in data collection and the quantitative analysis of national votes in European democracies provide an encompassing and differentiated overview of the fate of oppressed groups in direct democracy. Finally, identifying circumstances under which members of these groups can benefit from direct democratic votes in contrast to conditions that foster discrimination at the ballot yields important suggestions for the institutional design of direct democratic processes.

10.4 A Tyranny of the Majority?

Summing up this dissertation, neither the direct democratic bills that came to a vote nor the direct democratic outputs on the national level in European democracies between 1990 and 2015 support the notion of a clear-cut *Tyranny of the Majority* in the sense of constantly endangering oppressed groups' interests. In contrast, more pro-bills supporting oppressed groups reached the ballot than contra-bills did. The same holds for adopted bills – pro-outputs outnumbered contra-outputs. Therefore, oppressed groups are in fact able to mobilize a majority of voters to outvote a privileged minority on a regular basis. As a result, oppressed groups are not generally oppressed in direct democracy as well.

However, the concept of oppressed groups is nevertheless valuable for analyzing the implications of direct democracy. It enables the investigation of the fate of a variety of different groups. In doing so, its application reveals that there are some groups that face disadvantages at the ballot more often than others – either because contra-bills disadvantaging them outnumber pro-bills supporting them already at the bill-level, because pro-bills are less likely to win, because contra-bills are more likely to succeed, or a combination of all of these. These are members of the LGBTQ+ community, low SES groups, non-citizens, and political groups. As a result, a concept of oppressed groups in direct democracy should stress the importance of resources, rights and attitudes towards the oppressed group concerned by a bill to define which groups are facing disadvantages in direct democracy. As resources, rights and attitudes vary between countries and over time, this concept allows for flexibility in its adaption to different contexts. My results also call for support for LGBTQ+ groups, non-citizens, and low SES groups to reduce the disadvantages they face at the ballot. For example, a limit on campaign spending and reserved broadcasting time, coupled with financial and administrative support from a Ministry for initiatives by low SES groups or non-citizens could mitigate the effect of scarce resources. Another idea is to link direct democratic votes with citizens' assemblies to ensure that a variety of groups can voice their interests (Stojanović, 2023). To conclude, thus far, there is no general answer to the question of whether direct democracy represents a *Tyranny of the Majority*. Instead, the answer depends on the specific group and context in question.

In addition, contra-bills are in general as likely to succeed at the ballot as pro-bills are. The analysis of this wide variety of votes suggests that some institutional steps can be taken in order to increase supportive outputs while reducing potentially harmful ones. Specifically, these are binding vote results and the absence of quora requirements. By promoting these settings, the potential of direct democratic votes in general and for oppressed groups in particular can be leveraged: including as many people as possible in the making of political decisions, offering additional channels of influence and agenda-setting to those not well represented by representative institutions, and decreasing a perception of distance between the rulers and the ruled over. My encompassing analyses thereby address an important research gap and enable clear-cut recommendations for politics and political decision-makers.

Appendix

Appendix A: Codebook

Category	Guiding Questions (Code *pro-oppressed group (1)* if any of these questions can be answered with "yes" compared to the situation at the time of the vote/a potential counter-proposal)[26]
LGBTQ+	1.1) Does the bill propose measures that prohibit discrimination based on sexual orientation or gender identity? 1.2) Does the bill propose measures that introduce same-sex partnerships or marriages? 1.3) Does the bill propose measures that adapt the rights of same-sex couples to those of married people (e.g., regarding heritages, taxes)?
Rights of non-citizens (e.g., asylum, citizenship & franchise)	2.1) Does the bill propose measures that give more legal rights to non-citizens? 2.2) Does the bill propose measures that facilitate the way to citizenship (e.g., lowering of requirements, right to naturalization, supply of language courses, abolishment of decisions by popular vote)? 2.3) Does the bill propose measures that give more rights to immigrants/asylum seekers? Does it increase protection against deportation? 2.4) Does the bill propose measures to increase social welfare to non-citizens?
Non-citizens: fees & taxes	3.1) Does the bill propose measures that decrease fees for naturalization? 3.2) Does the bill propose measures that decrease taxes for non-citizens (e.g., by introducing flat rate taxation)? 3.3) Does the bill propose measures that decrease insurance fees for non-citizens?
Discrimination ban	4.1.) Does the bill propose measures that prohibit discrimination based on ethnicity, religion, sexual orientation, gender etc.?

---

26 Exceptions: 7.5, 10.1.

People with disabilities/ mental illness	5.1) Does the bill propose measures that prohibit discrimination based on disabilities? 5.2) Does the bill propose measures that benefit persons with disabilities (e.g., promoting equal living conditions, introduction of disability insurance, investments in homes/schools/ workplaces for people with disabilities, integration of pupils with disabilities into regular schooling, free public transport, financial support for costs related to disability, support accessible constructions)? 5.3.) Does the bill propose measures that give voice to persons with disabilities? 5.4) Does the bill propose measures that improve support for people dealing with mental health issues (e.g., supply of therapy, investments in psychiatric clinics, financial support in case of illness, introduction of obligatory health insurance with reasonable fees)?
Linguistic minorities	6.1) Does the bill propose measures that protect members of linguistic minorities? 6.2) Does the bill propose measures that support the understanding between different language groups? 6.3) Does the bill propose measures that support multilingualism (e.g., introduce teaching minority languages at school)? 6.4.) Does the bill propose measures that establish minority languages as (additional) official languages?
Religious minorities	7.1) Does the bill propose measures that give voice to representatives of religious minorities? 7.2) Does the bill propose measures that introduce teaching religious subject also for religious minorities? 7.3) Does the bill propose measures that prohibit discrimination based on religion? 7.4) Does the bill propose measures that enable religious minorities to gain public law status/decrease the monopoly of privileged religious groups? 7.5) Does the bill propose measures that discriminate members of certain religious minorities? (if yes code *contra-oppressed*) 7.6) Does the bill propose measures that improve the financial situation of religious minorities?

Gender	8.1) Does the bill propose measures that promote equality b/w men & women (e.g., defines that as "Staatsziel", abolishes unequal fees or taxes)?
	8.2) Does the bill propose measures that give voice to women representatives (e.g., inclusion of women groups in decision-making, introduction of gender quotas for political bodies)?
	8.3) Does the bill propose measures that prohibit discrimination based on gender or sexual identity?
	8.4) Does the bill propose measures that introduce gender-just language?
	8.5) Does the bill propose measures that particularly support disadvantaged women (e.g., introduction of pension benefits for time of childcare, support for single mothers)?
Rule of law / basic rights	9.1) Does the bill propose measures that guarantee basic political & social rights?
	9.2) Does the bill propose measures that guarantee legal protection or the right of a fair trial?
	9.3) Does the bill propose measures that enhance legal tools of minorities (e.g., right to sue against denied requests for citizenship)?
Low SES: fees & taxes	10.1) Does the bill propose measures that introduce/increase (education, healthcare, insurance, traffic, public service etc.) fees or costs? (if yes code *contra-oppressed*)
	10.2) Does the bill propose measures that decrease costs for housing/energy?
	10.3) Does the bill propose measures that decrease taxes in general or for low-income groups in particular? Does it promote progressive taxing instead of flat rate tax?
	10.4) Does the bill propose measures that decrease (education, healthcare, insurance, traffic, public service etc.) fees especially for low-income groups?
	10.5) Does the bill propose measures that introduce a minimum wage?
	10.6) Does the bill propose measures that introduce mandatory insurances with fees proportional to income, so that for example healthcare is not dependent on wealth anymore?
	10.7) Does the bill propose measures that empower trade unions and/or improve workers' rights?
Low SES: Public transport	11.1) Does the bill propose measures that increase the supply of public transport?
	11.2) Does the bill propose measures that decrease public transport fees?
	11.3) Does the bill propose measures that invest in public transport?
	11.4) Does the bill propose measures that invest in infrastructure for bikes/pedestrians?

Low SES: Education & daycare	12.1) Does the bill propose measures that introduce/increase supply/quality of public daycare (e.g., kindergarten, full time schools)?
	12.2) Does the bill propose measures that define education as "Staatsziel"?
	12.3) Does the bill propose measures that support low SES pupils (e.g., extension of primary school, making kindergarten obligatory, teaching two foreign languages at primary school)?
	12.4) Does the bill propose measures that abolish/decrease fees for education? Does it introduce/increase scholarships, especially for low-income groups?
	12.5) Does the bill propose measures that invest in education (e.g., building of schools, establishing of universities, smaller classes, support of schools in need)?
	12.6) Does the bill propose measures that help children with foreign mother tongue learning the official language (e.g., teaching in official language instead of dialect, additional courses)?
	12.7) Does the bill propose measures that support integration of pupils with disabilities?
	12.8) Does the bill propose measures that support parents in paying for daycare?
	12.9) Does the bill propose measures that increase the support for children in training?
Low SES: social welfare	13.1) Does the bill propose measures that give voice to representatives of welfare societies?
	13.2) Does the bill propose measures that define provision of equal living conditions as "Staatsziel"?
	13.3) Does the bill propose measures that guarantee basic social rights?
	13.4) Does the bill propose measures that support retired/sick people (e.g., introduction of mandatory insurance, financial support for it, increase supply/quality of care homes)?
	13.5) Does the bill propose measures that give financial support for people in need (e.g., families, unemployed)?
	13.6) Does the bill propose measures that support unemployed in findings jobs?
	13.7) Does the bill propose measures that guarantee local job/social welfare centers?
	13.8) Does the bill propose measures that broaden the entitlement to social welfare (e.g., for asylum seekers)?
	13.9) Does the bill propose measures that introduce/increase paid maternity leave?
	13.10) Does the bill propose measures that increase social spending in general?

Low SES: housing	14.1) Does the bill propose measures that define provision of equal living conditions/affordable housing as "Staatsziel"? 14.2) Does the bill propose measures that decrease housing or energy costs? 14.3) Does the bill propose measures that increase supply of cheap flats? 14.4) Does the bill propose measures to decrease rent in general or for people in need? 14.5) Does the bill propose measures that improve legal situation of tenants or decrease costs for trials about rent? 14.6) Does the bill propose measures that decrease taxes for tenants? 14.7) Does the bill propose measures that support handicapped-accessible constructions?
Low SES: healthcare	15.1) Does the bill propose measures that define provision of equal living conditions/healthcare as "Staatsziel"? 15.2) Does the bill propose measures that implement obligatory health insurance? 15.3) Does the bill propose measures that decrease fees for health insurance in general or for low-income groups? 15.4) Does the bill propose measures that invest in hospitals, nursing homes or ambulant care? 15.5) Does the bill propose measures that decrease treatment costs or taxes for people suffering from illness/accidents? 15.6) Does the bill propose measures that support people caring for their sick relatives at home or re-construct accessibly? 15.7) Does the bill propose measures that prevent sickness (e.g., support sport activities, ban on smoking, allow abortions in case of health risks for mother)?
Parliamentary opposition	16.1) Does the bill propose measures that protect or support parliamentary opposition? 16.2) Does the bill propose measures that increase rights or power of opposition?
Voting system	17.1) Does the bill propose measures that lead to a more proportional composition of parliament? (i.e., get rid of/weaken majoritarian voting procedures, get rid of certain % thresholds for parliamentary elections, increase number of parliamentary seats) 17.2) Does the bill propose measures that shorten legislative terms? 17.3) Does the bill propose measures that lower the voting/eligibility age? 17.4) Does the bill propose measures that decrease hurdles for voting (e.g., easier postal vote, e-voting)?

Division of power	18.1) Does the bill propose measures that increase checks on executive (e.g., introduction of committees of inquiry, decrease in rights of head of government, increase in decisions by popular vote, term limits for government members)?
	18.2) Does the bill propose measures that introduce/strengthen bicameralism?
	18.3) Does the bill propose measures that include division of power as constitutional principle?
	18.4) Does the bill propose measures that secure the independence of courts?
	18.5) Does the bill propose measures that establish coalition government?
	18.6) Does the bill propose measures that increase the media presence of (political) minorities? Does it propose measures against the media monopolies of certain political actors?

Appendix B: Additional Analyses

Table 38: Direct Democratic Bills and Outputs and Attitudes, 1990-2015, means of attitudes

	Pro-bills	Contra-bills	Pro-outputs	Contra-outputs
No neighbors of different race	0.0804	0.0765	0.0908	0.0766
No neighbors with mental problems	0.2085	0.1752	0.164	0.069
No Muslim neighbors	0.0507	0.0522	0.076	0.0296
No neighbors of different religion	0.0673	0.1135	0.0588	0.1002
No immigrant neighbors	0.1041	0.0908	0.1158	0.08
No homosexual neighbors	0.3066	0.3175	0.3206	0.3278
Jobs for men	0.3151	0.3377	0.3151	0.3211
Larger income differences	0.4419	0.4636	0.467	0.4228
Negative attitude towards group	0.3816	0.2664	0.4456	0.1677
Equal treatment and opportunities	0.8046	0.8058	0.8005	0.8085

Sources: own dataset, World Values Survey Round 2-6, European Social Survey Round 1-7

Table 39: Direct Democratic Bills and Outputs and Context, 1990-2015, means

	Pro-bills	Contra-bills	Pro-outputs	Contra-outputs
Tertiary degree	0.2321	0.1931	0.2231	0.1813
GDP growth/capita	0.0195	0.0114	0.0223	−0.0023
Ethnic fractionalization	0.2776	0.2610	0.2481	0.2466

Sources: own dataset, Eurostat, Worldbank, Historical Index of Ethnic Fractionalization Dataset

Table 40: Votes in Switzerland and Institutional Explaining Variables, Cramér's V

	Votes outside Switzerland (%)	Votes in Switzerland (%)	Cramér's V
Bottom-up votes	46.78	53.22	
Mandatory votes	40.00	60.00	0.3702***
Top-down votes	100.00	0	
Not binding	100.00	0	0.2772***
Binding	48.12	51.88	
Quorum	45.75	54.25	0.1532**
No quorum	61.32	38.68	

*** p < 0.01, ** p < 0.05, * p < 0.1; Source: own dataset

Table 41: Votes in Switzerland and Attitudinal and Socio-Economic Explaining Variables, means (ttests)

	Mean outside Switzerland	Mean in Switzerland	Difference in Means Significant?
No neighbors of different race	0.1405	0.0467	Yes, p < 0.01
No neighbors with mental problems	0.5475	0.0911	Yes, p < 0.01
No Muslim neighbors	Not asked outside CH		
No neighbors of different religion	0.1249	0.044	Yes, p < 0.01
No immigrant neighbors	0.1855	0.0526	Yes, p < 0.01
No homosexual neighbors	0.4794	0.1383	Yes, p < 0.01
Jobs for men	0.3232	0.3211	No
Larger income differences	0.4901	0.4076	Yes, p < 0.01
Equal treatment and opportunities	0.8015	0.8091	Yes, p < 0.1
Tertiary education degree	0.1783	0.2582	Yes, p < 0.1
GDP growth/capita	0.0236	0.0070	Yes, p < 0.01
Ethnic fractionalization	0.1853	0.3382	Yes, p < 0.01

Sources: World Values Survey Round 2-6, European Social Survey Round 1-7, Eurostat, Worldbank, Historical Index of Ethnic Fractionalization Dataset

Table 42: Direct Democratic Instrument and Institutional Explaining Variables, Cramér's V

	Bottom-up votes (%)	Mandatory votes (%)	Top-down votes (%)	Cramér's V
Not binding	0	0	100.00	0.7570***
Binding	71.55	23.01	5.44	
Quorum	66.67	25.49	7.84	0.1989***
No quorum	65.09	15.09	19.81	

*** $p < 0.01$, ** $p < 0.05$, * $p < 0.1$; Source: own dataset

Table 43: Direct Democratic Instrument and Attitudinal and Socio-Economic Explaining Variables, means (anova)

	Mean bottom-up	Mean mandatory	Mean top-down	Difference in Means Significant?
No neighbors of different race	0.0668	0.0607	0.1549	Yes, $p < 0.01$
No neighbors with mental problems	0.1500	0.1784	0.5137	Yes, $p < 0.01$
No Muslim neighbors	0.0617	0.0443	No cases	No
No neighbors of different religion	0.0725	0.044	0.1449	Yes, $p < 0.01$
No immigrant neighbors	0.0864	0.0799	0.1645	Yes, $p < 0.01$
No homosexual neighbors	0.2326	0.3002	0.4925	Yes, $p < 0.01$
Jobs for men	0.3037	0.3575	0.3455	No
Larger income differences	0.4344	0.4533	0.4725	No
Equal treatment and opportunities	0.8064	0.8039	0.8096	No
Tertiary education degree	0.2125	0.2481	0.2086	No
GDP growth/capita	0.0106	0.0237	0.0241	Yes, $p < 0.05$
Ethnic fractionalization	0.2878	0.2723	0.1812	Yes, $p < 0.01$

Sources: own dataset, World Values Survey Round 2-6, European Social Survey Round 1-7, Eurostat, Worldbank, Historical Index of Ethnic Fractionalization Dataset

Table 44: Binding Votes and Quora, Cramér's V

	Binding Votes (%)	Not binding Votes (%)	Cramér's V
Quorum	93.46	6.54	0.0534
No quorum	90.57	9.43	

*** $p < 0.01$, ** $p < 0.05$, * $p < 0.1$; Source: own dataset

Table 45: Binding Votes and Attitudinal and Socio-Economic Explaining Variables, means (ttests)

	Mean not binding votes	Mean binding votes	Difference in Means Significant?
No neighbors of different race	0.1834	0.0707	Yes, $p < 0.01$
No neighbors with mental problems	0.5542 (only one case)	0.1759	No
No Muslim neighbors	No cases		
No neighbors of different religion	0.149	0.0802	Yes, $p < 0.1$
No immigrant neighbors	0.1747	0.0904	Yes, $p < 0.05$
No homosexual neighbors	0.6083	0.2686	Yes, $p < 0.01$
Jobs for men	0.4801	0.3096	Yes, $p < 0.01$
Larger income differences	0.5175	0.4394	Yes, $p < 0.1$
Equal treatment and opportunities	0.8079	0.8061	No
Tertiary education degree	0.2342	0.2179	No
GDP growth/capita	0.0199	0.0148	No
Ethnic fractionalization	0.1563	0.2807	Yes, $p < 0.01$

Sources: own dataset, World Values Survey Round 2-6, European Social Survey Round 1-7, Eurostat, Worldbank, Historical Index of Ethnic Fractionalization Dataset

Table 46: Correlations between Attitudinal and Socio-Economic Variables I, correlation coefficients

	No neighbors of different race	No neighbors with mental problems	No Muslim neighbors	No neighbors of diff. religion
No neighbors with mental problems	0.8848***			
No Muslim neighbors	1.0000***	1.0000***		
No neighbors of different religion	0.6360***	1.0000***	No cases	
No immigrant neighbors	0.8973***	0.9623***	1.0000***	0.6047***
No homosexual neighbors	0.8419***	0.9809***	.	0.8658***
Jobs for men	0.3985**	0.4560**	.	0.4181*
Larger income differences	0.5273***	0.5436**	.	0.5739***
Equal treatment and opportunities	−0.4663*	No cases	No cases	−0.1249
Tertiary education degree	−0.8445***	−0.9148***	.	−0.7847***
GDP growth/capita	0.3022*	0.8827***	0.5020**	0.2065
Ethnic fractionalization	−0.6479***	−0.2195	0.8299***	−0.2325

*** $p < 0.01$, ** $p < 0.05$, * $p < 0.1$; Sources: World Values Survey Round 2-6, European Social Survey Round 1-7, Eurostat, Worldbank, Historical Index of Ethnic Fractionalization Dataset

Table 47: Correlations between Attitudinal and Socio-Economic Variables II, correlation coefficients

	No immigrant neighbors	No homosexual neighbors	Jobs for men	Larger income differences
No homosexual neighbors	0.8998***		.	
Jobs for men	0.2981**	0.4441**	.	
Larger income differences	0.5688***	0.5125***	0.6279***	
Equal treatment and opportunities	−0.5022**	−0.3014	−0.5637***	−0.8509***
Tertiary education degree	−0.8083***	−0.8033***	−0.4441***	−0.7757***
GDP growth/capita	0.4146***	0.4015***	0.2767**	0.1535
Ethnic fractionalization	−0.4055***	−0.3759***	−0.1658	−0.4823***

*** $p < 0.01$, ** $p < 0.05$, * $p < 0.1$; Sources: World Values Survey Round 2-6, European Social Survey Round 1-7, Eurostat, Worldbank, Historical Index of Ethnic Fractionalization Dataset

Table 48: Correlations between Attitudinal and Socio-Economic Variables III, correlation coefficients

	Equal treatment and opportunities	Tertiary degree	GDP growth/capita
Tertiary degree	0.3025**		
GDP growth/capita	−0.0267	−0.0154	
Ethnic fractionalization	0.1131	0.6040***	−0.1896*

*** $p < 0.01$, ** $p < 0.05$, * $p < 0.1$; Sources: Eurostat, Worldbank, Historical Index of Ethnic Fractionalization Dataset

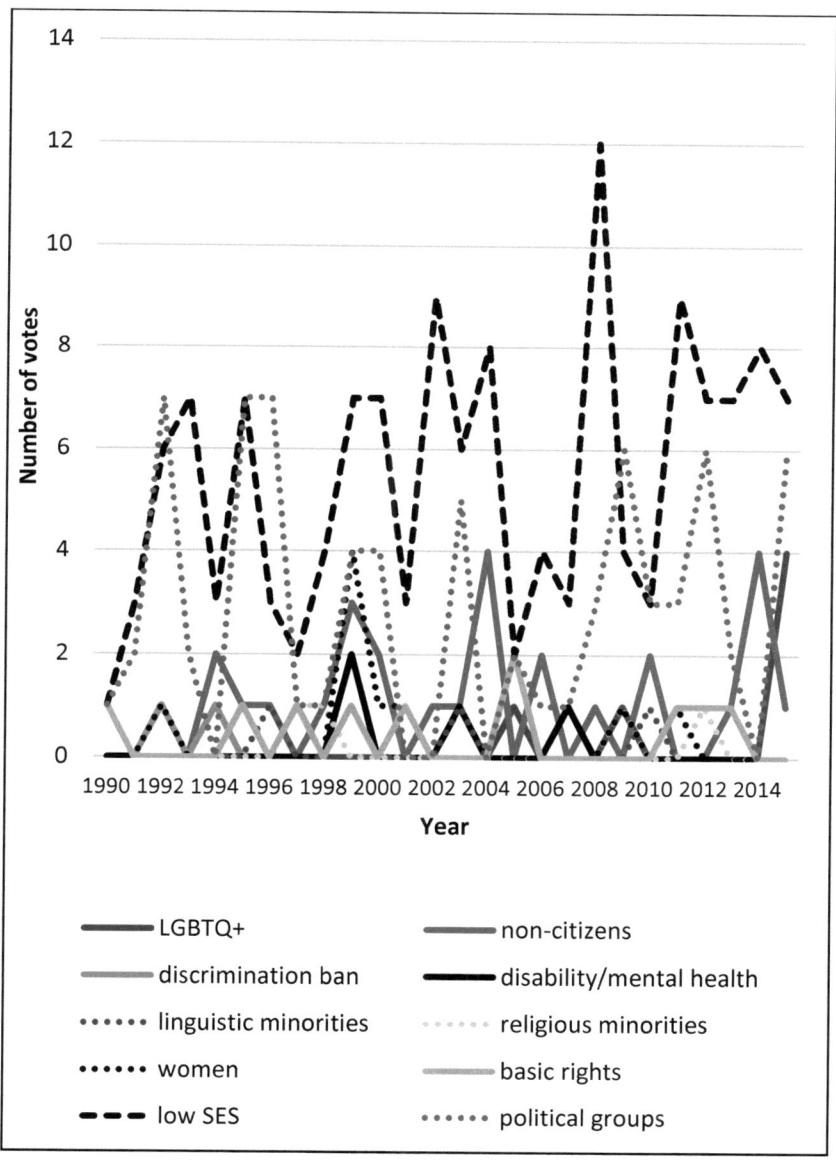

Figure 22: Number of Votes Affecting Different Oppressed Groups, 1990-2015. Source: own dataset

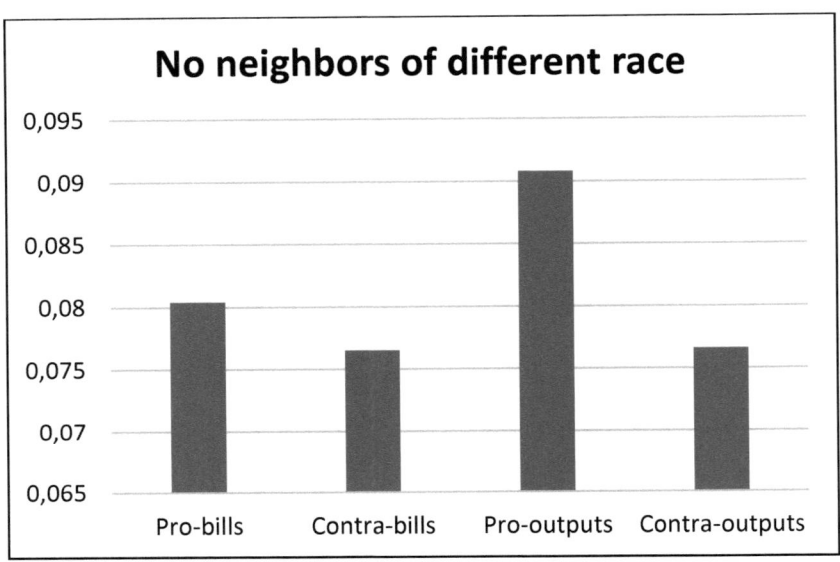

Figure 23: Means of Agreement "No neighbors of a different race".
Sources: own dataset, World Values Survey Round 2-6

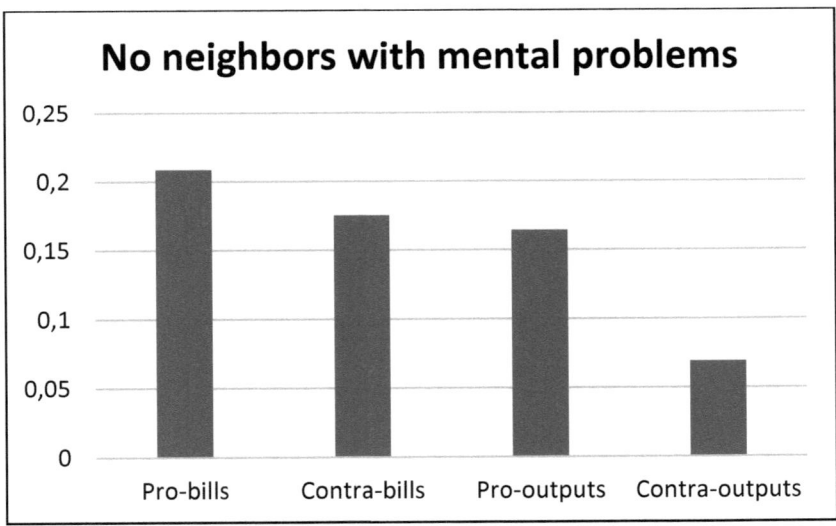

Figure 24: Means of Agreement "No neighbors with mental problems".
Sources: own dataset, World Values Survey Round 2-6

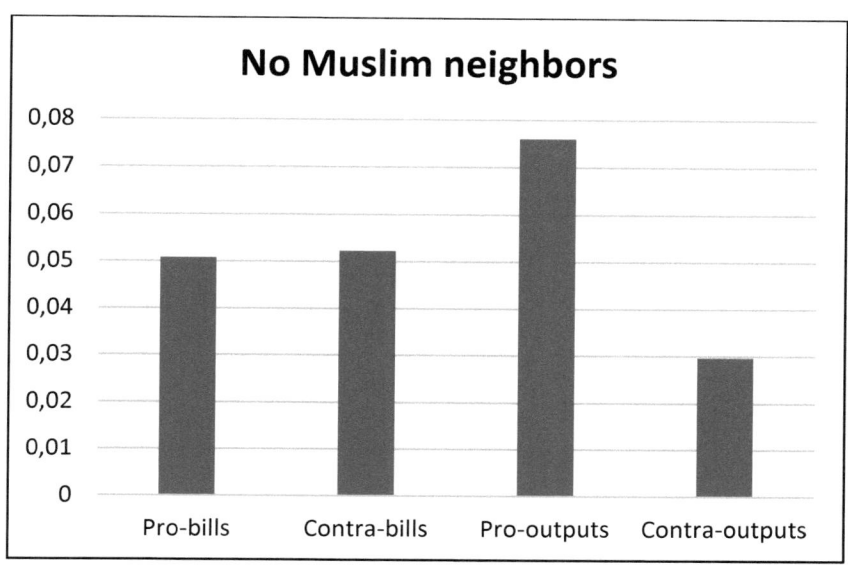

Figure 25: Means of Agreement "No neighbors of Muslim religion".
Sources: own dataset, World Values Survey Round 2-6

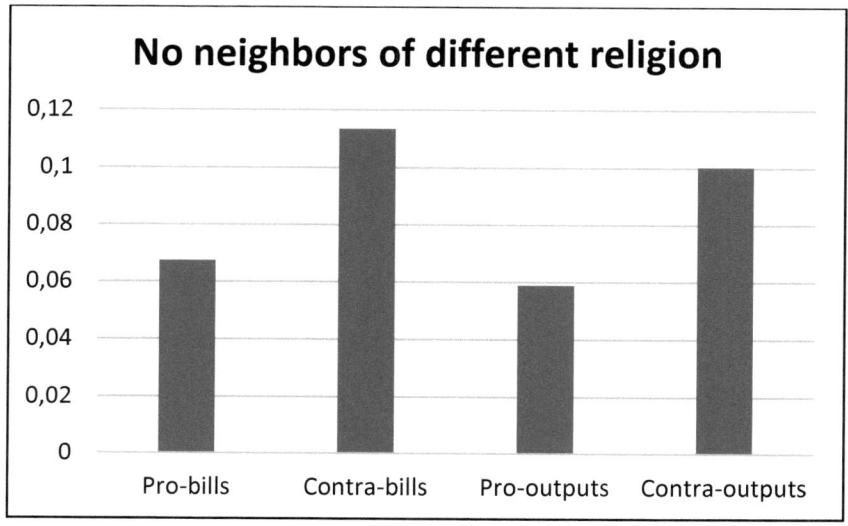

Figure 26: Means of Agreement "No neighbors of different religion".
Sources: own dataset, World Values Survey Round 2-6

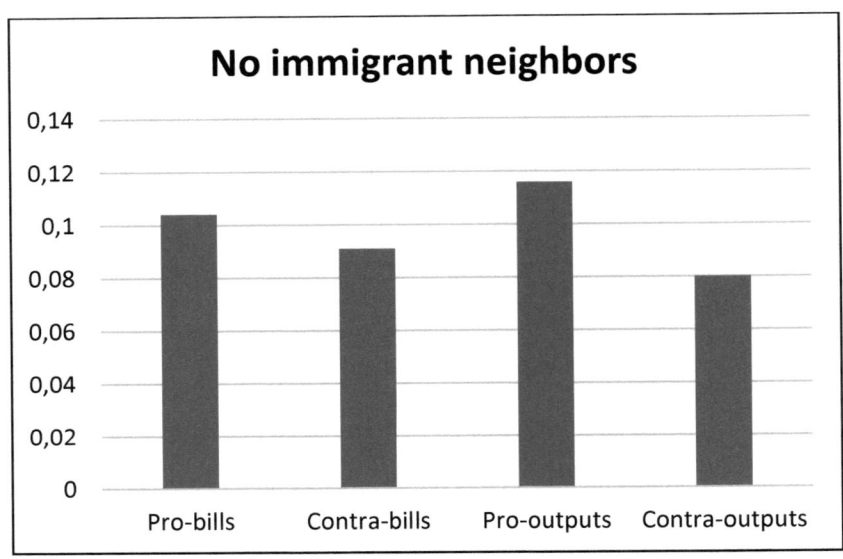

Figure 27: Means of Agreement "No immigrant neighbors".
Sources: own dataset, World Values Survey Round 2-6

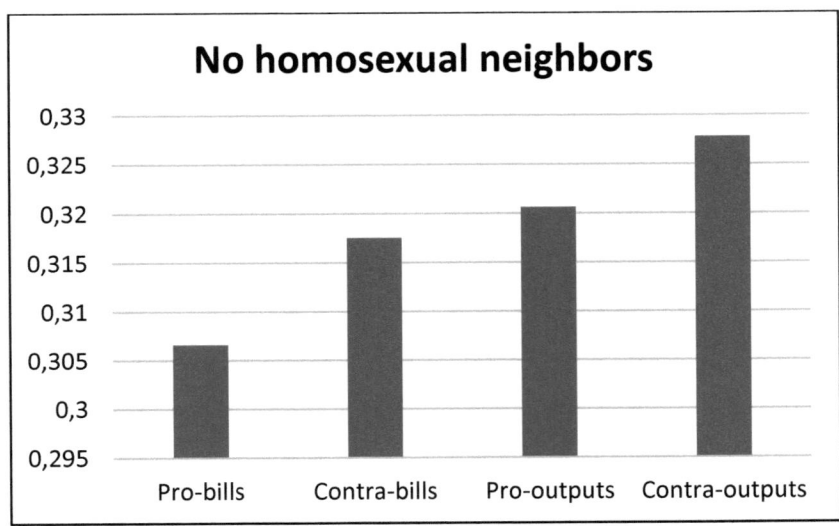

Figure 28: Means of Agreement "No homosexual neighbors".
Sources: own dataset, World Values Survey Round 2-6

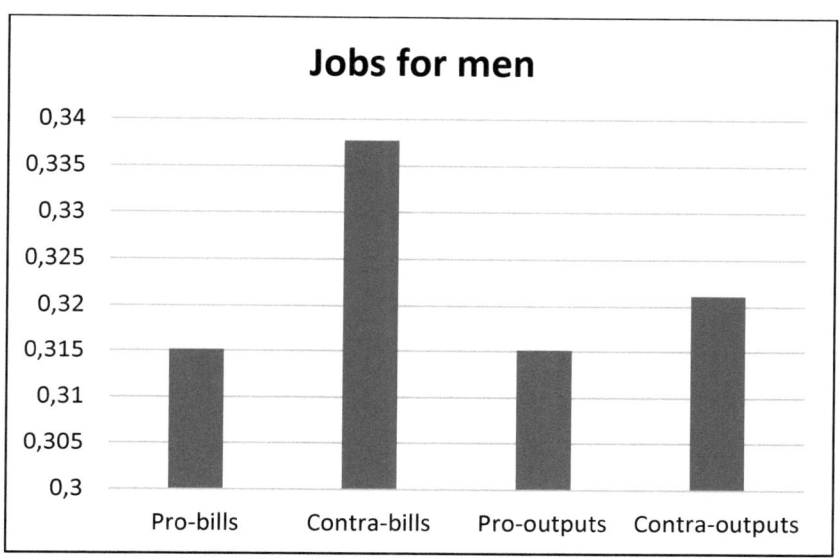

Figure 29: Means of Agreement "When jobs are scarce, men should be advantaged". Sources: own dataset, World Values Survey Round 2-6

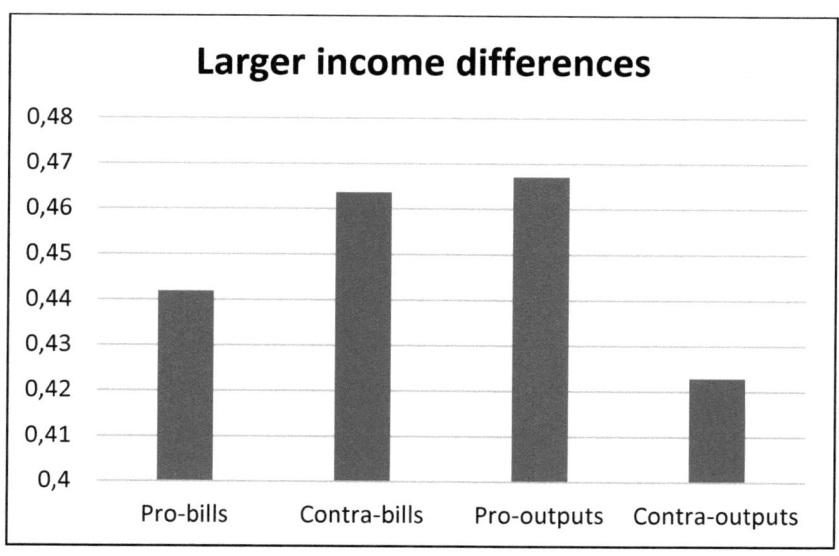

Figure 30: Means of Agreement "Larger income differences are necessary". Sources: own dataset, World Values Survey Round 2-6

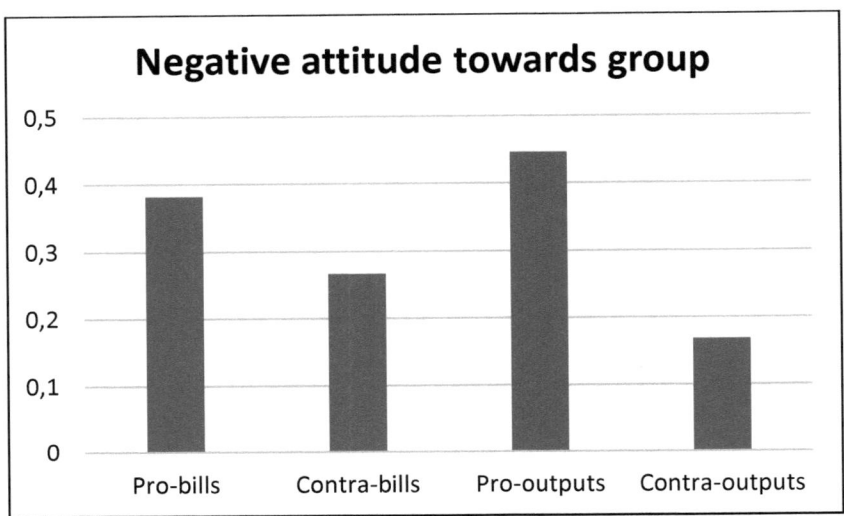

Figure 31: Means of Negative Attitude towards Affected Group.
Sources: own dataset, World Values Survey Round 2-6

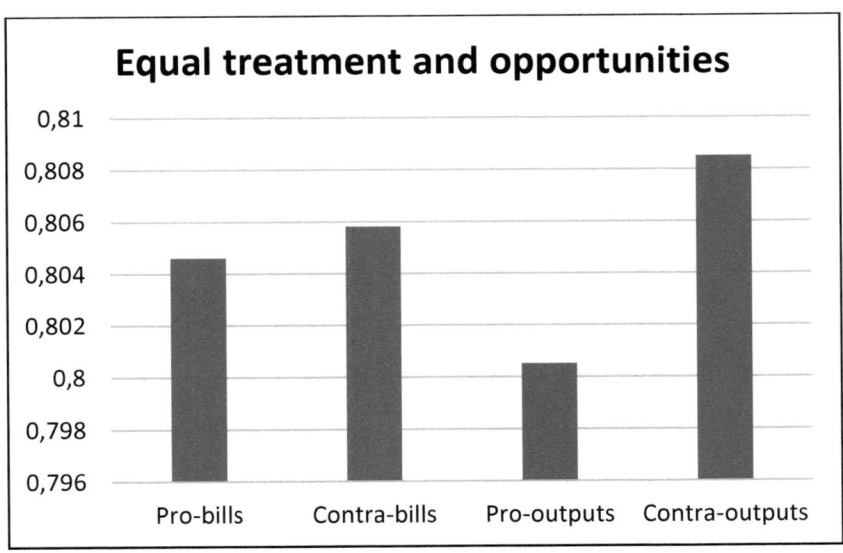

Figure 32: Means of Agreement "Important that people are treated equally & have equal opportunities".
Sources: own dataset, European Social Survey Round 1-7

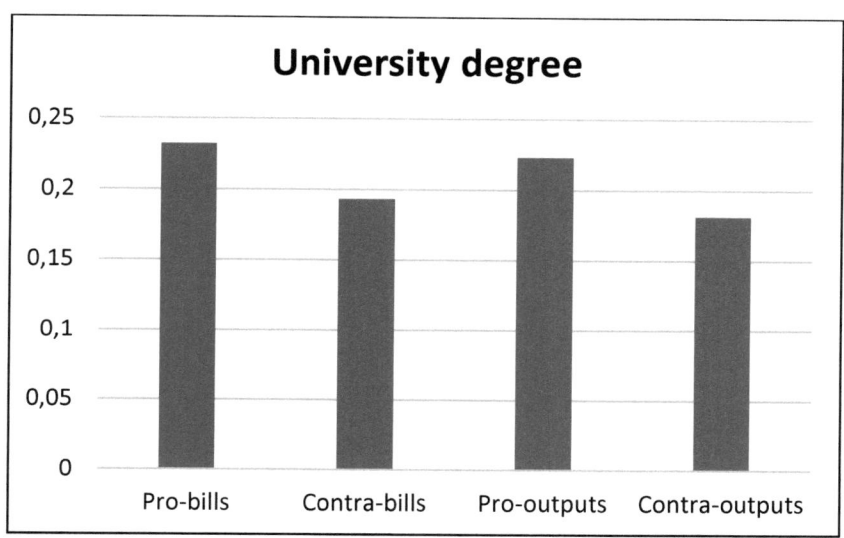

Figure 33: Means of Share of People with University Degree.
Sources: own dataset, Eurostat

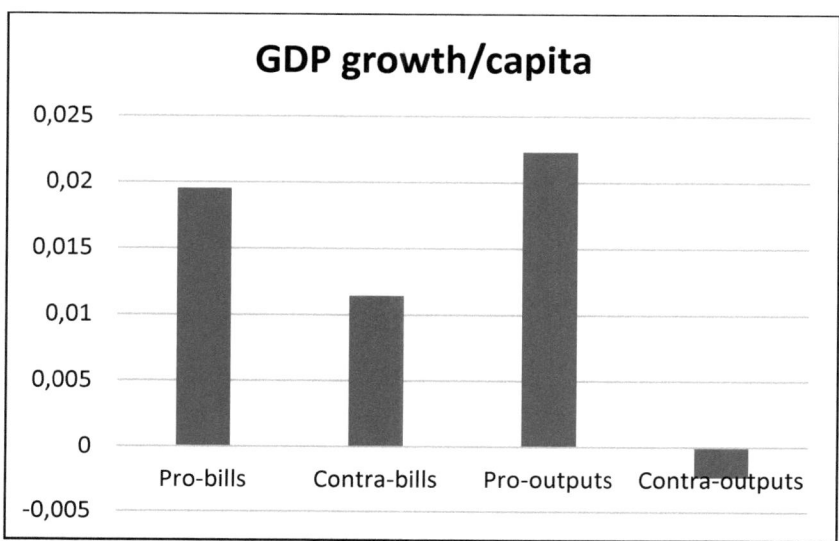

Figure 34: Means of Growth of GDP per capita.
Sources: own dataset, Worldbank

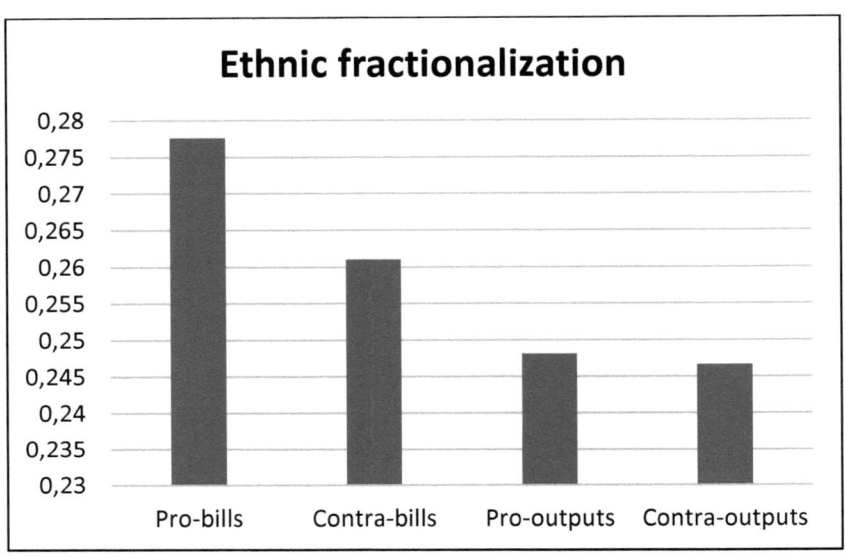

Figure 35: Means of Levels of Ethnic Fractionalization.
Sources: own dataset, Historical Index of Ethnic Fractionalization Dataset

Bibliography

Ackermann, K., Braun, D., Fatke, M., & Fawzi, N. (2021). Direct democracy, political support and populism–attitudinal patterns in the German Bundesländer. *Regional & Federal Studies*. https://doi.org/10.1080/13597566.2021.1919876.

Aguiar-Conraria, L., & Magalhães, P. C. (2010). Referendum design, quorum rules and turnout. *Public Choice*, *144*, 63–81.

Alesina, A., & Glaeser, E. (2004). *Fighting Poverty in the US and Europe: A World of Difference*. Oxford University Press.

Allen, P. (2021). Experience, Knowledge, and Political Representation. *Politics & Gender*. https://doi.org/doi:10.1017/S1743923X21000362.

Barber, B. (1984). *Strong Democracy. Participatory Politics for a New Age*. University of California Press.

Barry, B. (1975). Political Accommodation and Consociational Democracy. *British Journal of Political Science*, *5*(4), 477–505.

Batory, A., & Svensson, S. (2019). The use and abuse of participatory governance by populist governments. *Policy & Politics*, *47*(2), 227–244.

Bell, D. A. (1978). The Referendum: Democracy's Barrier to Racial Equality. *Washington Law Review*, *54*(1), 1–29.

Bellamy, R. (2018). Majority Rule, Compromise and the Democratic Legitimacy of Referendums. *Swiss Political Science Review*, *24*(3), 312–319.

Benedikter, T. (2012). Direct Democracy and Linguistic Minorities in Switzerland and South Tyrol—A Comparison. In W. Marxer (Ed.), *Direct Democracy and Minorities* (pp. 106–122). Springer VS.

Billig, M., & Tajfel, H. (1973). Social categorization and similarity in intergroup behaviour. *European Journal of Social Psychology*, *3*(1), 27–52.

Bochsler, D., & Hug, S. (2015). How minorities fare under referendums: A cross-national study. *Electoral Studies (Elsevier)*, *38*, 206–216.

Bolliger, C. (2007). Minderheiten in der direkten Demokratie: Die Medaille hat auch eine Vorderseite. In M. Freitag & U. Wagschal (Eds.), *Direkte Demokratie. Bestandsaufnahmen und Wirkungen im internationalen Vergleich*. (pp. 419–446). LIT Verlag.

Boswell, J. (2016). Deliberating Downstream: Countering Democratic Distortions in the Policy Process. *Perspectives on Politics*, *14*(3), 724–737.

Bowler, S., Denemark, D., Donovan, T., & McDonnell, D. (2017). Right-wing populist party supporters: Dissatisfied but not direct democrats. *European Journal of Political Research*, *56*(1), 70–91.

Brady, H. E., Verba, S., & Schlozman, K. (1995). Beyond Ses: A Resource Model of Political Participation. *The American Political Science Review, 89*(2), 271–294.

Christensen, H. S., Jäske, M., Setälä, M., & Laitinen, E. (2017). The Finnish Citizens' Initiative: Towards Inclusive Agenda-setting? *Scandinavian Political Studies, 40*(4), 411–433.

Christmann, A. (2012). *Die Grenzen direkter Demokratie. Volksentscheide im Spannungsverhältnis von Demokratie und Rechtsstaat.* Nomos.

Christmann, A., & Danaci, D. (2012). Direct Democracy and Minority Rights: Direct and Indirect Effects on Religious Minorities in Switzerland. *Politics and Religion, 5*(1), 133–160.

Dalton, R. J. (Ed.). (2004). *Democratic Challenges, Democratic Choices. The Erosion of Political Support in Advanced Industrial Democracies.* Oxford University Press.

Danaci, D. (2012). The Minaret Ban in Switzerland: An Exception to the Rule? In W. Marxer (Ed.), *Direct Democracy and Minorities* (pp. 155–164). Springer VS.

Di Bari, M. (2021). Direct Democracy and the Rights of Sexual Minorities. *Direito Público, 18*(98), 179–204. https://doi.org/10.11117/rdp.v18i98.5848

Dincer, O. C., & Lambert, P. J. (2012). Taking care of your own: Ethnic and religious heterogeneity and income inequality. *Journal of Economic Studies, 39*(3), 290–313.

Donovan, T. (2013). Direct Democracy and Campaigns Against Minorities. *Minnesota Law Review, 97*(5), 1730–1779.

Donovan, T., & Tolbert, C. (2013). Do Popular Votes on Rights Create Animosity Toward Minorities? *Political Research Quarterly, 66*(4), 910–922.

Drazanova. (2019). *Historical Index of Ethnic Fractionalization Dataset, Version 2.0.* https://dataverse.harvard.edu/dataset.xhtml?persistentId=doi:10.7910/DVN/4JQRCL.

Eder, C., & Magin, R. (2008). Direkte Demokratie. In M. Freitag & A. Vatter (Eds.), *Die Demokratien der deutschen Bundesländer* (pp. 257–308). Verlag Barbara Budrich.

el-Wakil, A., & McKay, S. (2020). Disentangling Referendums and Direct Democracy: A Defence of the Systemic Approach to Popular Vote Processes. *Representation, 56*(4), 449–466.

Elsässer, L., Hense, S., & Schäfer, A. (2021). Not just money: Unequal responsiveness in egalitarian democracies. *Journal of European Public Policy, 28*(12), 1890–1908.

Enders, C. K., & Tofighi, D. (2007). Centering Predictor Variables in Cross-Sectional Multilevel Models: A New Look at an Old Issue. *Psychological Methods, 12*(2), 121–138.

Ennser-Jedenastik, L. (2021). What drives partisan conflict and consensus on welfare state issues? *Journal of Public Policy, 41*(4), 731–751.

ESS6—Integrated file, edition 2.4 [Data set] (European Social Survey European Research Infrastructure (ESS ERIC)). (2018). Sikt – Norwegian Agency for Shared Services in Education and Research. https://doi.org/10.21338/ESS6E02_4.

ESS10—Integrated file, edition 2.1 [Data set] (European Social Survey European Research Infrastructure (ESS ERIC)). (2022). Sikt – Norwegian Agency for Shared Services in Education and Research. https://doi.org/10.18712/ess10.

Eule, J. N. (1990). Judicial Review of Direct Democracy. *The Yale Law Journal*, *99*(7), 1503–1590.

European Social Survey Round 1 Data (2002). Data file edition 6.6. (n.d.). NSD – Norwegian Centre for Research Data, Norway – Data Archive and distributor of ESS data for ESS ERIC. doi:10.21338/NSD-ESS1-2002.

European Social Survey Round 2 Data (2004). Data file edition 3.6. (n.d.). NSD – Norwegian Centre for Research Data, Norway – Data Archive and distributor of ESS data for ESS ERIC. doi:10.21338/NSD-ESS2-2004.

European Social Survey Round 3 Data (2006). Data file edition 3.7. (n.d.). NSD – Norwegian Centre for Research Data, Norway – Data Archive and distributor of ESS data for ESS ERIC. doi:10.21338/NSD-ESS3-2006.

European Social Survey Round 4 Data (2008). Data file edition 4.5. (n.d.). NSD – Norwegian Centre for Research Data, Norway – Data Archive and distributor of ESS data for ESS ERIC. doi:10.21338/NSD-ESS4-2008.

European Social Survey Round 5 Data (2010). Data file edition 3.4. (n.d.). NSD – Norwegian Centre for Research Data, Norway – Data Archive and distributor of ESS data for ESS ERIC. doi:10.21338/NSD-ESS5-2010.

European Social Survey Round 6 Data (2012). Data file edition 2.4. (n.d.). NSD – Norwegian Centre for Research Data, Norway – Data Archive and distributor of ESS data for ESS ERIC. doi:10.21338/NSD-ESS6-2012.

European Social Survey Round 7 Data (2014). Data file edition 2.2. (n.d.). NSD – Norwegian Centre for Research Data, Norway – Data Archive and distributor of ESS data for ESS ERIC. doi:10.21338/NSD-ESS7-2014.

Feld, L. P., Fischer, J. A. V., & Kirchgässner, G. (2010). The Effect of Direct Democracy on Income Redistribution: Evidence for Switzerland. *Economic Inquiry*, *48*(4), 817–840.

Feld, L. P., & Kirchgässner, G. (2000). Direct democracy, political culture, and the outcome of economic policy: A report on the Swiss experience. *European Journal of Political Economy*, *16*(2), 287–306.

Fraser, N. (1997a). A Rejoinder to Iris Young. *New Left Review*, *223*(1), 126–129.

Fraser, N. (1997b). *Justice Interruptus: Critical Reflections on the "Postsocialist" Condition*. Routledge.

Frey, B. S., & Goette, L. (1998). Does the Popular Vote Destroy Civil Rights? *American Journal of Political Science*, *42*(4), 1343–1348.

Gamble, B. S. (1997). Putting Civil Rights to a Popular Vote. *American Journal of Political Science*, *41*(1), 245–269.

Geißel, B. (2020). *Ungleichheit und direkte Demokratie Europa (Version 1.0.0)*. Universität Frankfurt am Main. https://doi.org/10.7802/2128.

Geißel, B., Krämling, A., & Paulus, L. (2019a). It Depends…Different Direct Democratic Instruments and Equality in Europe from 1990 to 2015. *Politics and Governance*, 7(2), 365–379.

Geißel, B., Krämling, A., & Paulus, L. (2019b). More or less equality? Direct Democracy in Europe from 1990 to 2015. *Zeitschrift Für Vergleichende Politikwissenschaft*, 13(4), 491–525.

Gerber, E. R. (1999). *The Populist Paradox: Interest Group Influence and the Promise of Direct Legislation.* Princeton University Press.

Gerber, E. R., & Hug, S. (2002). *Minority Rights and Direct Legislation: Theory, Methods, and Evidence.* http://www.unige.ch/ses/spo/static/simonhug/mrdd/joprr.pdf.

Gherghina, S. (2019). How Political Parties Use Referendums: An Analytical Framework. *East European Politics and Societies and Cultures*, 33(3), 677–690.

Gibson, J. L., & Gouws, A. (2000). Social Identities and Political Intolerance: Linkages within the South African Mass Public. *American Journal of Political Science*, 44(2), 278–292.

Gidron, N., & Hall, P. A. (2017). The politics of social status: Economic and cultural roots of the populist right. *The British Journal of Sociology*, 68(S1), S57–S84.

Gisselquist, R. M. (2014). Ethnic divisions and public goods provision, revisited. *Ethnic and Racial Studies*, 37(9), 1605–1627.

Grotz, F., & Lewandowsky, M. (2020). Promoting or Controlling Political Decisions? Citizen Preferences for Direct-Democratic Institutions in Germany. *German Politics*, 29(2), 180–200.

Guasti, P., & Bustikova, L. (2020). In Europe's Closet: The rights of sexual minorities in the Czech Republic and Slovakia. *East European Politics*, 36(2), 226–246.

Haider-Markel, D. P., Querze, A., & Lindaman, K. (2007). Lose, Win, or Draw?: A Reexamination of Direct Democracy and Minority Rights. *Political Research Quarterly*, 60(2), 304–314.

Hainmueller, J., & Hangartner, D. (2019). Does Direct Democracy Hurt Immigrant Minorities? Evidence from Naturalization Decisions in Switzerland. *American Journal of Political Science*, 63(3), 530–547.

Hajnal, Z. L., Gerber, E. R., & Louch, H. (2002). Minorities and Direct Legislation: Evidence from California Ballot Proposition Elections. *The Journal of Politics*, 64(1), 154–177.

Haselswerdt, J. (2020). Carving Out: Isolating the True Effect of Self-Interest on Policy Attitudes. *American Political Science Review*, 114(4), 1103–1116.

Haskell, J. (2001). *Direct democracy or representative government? : Dispelling the populist myth.* Westview Press.

Helbling, M., & Kriesi, H. (2004). Staatsbürgerverständnis und politische Mobilisierung: Einbürgerungen in Schweizer Gemeinden. *Swiss Political Science Review, 10*(4), 33–58.

Heußner, H. K. (2012). Minorities and Direct Democracy in the USA: Direct Legislation Concerning Minorities and Instruments of Minority Protection. In *Direct Democracy and Minorities* (pp. 123–144). Springer VS.

Hogg, M. A., & Abrams, D. (2003). Intergroup Behavior and Social Identity. In M. A. Hogg & J. Cooper (Eds.), *The SAGE Handbook of Social Psychology* (pp. 407–431). Sage Publications.

Inglehart, R., Haerpfer, C., Moreno, A., Welzel, C., Kizilova, K., Diez-Medrano, J., Lagos, M., Norris, P., Ponarin, E., & et al. (Eds.). (2014). *World Values Survey: Round Six—Country-Pooled Datafile*. JD Systems Institute. www.worldvaluessurvey.org/WVSDocumentationWV6.jsp.

Inglehart, R., Haerpfer, C., Moreno, A., Welzel, C., Kizilova, K., Diez-Medrano, J., Lagos, M., Norris, P., Ponarin, E., Puranen, B., & et al. (Eds.). (2014). *World Values Survey: Round Five—Country-Pooled Datafile*. JD Systems Institute. www.worldvaluessurvey.org/WVSDocumentationWV5.jsp.

Inglehart, R., Haerpfer, C., Moreno, A., Welzel, C., Kizilova, K., Diez-Medrano, J., Lagos, M., Norris, P., Ponarin, E., Puranen, B., & et al. (Eds.). (2014). *World Values Survey: Round Four—Country-Pooled Datafile*. JD Systems Institute. www.worldvaluessurvey.org/WVSDocumentationWV4.jsp.

Inglehart, R., Haerpfer, C., Moreno, A., Welzel, C., Kizilova, K., Diez-Medrano, J., Lagos, M., Norris, P., Ponarin, E., Puranen, B., & et al. (Eds.). (2014). *World Values Survey: Round Three—Country-Pooled Datafile*. JD Systems Institute. www.worldvaluessurvey.org/WVSDocumentationWV3.jsp.

Inglehart, R., Haerpfer, C., Moreno, A., Welzel, C., Kizilova, K., Diez-Medrano, J., Lagos, M., Norris, P., Ponarin, E., Puranen, B., & et al. (Eds.). (2014). *World Values Survey: Round Two—Country-Pooled Datafile*. JD Systems Institute. www.worldvaluessurvey.org/WVSDocumentationWV2.jsp.

Inglehart, R., & Norris, P. (2017). Trump and the Populist Authoritarian Parties: The Silent Revolution in Reverse. *Perspectives on Politics, 15*(2), 443–454.

Jacobs, K., Akkerman, A., & Zaslove, A. (2018). The voice of populist people? Referendum preferences, practices and populist attitudes. *Acta Politica, 53*(4), 517–541.

Jäske, M., & Setälä, M. (2019). Referendum and Citizens' Initiatives. In *Handbook of Democratic Innovation and Governance* (pp. 90–104). Edward Elgar Publishing.

Kim, J. H. (2019). Direct Democracy and Women's Political Engagement. *American Journal of Political Science, 63*(3), 594–610.

Kissane, B. (2012). Is the Irish Referendum a Majoritarian Device? In W. Marxer (Ed.), *Direct Democracy and Minorities* (pp. 145–154). Springer VS.

Kobach, K. W. (1993). *The Referendum. Direct Democracy in Switzerland*. Dartmouth.

Kohler, U., & Kreuter, F. (2012). *Datenanalyse mit Stata. Allgemeine Konzepte der Datenanalyse und ihre praktische Anwendung* (4th ed.). Oldenbourg.

Kousser, T., & McCubbins, M. D. (2005). Social Choice, Crypto-Initiatives and Policy Making by Direct Democracy. *Southern California Law Review, 78*, 949–984.

Krämling, A., Geißel, B., Rinne, J., & Paulus, L. (2022). Direct Democracy and Equality—A Global Perspective. *International Political Science Review*. https://doi.org/10.1177/01925121211058660.

Kriesi, H. (2005). *Direct Democratic Choice. The Swiss Experience*. Lexington Books.

Kymlicka, W. (1995). *Multicultural Citizenship. A Liberal Theory of Minority Rights*. Clarendon Press.

Lacey, J. (2021). On popular votes and the problems of self-government: A systemic case for ordinary popular vote processes. *Critical Review of International Social and Political Philosophy*. https://doi.org/10.1080/13698230.2021.1997249.

Lafont, C. (2020). *Democracy Without Shortcuts: A Participatory Conception of Deliberative Democracy*. Oxford University Press.

Landemore, H. (2020). *Open Democracy. Reinventing Popular Rule for the Twenty-First Century*. Princeton University Press.

Leemann, L. (2015). Political Conflict and Direct Democracy: Explaining Initiative Use 1920-2011. *Swiss Political Science Review, 21*(4), 596–616.

Lewis, D. C. (2013). *Direct Democracy and Minority Rights. A Critical Assessment of the Tyranny of the Majority in the American States*. Routledge.

Lima e Silva, G., & Silva, F. G. (2019). Between experience and structure: Social suffering, collective identities and justice in Iris Marion Young. *Digithum, 23*, 1–11.

Lupia, A., & Matsusaka, J. G. (2004). Direct Democracy: New Approaches to Old Questions. *Annual Review of Political Science, 2004*(7), 463–482.

Lutz, G. (2007). Low turnout in direct democracy. *Electoral Studies, 26*(3), 624–632.

Madison, J. (2008). The Federalist, 51. In L. Goldman (Ed.), *The Federalist Papers* (pp. 256–259). OUP Oxford.

Magin, R., Eder, C., & Vatter, A. (2008). Direkte Demokratie in den Bundesländern. Ein Vergleich der Institutionen und Anwendungsmuster. In A. Hildebrandt & F. Wolf (Eds.), *Die Politik der Bundesländer. Staatstätigkeit im Vergleich* (pp. 345–362). VS Verlag für Sozialwissenschaften.

Mancenido-Bolaños, M. A. V. (2020). Iris Marion Young's 'Faces of Oppression' and the Oppression of Women in the Responsible Parenthood and Reproductive Health Act of 2012. *Kritike, 14*(1), 98–121.

Mansbridge, J. (1999). Should Blacks Represent Blacks and Women Represent Women? A Contingent "Yes." *The Journal of Politics, 61*(3), 628–657.

Marcinkowski, F., & Donk, A. (2012). Winning without Victory? The Media Coverage of Minority Affairs in Swiss Direct Democratic Campaigns. In W. Marxer (Ed.), *Direct Democracy and Minorities* (pp. 194–211). Springer VS.

Marx, T., & Leininger, A. (2022). Reduzieren Zustimmungsquoren die Beteiligung an direktdemokratischen Abstimmungen? *Zeitschrift Für Vergleichende Politikwissenschaft*. https://doi.org/10.1007/s12286-022-00539-3.

Marxer, W. (2012). Minorities and Direct Democracy in Liechtenstein. In W. Marxer (Ed.), *Direct Democracy and Minorities* (pp. 165–180). Springer VS.

Matsusaka, J. G. (2014). Disentangling the direct and indirect effects of the initiative process. *Public Choice*, *160*(3), 345–366.

Merkel, W. (2011). Volksabstimmungen: Illusion und Realität. *Aus Politik Und Zeitgeschichte*, *61*(44–45), 47–55.

Merkel, W. (2015). *Nur schöner Schein? Demokratische Innovationen in Theorie und Praxis*. Friedrich-Ebert-Stiftung.

Merkel, W., & Ritzi, C. (2017). *Die Legitimität direkter Demokratie. Wie demokratisch sind Volksabstimmungen?* Springer VS.

Milic, T., Rousselot, B., & Vatter, A. (2014). *Handbuch der Abstimmungsforschung*. Verlag Neue Zürcher Zeitung.

Miller, D. (2016). Majorities and Minarets: Religious Freedom and Public Space. *British Journal of Political Science*, *46*(2), 437–356.

Moeckli, D. (2018). Referendums: Tyranny of the Majority? *Swiss Political Science Review*, *24*(3), 335–341.

Mollerstrom, J. (2015). Ethnic fractionalization and the demand for redistribution – Potential implications for the Nordic model. *Nordic Economic Policy Review*, 219–243.

Moore, R. T., & Ravishankar, N. (2012). Who loses in direct democracy? *Social Science Research*, *41*(3), 646–656.

Morel, L. (2001). The Rise of Government-Initiated Referenda in Consolidated Democracies. In M. Mendelsohn & A. Parkin (Eds.), *Referendum democracy.Citizens, elites, and deliberation in referendum campaigns*. Palgrave.

Morel, L. (2007). The Rise of 'Politically Obligatory' Referendums: The 2005 French Referendum in Comparative Perspective. *West European Politics*, *30*(5), 1041–1067.

Pállinger, Z. T. (2012). Direct Democracy, the Rule of Law and the Protection of Minorities: The Case of Hungary. In W. Marxer (Ed.), *Direct Democracy and Minorities* (pp. 91–105). Springer VS.

Parkinson, J. (2020). The Roles of Referendums in Deliberative Systems. *Representation*, *56*(4), 485–500.

Pateman, C. (1970). *Participation and Democratic Theory*. Cambridge University Press.

Pineda, V. S. (2020). Understanding Disability in Theory, Justice, and Planning. In *Building the Inclusive City: Governance, Access, and the Urban Transformation of Dubai* (pp. 23–45). Springer International Publishing.

Qvortrup, M. (2006). Democracy by Delegation: The Decision to Hold Referendums in the United Kingdom. *Representation*, *42*(1), 59–72.

Rahat, G. (2009). Elite motives for initiating referendums: Avoidance, addition and contradiction. In M. Setälä & T. Schiller (Eds.), *Referendums and Representative Democracy. Responsiveness, accountability and deliberation* (pp. 98–116). Routledge.

Rao, M., Raschky, P. A., & Tombazos, C. G. (2018). Political extremism and economic activity. *Economic Letters*, *170*, 59–62.

Rosenbluth, F. M., & Shapiro, I. (2018). *Responsible Parties. Saving Democracy from Itself*. Yale University Press.

Schäfer, A., & Schoen, H. (2013). Mehr Demokratie, aber nur für wenige? Der Zielkonflikt zwischen mehr Beteiligung und politischer Gleichheit. *Leviathan*, *41*(1), 94–120.

Schmidt, M. G. (2010). *Demokratietheorien. Eine Einführung.* (5.). VS Verlag für Sozialwissenschaften.

Scott, R. (2022). Does university make you more liberal? Estimating the within-individual effects of higher education on political values. *Electoral Studies*, *77*. https://doi.org/10.1016/j.electstud.2022.102471.

Serdült, U., & Welp, Y. (2012). Direct Democracy Upside Down. *Taiwan Journal of Democracy*, *8*(1), 69–92.

Setälä, M. (1999). Referendums in Western Europe—A Wave of Direct Democracy? *Scandinavian Political Studies*, *22*(4), 327–340.

Shayo, M. (2009). A Model of Social Identity with an Application to Political Economy: Nation, Class, and Redistribution. *American Political Science Review*, *103*(2), 147–174.

Simon, C. A., Matland, R. E., Wendell, D. G., & Tatalovich, R. (2018). Voting Turnout and Referendum Outcomes on Same-Sex Marriage, 1998–2015. *Social Science Quarterly*, *99*(4), 1522–1534.

Sommet, N., & Morselli, D. (2017). Keep Calm and Learn Multilevel Logistic Modeling: A Simplified Three-Step Procedure Using Stata, R, Mplus, and SPSS. *International Review of Social Psychology*, *30*(1), 203–218.

Stegmueller, D. (2013). How Many Countries for Multilevel Modeling? A Comparison of Frequentist and Bayesian Approaches. *American Journal of Political Science*, *57*(3), 748–761.

Stojanović, N. (2021). *Multilingual democracy. Switzerland and beyond.* ECPR Press/ Rowman & Littlefield.

Stojanović, N. (2023). Citizens' assemblies and direct democracy. In M. Reuchamps, J. Vrydagh, & Y. Welp (Eds.), *De Gruyter Handbook of Citizens' Assemblies* (pp. 183-196). De Gruyter.

Swift, T. (2019). *Lover*. Republic.

Tajfel, H. (1970). Experiments in Intergroup Discrimination. *Scientific American, 223*(5), 96–103.

Tempels, T., Blok, V., & Verweij, M. (2020). Injustice in Food-Related Public Health Problems: A Matter of Corporate Responsibility. *Business Ethics Quarterly, 30*(3), 388–413.

Thomeczek, J. P. (2021). Alles eine Frage von Kosten und Nutzen? Eine Aggregatdatenanalyse der Abstimmungsbeteiligung in den deutschen Bundesländern zwischen 1946 und 2019. *Swiss Political Science Review, 27*(2), 449–475.

Tocqueville, A. de. (2012). *Democracy in America* (E. Nolla, Ed.; J. T. Schleifer, Trans.). Liberty Fund.

Töller, A., & Vollmer, A. (2013). Wem nützt direkte Demokratie? Policy-Effekte direkter Demokratie und Folgerungen für die Forschung zu Deutschland. *Zeitschrift Für Vergleichende Politikwissenschaft, 7*(4), 299–320.

Trechsel, A. H. (2010). Reflexive Accountability and Direct Democracy. *West European Politics, 33*(5), 1050–1064.

Trüdinger, E.-M., & Bächtiger, A. (2022). Attitudes vs. Actions? Direct-democratic preferences and participation of populist citizens. *West European Politics*. https://doi.org/10.1080/01402382.2021.2023435.

Urbinati, N. (2014). *Democracy Disfigured. Opinion, Truth, and the People*. Harvard University Press.

Vatter, A. (2007). Direkte Demokratie in der Schweiz: Entwicklungen, Debatten und Wirkungen. In M. Freitag & U. Wagschal (Eds.), *Direkte Demokratie. Bestandsaufnahmen und Wirkungen im internationalen Vergleich.* (pp. 71–113). LIT Verlag.

Vatter, A., & Danaci, D. (2010). Mehrheitstyrannei durch Volksentscheide? Zum Spannungsverhältnis zwischen direkter Demokratie und Minderheitenschutz. *Politische Vierteljahresschrift, 51*(2), 205–222.

Vatter, A., Stadelmann-Steffen, I., & Danaci, D. (2014). Who supports minority rights in popular votes? Empirical evidence from Switzerland. *Electoral Studies, 36*, 1–14.

Weldon, S. (2006). The Institutional Context of Tolerance for Ethnic Minorities: A Comparative, Multilevel Analysis of Western Europe. *American Journal of Political Science, 50*(2), 331–349.

Welp, Y., & Ruth, S. P. (2017). The Motivations Behind the Use of Mechanisms of Direct Democracy. In S. P. Ruth, Y. Welp, & L. Whitehead (Eds.), *Let the People Rule? Direct Democracy in the Twenty-First Century* (pp. 99–119). ECPR Press.

Wenzelburger, G., Jäckle, S., & König, P. (2014). *Weiterführende statistische Methoden für Politikwissenschaftler. Eine anwendungsbezogene Einführung mit Stata*. De Gruyter Oldenbourg.

Williams, C. C., Forbes, J. R., Placide, K., & Nicol, N. (2020). Religion, Hate, Love, and Advocacy for LGBT Human Rights in Saint Lucia. *Sexuality Research and Social Policy*, *17*, 729–740. https://doi.org/10.1007/s13178-020-00429-x.

Williams, M. S. (2000). *Voice, Trust, and Memory. Marginalized Groups and the Failings of Liberal Representation.* (2nd ed.). Princeton University Press.

Young, I. M. (1989). Polity and Group Difference: A Critique of the Ideal of Universal Citizenship. *Ethics*, *99*, 250–274.

Young, I. M. (1990). *Justice and the Politics of Difference.* Princeton University Press.

Young, I. M. (2000). *Inclusion and Democracy.* Oxford University Press.

Zurlinden, M. (2015). *Religionsgemeinschaften in der direkten Demokratie. Handlungsräume religiöser Minderheiten in der Schweiz.* Springer VS.

Name Index

Christmann, A. 22, 29, 36, 41, 48, 58-62, 68, 70, 109, 141, 147, 149, 168, 200
el-Wakil, A. 35, 200
Fraser, N. 31, 201
Kymlicka, W. 23, 32, 35, 204
Landemore, H. 48, 63, 71, 154, 169, 204
Lewis, D. C. 21, 29, 36, 41, 43, 53, 55 f., 59, 64, 69, 147, 162-166, 172, 204
McKay, S. 35, 200
Merkel, W. 41, 47, 51, 68, 164, 205

Stojanović, N. 41, 48, 54 f., 63, 71, 92, 139, 145, 154, 164, 169, 172, 177, 206
Tocqueville, A. 21, 40, 161, 207
Vatter, A. 5, 22, 29, 36, 39, 41, 43, 55-59, 62, 68 ff., 92, 106, 141 f., 146, 149, 152, 163, 168 f., 172, 175, 200, 204 f., 207
Williams, M. 32 f., 73, 163, 208
Young, I. M. 23, 25 ff., 29-35, 41, 44 f., 49, 73, 157, 159, 161, 163, 173, 176, 201, 204, 208

Yves Schemeil

The Making of the World

How International Organizations Shape Our Future

2023 • 406 pp. • Paperback • 44,90 € (D) • 46,20 € (A)
ISBN 978-3-8474-2146-7 • also available as e-book in open access

International Organizations (IOs) were designed to provide global public goods, among which security for all, trade for the richest, and development for the poorest. Their very existence is now a promise of success for the cooperative turn in international relations. Although the IO network was once created by established powers, rising states can hardly resist the massive production of norms that their governments can be reluctant to respect without being able to discard them. IOs are omnipresent, and exert great influence on the world as we know it. However, rulers and ruled are hardly aware of such compelling and snowballing processes. Yves Schemeil uses his in-depth knowledge of IOs to analyze their current impact on international relations, on world politics, and their potential of shaping the global future.

www.shop.budrich.de